Beyond microfoundations:
Post Walrasian macroeconomics

Beyond microfoundations: Post Walrasian macroeconomics

Edited by

DAVID COLANDER
Middlebury College

Published by the Press Syndicate of the University of Cambridge
The Pitt Building, Trumpington Street, Cambridge CB2 1RP
40 West 20th Street, New York, NY 10011-4211, USA
10 Stamford Road, Oakleigh, Melbourne 3166, Austrailia

First Published 1996

Printed in the United States of America

Library of Congress Cataloging-in-Publication Data

Colander, David.

Beyond microfoundations: post Walrasian macroeconomics / David Colander.

p. cm.

Includes bibliographical references and index.

ISBN 0-521-55237-0

1. Macroeconomics. 2. Microeconomics. 3. Economics, Mathematical. 4. Walras,
Léon, 1834-1910.   I. Colander, David C.
HB172.5.B47   1996
330 - dc20   95-44891
                                                                      CIP

A catalog record of this book is available from the British Library.

ISBN 0 521 55237 0 Hardback

Contents

About the authors

John Bryant
Professor of Economics at Rice University

The author of many articles in macroeconomics, he was one of the first to develop a Keynesian model from a New Classical rational expectations foundation. His theoretical work on coordination introduced the technological complementarities of team production, which has impacted the study of industrial organization as well as Keynesian macroeconomics, and motivated the seminal experiments on coordination by Van Huyck, Batallio, and Beil. This work can be viewed as a game-theoretic formalization and extension of Rousseau's (1755) Stag Hunt parable used to motivate the social contract and is also influenced by the modern historian Fernand Braudel.

His applied work on coordination has included analyses of bank runs and of the multiplicity of equlibria arising from the intermediation of indivisible assets. He also helped develop the "Government Irrelevancy" literature, and jointly with Neil Wallace, helped develop the New Classical "New Monetary Economics" or "Legal Restrictions Theory of Money."

Prior to his appointment at Rice University, he was a senior economist at the Federal Reserve Bank of Minneapolis and an economist at the Board of Governors of the Federal Reserve System.

Robert Clower
Emeritus Professor of Economics, UCLA; Hugh C. Lane Distinguished Professor of Economic Theory at the University of South Carolina

A long-time contributor to the macroeconomic debate, he is most famous for his two papers "The Keynesian Counter-Revolution" (1965) and "A Reconsideration of the Microfoundations of Monetary Theory" (1967). A former editor of *Economic Inquiry* (1974-1980) and of the *AER* (1980-1985), and past President of the Western and Southern Economic Associations, he, and his iconoclastic views, have often been ahead of the wave of the profession's interest.

David Colander
Professor of Economics at Middlebury College

The Christian A. Johnson Distinguished Professor of Economics at Middlebury College in Middlebury, Vermont, he has authored, co-authored, or edited 30 books and over 80 articles on a wide range of topics. These include *Principles of Economics* (Richard D. Irwin), *History of Economic Thought* (with Harry Landreth) (Houghton Mifflin), *Why Aren't Economists as Important as Garbagemen?* (Sharpe), and *MAP: A Market Anti-Inflation Plan* (with Abba Lerner) (Harcourt Brace Jovanovich).

He received his Ph.D. from Columbia University and has taught at Columbia University, Vassar College, and the University of Miami as well as Middlebury College. He has also been a consultant to Time-Life Films, a consultant to Congress, a Brookings Policy Fellow, and a Visiting Scholar at Nuffield College, Oxford. He is listed in *Who's Who?* and *Who's Who in Education.*

He has been on the board of numerous economic societies and has been President of the Eastern Economic Association and Vice-President of the History of Economic Thought Society. He is currently on the editorial boards of the *Journal of Economic Methodology*, and the *Eastern Economic Journal*, and is on the Board of Advisors of the *Journal of Economic Perspectives.*

His latest work focuses on Marshallian general equilibrium, Post Walrasian economics, and the methodology appropriate to applied policy economics.

Harry Garretsen
Senior Economist for the de Nederlandsche Bank, the Dutch Central Bank, in Amsterdam

He received his Ph.D. degree in economics from the University of Gronigen, the Netherlands, and is the author of a book on the coordination problem and macroeconomic theory. Together with Hans van Ees he has published widely on New Keynesian and Post Walrasian themes in the *Journal of Post Keynesian Economics*, the *Journal of Macroeconomics,* and the *Journal of Economic Behaviour and Organization,* among others. His current research interests are capital market imperfections and aggregate economic fluctuations and path-dependency in economics.

Peter Howitt
Bank of Montreal Professor of Money and Finance at the University of Western Ontario

One of the few economists who has consistently maintained a Post Walrasian approach to macreconomics throughout his entire career, he has played an important role in keeping this Post Walrasian view in the profession's mind. He has had a distinguished career. Among other schools, he has taught at MIT, Hebrew University, and the University of Toulouse.

Included in his long list of activities are serving as associate editor of the *Canadian Journal of Economics*, a member of the Editorial Board of the *American Economic Review* and the *Journal of Economic Literature*, and President of the Canadian Economic Association. He has published over 75 articles and two books. His first article, "Walras and Monetary Theory" (1973), was a precursor of many of the ideas in this volume.

Robert J. Martel
Lecturer in Economics and Finance and Ph.D. candidate, Whittemore School of Business and Economics, University of New Hampshire

He previously taught at Bentley College and Boston University and has been a self-employed financial consultant and investment manager for the past 20 years. He is a Certified Financial Planner and a Chartered Financial Consultant. His contribution to this volume is based on his Ph. D. dissertation in New Keynesian economics.

Perry Mehrling
Assistant Professor of Economics at Barnard College and Columbia University

Early training at the London School of Economics alerted him to the fact that the Walrasian approach has little to say about money, and from then on all his work has involved the search for alternative foundations for monetary theory. His search for new directions has led him to the study of history of monetary thought, and he has a book forthcoming on the development of U.S. monetary thought from 1920-1960. He has also investigated the potential of alternative analytical formulations, as in his 1995 "Note on the Optimum Quantity of Money." He is attracted to the Post Walrasian approach by its potential for combining the insights of the older institutionalist school with the analytical tools needed to develop those insights into a proper theory.

Axel Leijonhufvud
Professor of Economics at the University of California at Los Angeles

Well known for his work on interpreting Keynes, he has been at the center of macroeconomic debates. He is the author of a wide variety of economic articles and books including *Keynes and the Keynesians: A Suggested Interpretation* (1967), *On Keynesian Economics and the Economics of Keynes: A Study in Monetary Theory* (1968), and *Information and Coordination: Essays in Macreconomic Theory* (1981).

David M. Reaume
Adjunct Associate Professor of Economics at the University of Alaska

He comes to a Post Walrasian economics via a 20-year career as an economic forecaster with the Board of Governors of the Federal Reserve System, Data

Resources, Incorporated, and his own consulting firm. His combination of extensive work in applied macroeconomics and a prior background in electrical engineering lends a perspective not often found in purely academic circles.

J. Barkley Rosser, Jr.
Professor of Economics at James Madison University
   The author of many articles on a variety of topics, as well as the author of a recent book on chaos theory and complexity that quickly went to a second printing. This book demonstrated the possibility of an essentially Post Walrasian approach applying across a wide range of areas of economics through the perspective of nonlinear dynamics. His earliest papers from the late 1970s dealt with problems in capital theory and nonlinear urban dynamics that exemplified his essentially non-Walrasian approach to economic theory.
   He is currently Book Review Editor for the *Journal of Economic Behaviour and Organization* and for the *Journal of Discrete Chaotic Dynamics*.

Hans van Ees
Associate Professor of Economics at the University of Groningen, the Netherlands
   He received his Ph.D. degree in economics from the University of Gronigen, the Netherlands, and is the author of a book on the microfoundations of macroeconomics. Together with Harry Garretsen he has published widely on New Keynesian and Post Walrasian themes in the *Journal of Post Keynesian Economics*, the *Journal of Macroeconomics,* and the *Journal of Economic Behaviour and Organization,* among others. His current research interests are capital market imperfections and aggregate economic fluctuations and path-dependency in economics.

Preface

For me, the ideas in this book started in graduate school in the early 1970s as I sat in macro courses. Much of the macro I was being taught did not make intuitive sense to me; it seemed to be lacking a micro core. I took Edmund Phelps's advanced seminar on microfoundations to fill in the needed microfoundations. In that seminar Phelps was going through new work, then just coming out, on microfoundations. That work was analytically impressive, but was, for me, intuitively unsatisfying; it did not resolve my problems with macro. At that point I decided that macro wasn't for me, and that I would specialize in micro issues. I chose a dissertation topic on optimal taxation.

A strange set of events pulled me back to macro. In 1974 I was playing around in my head with wild ideas, and I came up with a scheme to create property rights in prices – letting individuals trade rights to change prices – as a way to stop inflation. I reasoned that with inflation controlled by this plan, if there was any slack in the aggregate system, expansionary demand policy would be directed into increases in real output, not inflation. It was a simple scheme, but one I found intriguing; I sent it off to my dissertation advisor, Bill Vickery. He liked it and encouraged me to develop this work into a thesis. So I dumped my almost completed thesis on optimal taxation and started working on a thesis developing the ideas underlying this alternative conception anti-inflation policy. That work led me to a collaboration with Abba Lerner who was working on a similar idea; we wrote a book and a number of articles together outlining the plan and developing the underlying non-monetary theory of inflation that underlay it.

Since inflation was considered a macro topic, I found myself working in macro, despite my concerns with it. At that point I started seriously reading in the macro field, trying to make intuitive sense of both macro and micro foundations. I still couldn't do so; somehow it seemed that much of the intuitive sense that I was after was discarded in the formalist search for analytic models. Most macroeconomists returned the favor; they couldn't understand Abba's and my anti-inflation work; they couldn't see why such a scheme might be needed, or how it would work theoretically. Somehow – strangely, it seemed to me – whenever they considered our market anti-inflation plan, they considered it within a partial equilibrium framework, rather than within the general equilibrium framework that Abba and I used. Their Walrasian framework had no real role for money or for a nominal price level, and our plan was designed to control only that nominal price level. In short they had precluded our plan by assumption.

Working with Abba gave me the sense that there was much more to macroeconomics than was in the textbooks and standardly assigned articles. But my early work at trying to specify where my problems were with macro led nowhere. So I started to look into the nature of the profession to try to decide whether I, or the macro profession, had a serious problem. That consideration of the profession led me to Robert Clower, whose no-nonsense approach to economics fit my approach to a tee. He seemed to demand the same intuitive reasonableness of a theory that I was searching for. I read his work – understood some of it – and became convinced that he was on the right track. I reviewed a book of his saying that he told of a promised land, but didn't tell us how to get there; his wife thought my review outrageous; he and Axel Leijonhufvud thought it right on. At that point I returned to thinking about developing a macro theory that would fit my conception of the macroeconomy. It was a search for a general macro framework which could replace the standard Walrasian framework – one which was intuitively satisfying to me, and which other macro economists would understand. It was that search that led me to the Post Walrasian framework presenting in this volume.

Most of the other contributors to this volume were on a similar search; I met them at various conferences, seminars, or simply through correspondence. They had seen something I had written, or vice versa. We corresponded, argued with each other, and further developed the ideas. By the early 1990s it was clear to me that these ideas were coming together, although in a very informal way. Barkley Rosser's book on chaos and catastrophe theory, together with the work on complexity of the Sante Fe Institute, provided me with a glimpse of the underlying formal foundations of the Post Walrasian model. Those foundations would be in nonlinear dynamics and complexity. Macro functional relationships were similar to solitons – relatively stable functional forms whose stability depended on complex dynamics surrounding the function. They would not be inherently stable. Since stability depended on the dynamics, the dynamics had to be part of the core; comparative static models, no matter how complex, would not do. Within this Post Walrasian framework the interesting policy issues would concern alternative coordinating mechanisms; Abba Lerner's and my MAP proposal would have a potential role. That recognition that there was a formal structure of underlying theory that better fit my intuition led me to the decision to organize this book.

The actual impetus for the book came from the Eastern Economic Association. I was in charge of organizing sessions for the Boston meetings, and I set up a mini conference (a group of related sessions) in which most of the papers here were originally presented. The papers were then discussed, reworked, edited, and reworked again until we had a coherent book. Where it seemed necessary we added additional papers, but the core of the book derives from that mini conference.

The central idea underlying all the papers in this volume is that it is unacceptable to make assumptions that have no intuitive foundation in the world we observe around us, simply because those assumptions are required for analytic tractability. Models must intuitively fit the real world; if they don't, they are empty formalism. Specifically, you can't reasonably assume the market will coordinate economic affairs without specifying what you mean by the market and how market institutions are compatible with individual incentives. Coordinating the activities of billions of people is far too much for the invisible hand to accomplish alone; to do it a society needs institutions, and those institutions must be an integral part of macro analysis. The Walrasian approach to macroeconomics had eliminated the role for institutions and, in doing so, had eliminated its intuitive foundations.

In making these ideas into a book there are many people to thank. Michael Parkin, Kenneth Koford, and a variety of anonymous referees made helpful comments on the papers and suggestions for structuring the book. Helen Reiff played a major role in editing my papers, did the copyediting and proofing, and prepared the indices, Jenifer Gamber did the compositing, and put the book together. Scott Parris encouraged me at every point along the way of this project and saw it through to its completion.

The *Eastern Economic Journal* and the *Southern Economic Journal* gave permission to reprint articles which first appeared in those journals. I sincerely thank them all. Most of all, however, I want to thank the contributors who worked hard at satisfying my constant questioning, and put up with my pushing them to make the papers fit into a coherent whole.

The product is one which I think you, the reader, will find challenging, and interesting, in a way that few economics books today are. It gives you a sense of what Post Walrasian macroeconomics is, and, I hope, encourages you to think about issues within a Post Walrasian framework.

David Colander (Summer 1995)
New Haven, Vermont

CHAPTER 1

Overview

David Colander

It has been 25 years since the microfoundations of macro became popular. The changes that have occurred in macro in these 25 years have been substantial. The whole conception of macroeconomics has changed from a Keynesian aggregate fine-tuning conception to a New Classical, policy-ineffective, microeconomic conception, to a New Keynesian "who knows what theory or policy to use" conception.

This book is an introduction to a line of thinking about the macro economy that stands in bold opposition to much of the macroeconomic literature not only of the last 25 years, but of much of the work of 25 years before that – the work that led to the microfoundations work. The approach to macro presented in this volume significantly differs from much of both Classical and Keynesian thought – whether prefixed by new, neo, or whatever. Thus, it is in opposition not only to the New Classical and New Keynesian macroeconomics of the last 15 years, but also to the NeoKeynesian and neoclassical macroeconomics of the last 50 years.

Given such strong claims it is only natural that one wonders how, after 50 years of development, can there be such a fundamentally different approach to macro? I can best answer that with an analogy. Say you are at the base of two mountains whose peaks are above the clouds. You want to climb to the higher peak which means that you must choose one of the two. You do; you choose Mountain A – the Walrasian mountain; you start working your way up the slopes further and further, until finally you get above the clouds. When you do, you see that Mountain B – let's call it a Post Walrasian mountain – is the far higher one. That's what we believe happened in macroeconomics.

This analogy should help explain why a dramatic new approach may be needed to further our understanding of macro issues and why a discussion of that new approach involves the foundations of economic analysis, not extensions of existing work. Whereas most of the debate in macro over the last 50 years has concerned whether we should follow this path or that path, the papers in this volume will be arguing that the paths aren't the problem; the problem is the mountain – the core Walrasian foundation of macro theory.

The mountain analogy is also useful in explaining the profession's hesitancy to use the approach we advocate. It isn't easy to climb down a mountain, and start again up another mountain. The profession has already climbed so far up the Walrasian mountain, that there is a natural tendency to continue the climb, and to say to yourself – that's high enough. But most economists know, deep down, that it isn't high enough, although institutional incentives (like getting tenure and getting published) have, until recently, kept them from either accepting, or acting upon, what they know. Institutional incentives are now changing; most Walrasian paths have been followed to dead ends; and there is some very fancy math and game theory to apply to the Post Walrasian approach which offer large numbers of dissertation topics. Thus, we are hopeful that a number of younger economists will listen to our plea to move to the Post Walrasian mountain. (Older economists probably have too much invested in the Walrasian approach, and are not spry enough for the alternative climb.) To encourage fellow economists to accept that climb, I would point out that climbing the Post Walrasian mountain will go much faster since, in making that climb, many of the same techniques we have used in climbing the Walrasian mountain may well be relevant; it is the framework that is not.

1.1   Distinguishing characteristics of Post Walrasian macro

We've called the alternative approach to macro that we are advocating *Post Walrasian* to set it in distinct opposition to modern Walrasian or neoWalrasian work.[1] Before deciding on the term Post Walrasian, we explored many other terms: Marshallian macro, New Institutionalist macro, and Coordination macro. All had some votes, but, ultimately, we came to the conclusion that "Post Walrasian" is the best term because it most clearly directs economists to the distinguishing characteristics of our approach. These distinguishing characteristics are multiple equilibria and complexity, bounded rationality, and institutions and non-price coordinating mechanisms.

1.1.1   *Multiple equilibria and complexity*

Post Walrasian macro conjectures that the solution to a system of simultaneous equations as complex as is necessary to describe our economy has multiple equilibria and complex dynamics. This means that the aggregate economy cannot be meaningfully analyzed in the way that Walrasian economics analyzes it – within a comparative static model that assumes the existence of a unique aggregate equilibrium which is unaffected by dynamic adjustment processes. For a Post Walrasian, the interesting aspects of macroeconomics have all been assumed away by the Walrasian construction of the problem.

1.1.2 Bounded rationality

Post Walrasian macroeconomics conjectures that the macro economy is so complex that rational decision making in the context of a Walrasian-type general equilibrium system taken as a whole is impossible. This is in distinct contrast to Walrasian macroeconomics which conjectures that individuals can rationally deal with the complexity of the economic system and can process information sufficiently fast so that the resulting aggregate equilibrium reflects, in some way, a reasonable amalgam of their collective desires.

Post Walrasian macroeconomics does not give up rationality; it simply gives up global rationality as being beyond the processing capabilities of individuals. For Post Walrasians rationality has more local characteristics; it is bounded, not global, rationality.

1.1.3 Institutions and non-price coordinating mechanisms

The real world does not exhibit the chaotic results that would be the likely result of the two previous Post Walrasian conjectures. Walrasian advocates argue that this observation suggests that the Walrasian conjectures of unique equilibria and non-complex dynamics are the correct ones. Post Walrasians disagree; they see the reason why the aggregate economy is relatively stable is the existence of multilayered institutions – conventions, legal and social, that impose restrictions on individual actions – which limit individual actions within ranges. These institutions impose the stability that exists in the system and reduce the complexity of decision making for individuals. Thus, institutions play a central role in Post Walrasian macroeconomics whereas they are seen as simply frictions in Walrasian macroeconomics. In Post Walrasian macro, institutions provide systemic stability and, thus, must be an integral part of the analysis.

These three defining characteristics are, of course, interconnected; the reason there are multiple equilibria is the economy's complexity, and the reason institutions exist is to reduce the complexity for individuals, and to reduce the number of equilibria the economy can reach.

1.2 The Post Walrasian indictment of Walrasian macro

The Post Walrasian indictment of Walrasian macro is that it has not taken the complexity of the aggregate economy seriously either in its assumptions of individuals' ability to deal with that complexity, or in the structure of its models. When considering the macro economy's complexity Walrasian macro economists have always blinked – and fudged the intuition behind the math – by which I mean they have structured the formal specification of the problem so as to come up with a unique analytic solution using a system of comparative static equations with linear dynamics. Walrasian economists have always chosen to avoid dealing with that complexity, making Walrasian economics the equivalent of what Kenneth Boulding called "the celestial mechanics of a non-existent world."

Both Keynesians and Classicals have fudged, which has resulted in a wonderful charade. The two groups debate the relative merits of their respective fudges – Keynesians calling the Classical market-clearing fudge inconceivable, and Classicals calling Keynesians' fixed wage or price fudge *ad hoc*. Post Walrasians call both fudges unreasonable and *ad hoc* because the underlying analytic model of both is unreasonable and *ad hoc*; they are both on the wrong mountain.

Taking the complexity of the aggregate economy seriously undermines much of the theorizing that has been done in macro over the last 50 years. It means walking down the Walrasian mountain. For example, how can one look for rational micro foundations in a world that is so complex that on pure analytic grounds just about anything can happen. Yes, if one is careful enough to spell out an otherworldly (or, at least, other-islandly) story, one can come to an analytic solution that bears some relation to what we observe; but, for most, that analytic solution is intuitively unsatisfying as a description of the actual economy. Only people dealing in the same otherworldly world are interested in it. Yes, we can get graduate students to deal in that otherworldly world – if they are given no other choice – but is it one they would want to deal with if we didn't hold such "job or no job" power over them? We think not. Somehow, we need a more worldly macroeconomics – one that has a closer intuitive relation to the world within which we live.

The above argument is not about abstraction, or mathematics; it is about the intuitive foundations of the abstractions being made. Thus, while many past critics of Walrasian economics have based their criticism on the excessive mathematical nature of Walrasian models, I want to be clear that that is not the Post Walrasian criticism; if anything, the Post Walrasian criticism is that the mathematics used in Walrasian macroeconomics is too simple to correspond to the complex reality. The Post Walrasian critique of Keynesian and Classical models is that while they look impressive to non-mathematicians, to true mathematicians they are unsatisfying as descriptive of our economy. Thus, in Post Walrasian theory, you will see much discussion of mathematical tools that are at the outer edge of most economists' bag of tools – tools such as chaos theory and nonlinear dynamics.

The justification often given for the simple mathematics used in Walrasian macro is the need to have policy relevance. But to create a formally unsatisfying policy model that doesn't correspond to the way a reasonable policy maker sees the economy working can only lead to unsatisfying policy. About the only reason I can think of for doing so is to give the policy analysis an inappropriate aura of science. I am not claiming that that is the conscious reason it was done, but I do believe that it is likely an unconscious reason pushing for such inappropriate mathematization. Thus, the Post Walrasian critique is an attack on Walrasian theory from both sides. On the one hand, if one wants to deal meaningfully with the mathematics, one had better significantly beef up one's mathematical tools in one's formal models. On the other hand, it argues that if one wants to deal meaningfully with policy, one had better beef up one's understanding of institutions. Walrasian theory has tried to walk the middle road, and the result has been an unsatisfying split – from both a theoretical and a policy perspective.

The views expressed above are shared, in varying forms, by all the authors in this volume, although many of the authors are more politic than I, and would not have put it so bluntly (and a couple of the authors are even less politic than I, and would have put it more bluntly). While they agree in general, the authors differ substantially about specifics. To condemn Walrasian macro is the easy part; deciding what to put in its stead is the hard part. This volume touches on the hard part, but, to be honest, it concerns mostly the easy part. By that I mean that the work presented here is suggestive rather than defining. Thus, what you will be presented with in this volume is not a research program, but instead a call for the establishment of one, and the outline for what that research program might look like.

It essentially is a crying out of a group of macro economists to the profession to work towards designing a macro model that is intuitively reasonable, but is still within the mainstream tradition. It is a cry for reasonable assumptions because the assumptions made by traditional macro theories – Keynesian and Classical – either define away most of the interesting issues in macro, or assume that individuals act in unreasonable ways. For example, how can you use a model of macro that has no role for money – a model in which the costs of inflation are trivial – to capture policy issues in an economy in which economic policy makers, and their economic advisors, see inflation as the biggest evil, and contractionary monetary policy as the best way to stop inflation?

1.3   Antecedents to Post Walrasian macroeconomics

The ideas in Post Walrasian macro have been around for a long time and I want to be clear that the contributors of this volume are making no claims that the ideas expressed here are new. Many economists have known the other mountain is there, and at times mainstream economists have talked as if they were on this alternative mountain. Thus, it is not surprising that there are many possible antecedents to Post Walrasian work in both Classical and Keynesian schools of thought. For example, some will argue that early Classical economists, such as Dennis Robertson, or Frederick Hayek, understood the importance of complexity, and that Keynes's work undermined their attempt to deal with it. Others will argue that it was Keynes who really understood complexity, and that the neoWalrasians undermined Keynes. Certainly some non-mainstream interpreters of Keynes, such as Mary Timlin, Paul Davidson, and G.L.S. Shackle, have been talking about a Post Walrasian mountain, not a Walrasian mountain.

In addition, many of the contributors to this volume have been working in this Post Walrasian tradition for a long time, although their work and contributions often have been misinterpreted. Robert Clower and Axel Leijonhufvud's work is best known. What makes their work take on a new relevance is the New Classical challenge to Keynesian macroeconomics, which has undermined the neoKeynesian macro model. Their earlier work offers a reasonable Keynesian response to the New Classical challenge.

How can their work be a response to New Classical economics when it was done before New Classical economics was even known? I believe it is because they understood the New Classical arguments long before Robert Lucas formulated them, but they dismissed the New Classical response as unreasonable. They tried to deal with the issues in a more substantive way, but because their work challenged the foundations of Walrasian economic thinking, the profession shied away from, and misinterpreted, it. For whatever reason, while the Post Walrasian arguments have been made before, they have not been heard by the profession.

This book will not deal with these antecedent issues – it really doesn't matter who originated the ideas; what matters is that they are reasonable, and that they make intuitive sense. The argument in this volume is that, whoever developed it, the Post Walrasian approach to macro is a more reasonable way to analyze the aggregate economy than is the Walrasian approach.

1.4   Non-Walrasian and Post Walrasian macro

The issues being raised in this volume are, more and more, being raised by modern economists. Some of the best, such as Michael Woodford, or J.-M. Grandmont, have dealt with these problems in their models, and have created what might be called non-Walrasian models. Their work accepts the existence of multiple equilibria, and they seriously try to analyze how an economy might deal with these. But compared to the work presented in this book, they have gone only part way toward the Post Walrasian vision of the complex economy.

Their non-Walrasian approach is still trying to keep a foot on the Walrasian mountain – maintaining the assumption of global rationality. They do not see institutions as giving systemic rationality to the economy, and are still looking for a non-sequentially determined aggregate equilibrium. Post Walrasian macro sees the economy as too complex for such a non-Walrasian solution to exist. It looks for a hierarchical system of sequentially solved equations – equations that on the lowest levels may have a unique aggregate equilibrium. That uniqueness is, however, institutionally determined; it is not inherent in the system independent of the institutions.

The Post Walrasian next step is that if there are a multiplicity of equilibria out there, then individuals would have to have some way to deal with deciding which of those multiple equilibria existed. The complexity of solving everything simultaneously would exceed the computing capabilities of not only macro economists, but also of the individuals in the economy, and alternative ways of solving the problems would be found. The way posited in Post Walrasian economics is that individuals accept conventions, and these institutional constraints upon their actions. These imposed institutional constraints create the sufficiently stable environment within which individuals can operate. If individuals were globally rational, the economy would be unstable. Notice the major change in the approach and view of rationality. In Walrasian economics institutional constraints on individuals prevent the attainment of optimality; in Post Walrasian macroeconomics the constraints are systemic requirements for stability. Without the institutional constraints, there would be no functioning economy.

This difference in view creates a major difference in the research program. In the Post Walrasian program the micro and macro problems must be solved simultaneously. One cannot assume competitive markets exist independently of individuals' incentives to set them up, or from observation. One needs a theory of institutions, of which markets are one, before one can analyze what markets do. To say the market will solve a problem is meaningless since it is unclear what the market is.

1.5   Rational expectations and Post Walrasian macro

The differences in approach go back to the original work on rational expectations. That work involved a research project considering the corn/hog model of fluctuations. Richard Muth and Herbert Simon, who were both working on it, felt that the standard answer – of expectations being based on last year's price – was too simplistic, but they disagreed on what the alternative should be. Simon argued that the institutions that existed would play a central role in the appropriate model. Muth disagreed; he argued that process and institutions did not matter: We should assume that the market would achieve equilibrium. His argument for doing so was simple and sound: Farmers aren't stupid; they have access to the best information, which includes economists' predictions, so if the supply demand model is the correct one, they have access to it, and hence will use the expectations of economists' model in making predictions.

Interestingly, Muth's proposed solution did not gain widespread acceptance, and was little known for 10 years after he published it. My suspicion why it did not gain widespread acceptance is that it just did not fit in with most economists' intuition. They, for some reason, did not consider the inconsistency of their use of a unique, fully deterministic, supply demand model with an expectation that was inconsistent with that model.

The concept of rational expectations became well known in the 1970s when Robert Lucas and Leonard Rapping used it to solve a Walrasian general equilibrium macro model. This is, of course, a wonderful irony – economists were unwilling to use the rational expectations assumption in partial equilibrium models, but were willing to use it as a method of incorporating expectations into a general equilibrium system – a system requiring much more information processing. I suspect the reason why it was found acceptable there and not in single market analysis was the almost total intractability of the general equilibrium system without that assumption. Simon's goal – trying to specify a reasonable process in a single market – might have been a reasonable goal; the general equilibrium corresponding goal – trying to specify a reasonable process in a multitude of interrelated markets – was almost beyond comprehension. It was likely non-computable.

The rational expectations argument was very compatible with Classical economic thinking – markets work, and the assumption let one show formally that markets work.[2] It presented a fundamental challenge to Keynesians using a general equilibrium model; to use that model with any assumption other than rational expectations runs into logical consistency problems. An answer to the problem was earlier suggested by Alan Walters (1971). He pointed out that Muth's reasoning called only for "model consistent" expectations. Thus, there was nothing inherently rational about the rational expectations used by New Classical economists. What that meant was that if economists' model was not a supply demand model, but was, instead, a complex model that had no solution, any type of expectations could be rational expectations. Thus, to avoid the logical problem, all Keynesian economists had to do was to give up their model that had a unique equilibrium deterministic solution. It is that solution that Post Walrasians suggest. If Keynesians accept it, it means that their model is as logically consistent as the New Classical macro model.

The Post Walrasian answer to the rational expectations challenge is to agree that "model consistent expectations" are reasonable, but that to argue that the Walrasian general equilibrium model is not reasonable. With this answer one is brought back to Simon's approach to dealing with expectations – institutions and process are centrally important in the analysis of the economy.

Theoretically, this new work places macro in a strategic game-theoretic, rather than a functionally deterministic, setting. But it is a complicated layered game that is far too difficult to solve analytically. Yet, for an economy to work, that gigantic game must be solved in one way or another, and that means that coordinating devices – institutions – must be developed to reduce the number of potential equilibria to a manageable number. Macroeconomics cannot be studied or understood without an understanding of these coordinating devices and the limitations these coordinating devices place on individual decision making.

1.6   Post Walrasian macro and New Keynesian macro

The term New Keynesian has been much discussed in the early 1990s. Unfortunately, much of what goes under the name New Keynesian makes the same leap of faith as does New Classical economics. In order to make its microfoundations tractable, many New Keynesian researchers have been forced to make "representative individual" assumptions using partial equilibrium analysis to consider the problems facing the aggregate economy. This representative individual approach implicitly accepts the unique aggregate equilibrium assumption, and sees macro problems as being created by deviations from that equilibrium.

The Post Walrasian approach advocated in the papers in this volume sees the macro problem differently than do the standard approaches. It rejects the representative individual assumption, and the unique equilibrium assumption. There are many alternative equilibria that the economy can reach; institutions limit those equilibria and create systemic stability, but in doing so they impose constraints on the individuals in the economy. Those systemic macro constraints must be considered in analyzing the representative individual considered outside the context of the aggregate within which that individual exists. One cannot assume them away. Thus the representative agent of the Post Walrasian macro is an agent who is constrained by institutional considerations. Spelling out those constraints is one of the tasks Post Walrasians have set out for themselves.

For modeling purposes, the Post Walrasian approach means there is an extra component of the production function that might be called a coordination component. This extra component eliminates the one to one relationship between inputs and outputs that exists with the standard aggregate production function. Given different degrees of coordination, the same physical inputs can yield quite different aggregate outputs. Some of the most important of the coordinating mechanisms in the economy are those that affect expectations.

1.7   Post Walrasian economics is a theoretical and methodological revolution, not a policy revolution

The Post Walrasian view that extra-market coordination mechanisms are necessary to bring about a desirable equilibrium may make it seem that Post Walrasian economics belongs on the activist side of the political spectrum. That is not the case. How to come to any policy decision depends on one's theory of how society deals with complexity, and there is no simple answer to that question. The Austrian spontaneous generation of institutions is one approach, and the Institutionalist indicative planning approach is another. Both can fit in a Post Walrasian framework. The lack of any policy views automatically flowing from Post Walrasian macro can be seen in the authors represented in this volume. Their political views span the political spectrum; some follow from a New Classical laissez-faire approach, some follow a Keynesian activist approach, and some follow an eclectic approach. I don't even know what the macro policy views of a number of the contributors are. Nor do I care.

The Post Walrasian macro revolution is about how one approaches and analyzes the macro economy, not about what specific policies that analysis leads to. This distinguishes it from the Keynesian and New Classical revolutions which had either implicit, or explicit, policy agendas. I suspect that those agendas influenced their analyses – helping these researchers justify their intuitively unsatisfying assumptions: The assumptions had to be OK because they led to the right policy conclusion. It is precisely that connection between policy and model that I believe was wrong with the earlier approaches. Policy views should follow from, not lead to, economic models.

1.8   Description of the papers in the volume

The volume is divided into four sections. The first section deals with the conceptual foundation of Post Walrasian macroeconomics – the vision behind the approach. It includes three conceptual "thought pieces" that will be of interest to a broad group of economists, even those who do not see themselves as macro specialists. The second section contains three papers that deal with historical and analytical foundations of the macrofoundations approach. Those, too, should be of general interest.

The third section provides some specific complaints about Walrasian models and provides some alternative Post Walrasian models. These papers are at a slightly more technical level of discussion, but the authors avoid highly technical discussions and provide papers that give an interested reader an idea of what the technical approaches are, and how they relate to the Post Walrasian conception, rather than extend Post Walrasian theory. The final section relates Post Walrasian theory with Phelps's new structuralist theory, which is representative of the best of the modern development of Walrasian theory and policy. The book concludes with an annotated bibliography that should be useful to anyone planning to do research in this area.

1.8.1   The Post Walrasian vision

The leadoff paper in the volume, by Robert Clower and Peter Howitt, provides a general critique of the Walrasian (they call it neoWalrasian) approach. They argue that you can't just throw in institutions as you need them to make your other equations work. You must have a theory that incorporates the institutions you include in your analysis in a meaningful analytic and empirical way. In the paper they relate the Post Walrasian work to Clower's earlier writings, and contrast a Post Walrasian approach to money with modern Walrasian approaches.

The Clower and Howitt paper nicely spells out the reasoning that underlies Post Walrasian macro. In doing so it focuses in on one of the most important systemic macro constraints on the economy – the monetary system. What Clower and Howitt argue is that the study of the institutions of a monetary economy is inseparable from the study of the nature, structure, and decision process of firms. They argue that "to make sense of everyday phenomena of money and markets we must reject both the neoWalrasian fiction of institution-free economies and the comparably factitious Coasian conception of firms (p. 23)." They then go on to attack two approaches to monetary theory – search-theoretic and cash-in-advance approaches – that fail to incorporate a systemic role of markets and firms. The point they make is a simple, but fundamental, one: Markets and monetary institutions do not simply exist; they are created by firms, individuals, and governments, and any theory that does not incorporate that simple fact will not relate to the economic reality we observe.

The second paper, "Toward a Not-Too-Rational Macroeconomics," by Axel Leijonhfvud, argues along somewhat similar lines as the first, but provides a slightly different twist to the reasoning: Leijonhufvud argues that we have "the relationship between the system and its elements – that is, between the economy and its individual agents – backwards (p. 42)." He argues for a bottoms up, or macrofoundations, approach as opposed to a top down, or microfoundations, approach.

In the bottoms up approach, the total is greater than the sum of the parts, and the total cannot be understood without understanding the interactions. Referring back to his early work, he argues that the coordination problem was too extreme for his initial income-constrained individual coordination to occur, and that, instead, some system with buffer stocks of liquid assets to establish a corridor of stability for the economy was necessary to make it plausible. He argues that an economic system with such a core of stability will work quite well under most circumstances, but will work badly under some (extreme) conditions. He further argues that "choice theory [the core of micro] has been 'a snare and a delusion' for us all (p. 52)."

The economic problem must take account of (1) the complexity of our economy and answer the question of "how believably simple people cope with incredibly complex situations (p. 40)"; (2) the fact that social interaction does not always produce perfectly rational results; and (3) the perception that any tractable model will at best be suggestive. He argues that taking that complexity seriously will lead to the conclusion that the aggregate economy is almost infinitely complex, and that acceptance of his approach means that much of macroeconometrics will be replaced by statistical work in which theory plays a more limited role.

The third paper, by David Colander, argues that there are two fundamentally different visions of macro – a Walrasian micro foundation vision and a Post Walrasian macrofoundations vision. The Post Walrasian vision requires a variety of coordinating mechanisms in addition to the abstract Walrasian market to coordinate individual decisions effectively. The Post Walrasian approach means taking these other coordinating institutions seriously.

These three papers are quite different from one another in their scope, reasoning, and approach, but they are amazingly similar in the vision of macroeconomics they put forward. They all reject the standard Walrasian approach and argue that it must be replaced with one that takes seriously the proposition that institutions are coordinating mechanisms. Combined, they give one a sense of what is meant by "Post Walrasian vision" as compared to the standard Walrasian microfoundations vision.

1.8.2   The analytic and historical context of Post Walrasian macro

The second section consists of three papers that place the Post Walrasian approach in analytic and historical context. The first paper, by Perry Mehrling, looks at the evolution of macroeconomics with an eye to the relationship between the standard textbook model (IS/LM) and the Walrasian model of competitive equilibrium. He argues that the adoption of Walrasian competitive equilibrium as the long-run model for macroeconomics ultimately doomed any attempt to develop both a proper economic dynamics and a proper theory of money. In effect, the Walrasian approach captured the imagination of macroeconomists and in so doing doomed macroeconomics, though it took several decades for the full effects to work themselves out. It is only now, when economists have finally come to understand what the Walrasian approach can and cannot do, that it has become possible to dissociate macroeconomics from the Walrasian model. Post Walrasian economics could not be born until it was clear that Walrasian economics had come to an end.

In the second paper, Barkley Rosser considers some of the analytic foundations of Post Walrasian theory. Rosser argues that if an analytic foundation to macroeconomics exists, it is most likely to be found in chaotic dynamics, not in simplistic dynamics. This is not to say that macro systems are not deterministic in some complicated manner; it is only to say that the manner in which they are deterministic involves second, third, and n^{th} order differential equations which can lead to possible sudden jumps in the system; small changes in a parameter can bring about large changes with seemingly unrelated outcomes.

He points out the importance of extra-market coordination devices and argues that likely equilibria of the model will not only be multiple, but may well be chaotic. He then surveys some of the underlying analytics for Post Walrasian macro. Models with such complex functional relationships often demonstrate sensitive dependence on initial conditions, so that a slight change in the starting point can cause a quite different outcome. They become essentially path-dependent. In the paper Rosser spells these issues out. He first discusses how the complicated nature of the economy makes it impossible for equilibrium rational expectations models to hold. Next, he discusses chaos theory and the history of work in chaotic dynamics in economics. He then moves on to complexity beyond chaos, other nonlinear dynamic macro models without unique rational expectations equilibrium and possibly possessing discontinuous dynamics. He concludes with a discussion of issues involved in overcoming chaos, and the role that policy might have in a chaotic system.

The third paper, by David Colander, gives a different sense of the origins of Post Walrasian macro. He suggests that it was all in Marshall after all. Colander argues that the reason Marshall stuck with partial equilibrium was not that he did not understand the interrelationships among markets, or have the mathematical ability to construct a general equilibrium system along Walrasian lines; it was because Marshall felt that doing so would not provide a useful, workable model. Instead, Marshall felt that general equilibrium issues should be dealt with informally until the math appropriate for them was developed. That has only recently happened.

1.8.3   Modeling a Post Walrasian economy

The papers in the first two sections are all quite readable, and should provide one with a sense of the historical and analytic underpinnings of Post Walrasian theory. But they are not the type of work that most tenure committees are likely to consider substantive research. (Whether such pieces should be considered substantive is another question; the reality is that they often are not so considered.) In the current institutional structure one earns one's tenure working on more technical issues. Since an important purpose of this book is to encourage young researchers (and old ones too) to think about issues, and work, within a Post Walrasian framework rather than in a Walrasian framework, the third section discusses the problem of building up a formal Post Walrasian model. While the subject matter is, by nature, of a more technical nature than that in the first two sections, the technical level of the papers has, by design, been kept low. The purpose of this volume is not to extend the technical aspects of the Post Walrasian research; the purpose is to make the ideas accessible to a broader group of economists, and to encourage other researchers to work within this framework.

The first two papers of this section consider some technical issues relating to modeling the macro economy that are relevant to Post Walrasian macro. In the first paper Robert Martel looks specifically at the problem of aggregation, and the difficulty of extending "representative individual" reasoning to the aggregate economy. He argues that where there is interaction among individuals to the extent that social economic behavior is not the sum of the individual behaviors, the macro researchers cannot use the representative individual assumption.

The heterogeneity of agent responses inherent in broad markets creates endogenous distributional effects which can cause equilibrium outcomes that are quite different from those predicted by a representative agent model. He concludes that the mythical auctioneer and representative agent have only served to obscure our understanding of the higher-order complexity intrinsic to macroeconomic systems.

The next paper, by David Reaume, considers some of the same issues, but from a different standpoint. Reaume, who is trained as both an economist and an engineer, discusses systems theory and what implications it might have for macroeconomic theorizing. He argues that complex systems are not subject to simple, functional form specification, and that the problem is compounded when the aggregation problems are taken into account. He then goes on to look at a particular problem, that of approximating functional forms via a Taylor's series, a typical approximation procedure used. He shows that this approximation procedure can lead to significantly incorrect results. He concludes the paper with the observation that the Post Walrasian approach of relaxing the assumptions of super rationality and environmental simplicity has all the makings of a new paradigm in macroeconomics.

The third paper in this section, by John Bryant, considers the issue of team coordination and the game-theoretic approach to macrofoundations. Bryant shows how the team production concept can provide a foundation to a production analysis that includes coordination. It is that specification of a more complicated conception of aggregate production that lies at the heart of the Post Walrasian approach to modeling the macro economy. In the paper Byrant shows a number of structures that can lead to coordination failures. He argues that there is substantial doubt whether "strategic uncertainty" should be modeled probabilistically, and whether it is logically consistent to do so. He concludes by emphasizing his major theme "that the team coordination approach emphasizes the potential importance of macroeconomic context and institutions for economic behavior, in contrast to classical economics, a major thrust of which is to downplay their significance (p. 169)."

The fourth paper in this section, also by John Bryant, shows another approach to the technical work. Addressing the problem within a game-theoretic framework, as he did in the previous paper, Bryant considers the issue of coordination failure as a game of chicken and strategic decision making. In doing so he shows how one can formulate macro problems in an analytic way, while keeping the analysis relatively simple.

1.8.4   *The Post Walrasian approach vs. the Phelps new structuralist approach*

The final section consists of two papers that relate the Post Walrasian approach to Phelps's new structuralist approach which has been much discussed in the profession. These papers are useful because both the Post Walrasian and Phelps's new structuralist approach are reactions to the same problems of the failure of the standard Keynesian and Classical models to give us a reasonable framework with which to understand developments in the macro economy. Phelps's is an attempt to do so within a Walrasian tradition; it is about as far as one can go within a Walrasian framework.

In the first paper in the section Hans van Ees and Harry Garretsen consider Phelps's theoretical framework. They point out the potential adhocery with respect to the alleged uniqueness of equilibria that runs throughout the Phelps's books. While it is reasonable that multiple equilibria will occur in Phelps's model, Phelps assumes the possibility away because of analytic necessity. Phelps recognizes what he is doing, and, laudably, states that he is assuming "a divine hand guiding the economy to that solution exhibiting the largest output level (p. 198)." It is precisely such an approach that drives a Post Walrasian up the wall; assumptions of divine intervention may have a place in theology; they have no place in economy theory. (Actually Phelps is to be commended for making his assumption of divine intervention explicit. Many Walrasian theories hide it in the math.) The Post Walrasian position is that if multiple equilibria are possible they must be dealt with. Post Walrasians choose to deal with them by incorporating institutions that choose among alternative equilibria, but in doing so place constraints on individuals in the economy. This is why in Post Walrasian macro an analysis of those institutions must be part of the theory. In the second part of their paper Van Ees and Garretsen couch the formulations of economic policy in such a theory. The Walrasian tradition, of which Phelps is a part, doesn't do that. Van Ees and Garretsen point out that the implications of this assumption are fundamental and go beyond Phelps's interesting analysis because the New Classical reliance on the natural rate path of output and employment is dependent on assuming away multiple equilibria.

Whereas van Ees and Garretsen discuss Phelps's views from a theoretical perspective, the final paper in the section, by Colander and van Ees, discusses Phelps's book from a policy standpoint. This paper compares the policy proposals that follow from the Post Walrasian approach with the policy prescriptions that follow from Phelps's new structuralist analysis of the economy. It points out that while there are substantial areas of overlap, there are also substantial differences. Specifically, the Post Walrasian approach offers many more transmissions mechanisms for policy than does Phelps's, and comes to far less certain conclusions. Whereas Phelps's new structuralist approach focuses policy directly on the affected market, the Post Walrasian approach sees policies having potential effects quite separate from their initial effect. In the Post Walrasian approach unemployment can be reduced by means separate from means that reduce the real wage.

1.8.5   Annotated bibliography

The book concludes with an appendix by Hans van Ees and Harry Garretsen consisting of an annotated bibliography. This Post Walrasian research project is in its infancy; a major purpose of this volume is to introduce the ideas to others, and to encourage researchers to start thinking about, questioning, and extending the approach. We felt that a selected annotated bibliography would assist people in that effort. In their paper the authors divide the literature into Surveys, Coordination Failures, Sources of Inspiration/Forerunners, Equilibrium Coordination Failures, Endogenous Fluctuations, Non Linearities and Business Cycles, Indeterminancies and Self-fulfilling Expectations, Aggregate Coordination Failures, and Social Institutions and Coordination. For anyone thinking of beginning research in this area, this paper will be an invaluable resource.

1.9   Conclusion

The papers presented in this volume are certainly not going to settle the debate about macro. Nor will they provide a significant theoretical advancement in Post Walrasian approach; such advancements more appropriately belong in specialized journals. Instead, they are designed to offer the general economist a sense of this new approach and its implications. They do that, and more, and I think most economists will find them well worth the read.

Endnotes

1. In Colander (forthcoming) I spell out the reasons why I believe the term Post Walrasian is appropriate.
2. This should not be surprising. If one starts with a model incorporating assumptions that markets work, and that expectations will lead them to equilibrium, it would be impossible to come up with any other conclusion.

References

Colander, D. (forthcoming). "Beyond New Keynesian Macroeconomics: Post Walrasian Macroeconomics." In R. Rotheim, ed., *Post Keynesian Perspectives on New Keynesian Macroeconomics*. Aldershot, England: Edward Elgar.
Clower, R.W. (1969). "A Reconsideration of the Microfoundations of Monetary Theory." In R. W. Clower, ed., *Monetary Theory: Selected Readings*. Harmondsworth: Penguin.

Clower, R. W. and A. Leijonhufvud (1975). "The Coordination of Economic Activities: A Keynesian Perspective." *American Economic Review* 65: 182-88.

Davidson, P. (1978). *Money and the Real World*, 2nd ed. London: MacMillan

Leijonhufvud, A. (1968). *On Keynesian Economics and the Economics of Keynes: A Study in Monetary Theory.* New York: Oxford University Press.

Lucas, R. E., Jr. and L. Rapping (1949). "Real Wages, Employment and Inflation." *Journal of Political Economy* 77: 721-54.

Muth, J. "Rational Expectations and the Theory of Price Movements." *Econometrica* 29: 615-35.

Shackle, G.L.S. (1953). *Expectations, Investment and Income*, 2nd ed. Oxford: Oxford University Press.

Simon, H. (1978). "On How to Decide What to Do." *Bell Journal of Economics* 9: 494-507.

Timlin, M. (1942). *Keynesian Economics*. Toronto: University of Toronto Press.

Walters, A. A. (1971). "Consistent Expectations, Distributed Lags, and the Quantity Theory." *Economic Journal* 2:155-80.

PART I

THE POST WALRASIAN MACROECONOMIC
VISION

CHAPTER 2

Taking markets seriously: groundwork for a Post Walrasian macroeconomics

Robert Clower and Peter Howitt

In the modern textbook, the analysis deals with the determination of market prices, but the discussion of the market itself has entirely disappeared. This is less strange than it seems. Markets are institutions that exist to facilitate exchange; that is, they exist in order to reduce the cost of carrying out exchange transactions. In an economic theory which assumes that transaction costs are nonexistent, markets have no function to perform, and it seems perfectly reasonable to develop the theory of exchange by an elaborate analysis of individuals exchanging nuts for apples on the edge of the forest or some similar fanciful example.

Ronald Coase (1988:7-8)

Marshall's definition of economics as "a study of mankind in the ordinary business of life" is hopelessly ambiguous; but it effectively highlights one central difference between economics and physical sciences: The subject matter of economics is the stuff of everyday experience. Unfortunately, familiarity sometimes encourages us to treat familiar facts as self-evident truths rather than habits of mind and so unconsciously to inject these "truths" into formal theoretical arguments where they do not belong. Outwardly valid theoretical findings that emulate superficial technical aspects of exact sciences then become problematic because they derive not from explicit assumptions but rather from a confusion of habits of thought with rational analysis (cf. Born, 1962: 226). Because the confusion thus introduced is a matter of conceptual dissonance rather than logical inconsistency, the vacuousness of much supposedly "settled" theory is thus masked.

A case in point is the phenomenon of monetary exchange. Although it is now commonly acknowledged that no kind of exchange intermediary or, in common parlance, "money," can be introduced into conventional general equilibrium theory without violating its logical underpinnings (Debreu, 1959: 28), that is precisely what is done by every currently popular "theory of money," whether it puts "money" into the utility function (Patinkin, 1965) or production function (Fischer, 1974), invokes overlapping generations (Wallace, 1980) or cash-in-advance (Lucas, 1980), or even if it specifies an explicit structure of transactions costs (Heller-Starr, 1976). Although in most cases an attempt is made to motivate the holding of money by invoking some kind of transactions cost, the existence of such costs is ruled out by the assumption (explicit or implicit) that "the auctioneer" establishes the terms of all planned trades without cost to any agent.

To be sure, not everyone writing on the foundations of monetary theory has ignored the contradictions implicit in neoWalrasian monetary economics. In the past two decades, such writers as Feldman, Ostroy-Starr, Jones, Harris, Oh, Kiyotaki-Wright, and Aiyagari-Wallace have rooted their work in a search-theoretic foundation that takes explicit account of some costs of trading. These theories go to the opposite extreme from neoWalrasian theory by eliminating the central auctioneer that costlessly organizes trade, assuming instead that trade is a costly, do-it-yourself activity that takes place without the benefit of any form of market organization. The problem with these search-theoretic accounts of money is that they, like general equilibrium theory, fail to recognize that trading in a monetary economy is neither a costless centralized activity, nor chaotic and unorganized, but is instead organized by a decentralized network of business firms that use real resources and strive to earn profits.

What we are arguing is that the incompatibility of neoWalrasian theory with the "money" of everyday life is inseparable from another well known shortcoming of that theory, its incompatibility with the business firms of everyday life. As in the case of money, this incompatibility has not stopped writers like Debreu (1959) from incorporating firms (Debreu calls them "producers") into their mathematical structures and thereby achieving an illusive appearance of reality. Again, as in the case of money, the incompatibility arises from the absence of any transaction costs of a recognizable form in the neoWalrasian conceptualization of how trading occurs.

Our argument bears a superficial resemblance to that of Coase (1937), who has argued that a useful theory of the firm requires incorporation of transaction costs into orthodox theory. In truth, however, our critique of search-theoretic accounts of money constitutes a rejection of Coase's view of the nature of the firm. Coase's theory of the firm makes the same mistake as search theory in taking the existence of organized markets ("the price system") for granted as an implicit "maintained hypothesis." The central proposition of Coase's theory is that firms constitute an alternative structure that can substitute for markets as an organizational form for coordinating economic activities. It thus begs the question of who would organize markets in the absence of firms.

In this paper, as in other papers that we have (singly or jointly) prepared in recent years (Clower and Howitt, 1992; Clower, 1994; Howitt, 1993), our central object is to argue that to make sense of everyday phenomena of money and markets we must reject both the neoWalrasian fiction of institution-free economies and the comparably factitious Coasian conception of firms. In short, we must deal with markets and firms as economic rather than grammatical entities and, contra Coase, regard firms not as substitutes for but as complements to (more accurately, as organizers and operators of) markets.

A secondary – but closely related – object of our paper is to argue that the so-called "problem of microfoundations for Keynesian economics" has been misconceived, that the real problem is not one of microfoundations for macroeconomics, but to establish a coherent (by which we mean communicable, hence teachable) theoretical foundation for *economics*, which in our view ends up coming to much the same thing as our primary aim: to introduce analytical routines into economic theory that will enable us to make sense of ubiquitous aspects of everyday experience.

2.1   A critique of mechanistic approaches to money

We start with a critique of mechanistic approaches to money, by which we mean approaches based on choice-theoretic, rather than institution-theoretic, foundations, and which introduce *ad hoc* interaction mechanisms to guarantee that individuals will automatically "choose" to hold "money." What makes these theories "mechanistic" is the peculiar procedure, now common in economic theory, of injecting institutional details only as needed for a desired result, with little regard for conceptual coherence, and with no attempt to persuade the reader that the interactions implied by such institutional details constitute an empirically significant and analytically salient aspect of advanced economic systems. In short, these models seek to "explain" phenomena not by arguing that they are the natural outcome of interactions in real-world systems, but by showing that something remotely reminiscent of the facts to be explained can be described using the "neoWalrasian code" of constrained optimization.

We focus here on the two mechanistic approaches – search-theoretic and cash-in-advance models – that presently appear to dominate academic discussion of so-called monetary theory, although the once popular overlapping generations model would have provided an even easier target. The search-theoretic model (representations by Kiyotaki and Wright (1989; 1990; 1991) and by Aiyagari and Wallace (1991) are probably the best known examples) has its origin in much the same stylized depiction of tastes and endowments as Jevons

(1875) deployed to highlight the so-called problem of double coincidence of wants. In these representations, the double coincidence problem is "solved" (George Stigler would have said "murdered") by imposing strong restrictions on the number of commodities that any one agent can trade (agents consume just one good and trade just one other good), and by supposing that through some *deus ex machina* traders are matched pairwise (thus when two parties meet they either trade whatever they hold or they part; there can never exist bargaining over terms of trade,[1] much less "competition" among or between potential traders).

These theoretical fabrications bear almost no connection to the world of experience, in which the double coincidence problem is *abated* (it is never solved in a literal sense because in all voluntary trades, e.g., at supermarket checkout counters, one party must necessarily possess what the other party wants, and vice versa) not by forced pairing of trading partners but through the organization by income-seeking agents of specialized trading arrangements that offer (for an implicit or explicit price) other potential agent-traders convenient facilities for acquiring desired commodities in exchange for other commodities on terms that are specified by the organizer of the market facility. So the problem becomes one not of finding a trading "needle" in a "haystack" of possible trading partners, but simply one of learning the whereabouts of a suitable "market" (self-seeking market organizers have a powerful inducement (cf. Stigler, 1961) to inform potential customers, through one or another form of advertising, both of their whereabouts and of the commodities which they stand ready to trade).

So in experience we find that trading opportunities are given not randomly by nature, or forced upon agents by "authority," but are given instead by business firms: wholesalers, retailers, brokers, jobbers, manufacturers, banks, commodity exchanges, auction houses, employment agencies, mail order businesses, shopping malls, newspaper publishers, accountants, doctors, lawyers, interior decorators, hairdressers, jewelers, and so forth, that find it profitable to organize markets in such a way as to make trading relatively convenient and inexpensive for other transactors. Thus when one contemplates acquiring a consumption good one is not forced to search randomly among all humanity for someone in possession of the good and willing to part with it. Instead, one seeks a firm that can be trusted to have a variety of goods on display and available for purchase on predictable terms. One can also have assurance of the quality of goods to be delivered, advice concerning their use, and sometimes a promise of repair service and availability of replacement parts. The reason one finds such services provided is not that they are costless, or that firms offer them gratuitously, but that the provision of services for a price is in the financial interest of the firm.

The pernicious intrusion of familiar notions that violate the terms of theoretical discourse can be seen in the attempt to use these search-theoretic models to account for real economies in which trading activities are extensive and pervasive. For on reflection it is evident that significant trade would be unlikely to occur in a world of indivisible goods, positive production costs, and do-it-yourself shopping (consider the trading problems of East Europeans and Russians following the collapse of centrally directed economies in the Soviet sphere of influence). The problem of finding outlets for the sale of labor services is of particular interest here.

As writers like Hicks have long and often observed (Hicks, 1989: 29), most transactions in a monetary economy are not spot but credit transactions involving explicit or implicit contracts in which one side promises to deliver future goods or services. This is perhaps most evident in trades involving labor services, where some degree of future commitment is almost always involved on both sides. But it also involves markets for consumer goods, where retail organizations implicitly offer their customers future delivery on demand, and in markets for industrial goods, where long-term supply relationships are crucial to the smooth operation of manufacturing processes. Such long-term relationships could not be maintained in the institutional vacuum of search theory. Family, village, and tribe provide some of the required institutional framework, but for the extensive exchange relationships characteristic of modern economies one needs the services of business firms that spend large sums on establishing and maintaining reputations for fair and efficient dealing; in short, firms that make markets.

The importance of business firms being willing to enter into long-term commitments with customers is most easily recognized when one takes into account an important aspect of the cost of trading that is ignored in mechanistic (in particular in all neoWalrasoid) models, namely that trades invariably entail set-up costs that are incurred with each discrete transaction but whose magnitude is largely independent of amounts traded at any given instant. In particular, there is a set-up cost involved in establishing a trading relationship, which would have to be incurred over and over if relationships were fleeting (as in a world without established trading facilities). Set-up costs are associated with learning about the location and business practices of prospective trading partners, what kinds of goods are regularly stocked, the likelihood of stockouts, how long lineups are at the cash register, how conveniently goods are displayed, how one will be treated if goods purchased are found to be defective, how easily one can conduct bargaining formalities, and so on.

Most markets are, in fact, what Okun (1981) calls "customer markets," in which transactions are made on the basis of repeat business between a firm and its clientele. To succeed, firms must "establish" themselves as reliable sources of advantageous trading opportunities – sufficiently reliable and advantageous, at least, to make it purposeful for prospective customers to incur the set-up cost of arranging to do business with them. Such establishments are what constitute organized markets, and their absence from mechanistic accounts of money indicates that these accounts are attempting to describe a world in which, although something the theorist labels "money" is said to "exist," the absence of any plausible representation of essential market institutions indicates that what the theorist calls money is strictly a figment of the theorist's imagination.

Advocates are prone to defend mechanistic theories by saying that they are simply engaged in "abstraction," that they are abstracting from most of the institutional details of everyday transactions in order to highlight "essential" aspects of the phenomenon they wish to investigate, namely monetary exchange. If it seems unlikely that exchange will occur at all when such models are given realistic specification, then too bad for realism; if analysis is inconsistent with commonplace experience, the problem is neatly "solved" by abstracting from the source of inconsistency!

Personally we have no doubt that abstraction is an essential aspect of theory. The problem with mechanistic models of money is not that they abstract from, but that they aggressively distort, reality; instead of highlighting, mechanistic models hide essentials of the phenomena investigated. By postulating worlds of money without markets, they ignore history (see, e.g., Postan, 1944) which indicates that the rise of money economies is coincident with the rise of market economies.

By abstracting from institutions that create and sustain markets, mechanistic models ignore the obvious fact that every monetary economy is one where markets are organized by business firms, and the bulk of all exchange transactions are with firms, not with other individuals. What is thus ignored cannot be dismissed as minor or superficial. If we grant that the typical firm is a collection of (one or more – usually many more than one) markets, then we cannot help but acknowledge that the problem of "explaining" the origins of monetary exchange is outside the purview of mechanistic models. Among other things, the firms that organize markets in real life typically function on the basis of one or another form of trade credit, and no modern exchange system exists in which the stock of bank and fiat money is not swamped by other media of exchange. Since the start of this century, indeed, most competent students of money have learned to distrust any analysis that fails to recognize the dominance of "media of exchange" created by nonfinancial and nongovernmental institutions. Thus one is led to a very different definition of money, not just empirically, but in terms of theoretical constructs, once one takes into account the crucial role of business firms in establishing markets. Indeed, the effect is fundamental, for we then recognize that the reason why most individuals routinely use money is not that they are balancing choice alternatives in a maximizing mode, but are simply responding to the unwillingness of firms to deal on any other basis (money is "a passport for entry" into the market sector of the economy). In effect, the problem of accounting for monetary exchange is just the problem of explaining why the firms that make markets do not routinely deal in direct barter of goods for goods.

We suspect that much of the confusion concerning money is attributable to the deceptive solution that Jevons and Menger long ago gave by reformulating "the problem of money" as "the problem of double coincidence of wants," an expression that finds its way into most introductory books on economics and is given its final formulation in search theory. This formulation is misleading for at least two main reasons. First, in a market economy there is nothing coincidental about the pattern of goods held by the firms that make markets; their very survival requires them to hold a predictable array of goods for sale. Second, even if it could be shown that monetary exchange solves a social problem of "double coincidence," it is another thing altogether to show that the firms that make markets find it in their self interest to adopt and sustain that institution. Menger's concern with why people routinely accept token money in exchange for useful objects (1892) comes close to the truth by focusing on self interest, but his proposed answer, that money is "saleable," raises more questions than it answers, because it fails to address the ultimate conundrum: Why do firms organize their affairs in such a way as to make a limited number of objects routinely saleable?

The central obstacle to explaining the origins of monetary exchange lies in a phenomenon emphasized by Edgeworth (1888): firms that hold trade inventories enjoy economies of scale. As firm size expands, then as long as there is some degree of independence between the trading decisions of their customers, firm inventories need not expand proportionately to maintain a given probability of stockout. As one of us has observed elsewhere (Clower, 1977), economies of scale suggest that the most profitable form of trade should be organized multilateral barter, in which firms stock all goods in large quantities and allow customers to trade directly (pairwise) whatever they have for whatever they want. Even if some diseconomies of large scale organizations eventually set in, the problem remains: Why do we not in experience observe a small number of very large competing firms, each willing do business in all tradeable objects, with no single commodity playing a special role as "money"?

This problem has not been ignored entirely in the literature. Hicks (1989: 28-9) recognized the importance of trading firms and organizations in his writings on money. Alchian (1977) argued that there is a diseconomy of scope involved in a business firm trying to acquire the specialized knowledge needed to provide trading services in all tradeable objects, and that this diseconomy induces firms to specialize in a small number of tradeable objects, exchanging them directly for something that is known to be accepted by numerous other specialist firms. His account begs the question why firms cannot hire specialists to work under the umbrella of large multilateral trading enterprises, and why such enterprises would find monetary exchange advantageous. Chuchman (1982) has come closest of all writers to addressing squarely the evolution of specialist traders, although his work has relatively little to say as to why these traders are led to create institutions of monetary exchange. Our own ideas as to the appropriate solution are close to the those sketched in Clower (1977), which we are currently seeking to amplify. But the point is that none of these approaches to the problem has much to do with the "double coincidence problem."

The empirical vacuousness of search-theoretic models of money, a direct reflection of their mechanical concern with what Patinkin has called individual rather than market "experiments," is evidenced with equal or greater force in so-called cash-in-advance models, which we now consider briefly.

Cash-in-advance models were first adumbrated by Marshall (1875: 175-76; cf. also Clower, 1967) and first tentatively formalized by Patinkin (1949); but such models are now commonly associated mainly with the work of Lucas (1980 and later) which was motivated by an earlier "dichotomized" budget constraint model of Clower (1967). In the absence of credit substitutes for cash as media of spot exchange (such substitutes are explicitly ruled out in Clower's 1967 paper), the Lucas model requires that prospective buyers have cash in advance to exert an effective demand, hence the sobriquet "cash-in-advance" economy or model. This can be misleading, because the approach is easily modified to accommodate alternatives to cash finance so that agents without cash "in advance" can still exercise effective demands (Sargent, 1987). Indeed, as Kohn (1991) has argued, one can suppose that all spot purchases are financed with trade credit rather than cash.

If "money" is interpreted as means (media) of payment rather than ultimate means of settlement (Clower, 1971: fn. 9; Kohn, 1991: 71-72), then trade credit is every bit as much "money" as are bank deposits. Likewise, if money is treated as a "temporary abode of purchasing power" – an expression used by Foster and Catchings in the 1920s, but (cf. Johnson, 1962: fn. 2) popularized by Friedman in the 1960s – then the equivalence of trade credit and bank deposits is made even more evident by virtue of the fact that most business firms hold purchasing power in the form of accounts receivable following delivery of supplies of goods to regular customers. At the present time, indeed, it appears that bank deposits serve mainly as clearing "reserves" for settling interbusiness trade debts, not as means of payment as traditionally conceived. This observation receives strong support from deposit turnover data on U.S. insured demand deposits (Table 1.23 in FRB Bulletins), indicating that in 1992 an average stock of $0.316 trillion in demand deposits "financed" $263 trillion in settlements (deposit turnover rate of 833 annually).

A common objection to cash-in-advance models is that they are formally just a highly restrictive special case of the earlier, purportedly more general, money-in-the-utility-function model of Patinkin (Feenstra, 1986). Since the Patinkin model was based on a mechanical "stochastic payments process" that in his (*Value and Capital*-based) conceptual scheme had no economic foundation, this criticism is best treated as a tacit "pox on both houses" rather than an invidious comment favoring Patinkin over Lucas.

Like search-theoretic models, modern cash-in-advance models are motivated more by considerations of analytical convenience than concern with empirical verisimilitude or enhanced intellectual comprehension of money exchange. Correspondingly, they offer nothing in the way of useable foundations for monetary theory: no guidance as to why households and firms hold means of payment, no guidance as to what objects should be regarded as money, no guidance about the timing of transactions or about the turnover velocity of financial and other commodity inventories. Here, as in search-theoretic models, highly fanciful, essentially arbitrary "institutional" exchange arrangements – chosen apparently with an eye to "proof" of preconceived conclusions – are simply imposed. In keeping with their mechanistic orientation, reference is seldom if ever made to the bankers, brokers, and other middlemen who comprise the institutional muscle of every market economy, much less to the logistical, informational, and incentive-compatibility problems that these middlemen resolve.

2.2   The problem with Keynesian macroeconomics

The failure of economic theory to deal seriously with the actual mechanisms and agencies through which economic interactions occur in real-world economies helps to account not just for the vapid nature of modern monetary theory, but also for the failure of Keynesian economics to generate a progressive research program. It is hardly surprising that a profession with no clear analytical conception of the institutional workings of a modern economy, and no idea that one is even needed, should be unable to expand and elaborate on the insights of someone claiming that those workings are fundamentally flawed. Keynes's chances of success were further diminished by his own inability to formulate such an analytical conception.

In "The Keynesian Manifesto" of 1934,[2] Keynes (1934: 486-87) contrasted the position he proposed to espouse in his forthcoming *General Theory* – namely, "the existing economic system *is not*, in any significant sense, self-adjusting (1934: 486-87)" – with what he calls "the self adjusting school," whose adherents "...believe that the existing economic system is, in the long run, a self-adjusting system, though with creaks and groans and jerks...."   As one can easily verify through literature from that era (e.g., Robbins, 1934: 186; Douglas, 1935: 85-90), Keynes's delineation of the two opposing schools was assuredly valid at that time. The two schools are less in evidence in modern literature, where the contrast takes the form of the suggestion (initially prompted by Hansen, Klein, Modigliani, and other early proponents of the "rigid wage rate" version of Keynesian economics)[3] that the economic system would be self-adjusting if (contrary to experience) wages and prices would adjust rapidly enough to maintain continuous equality between demand and supply in all markets (Mankiw, 1992: 11-12; Abel and Bernanke, 1995: 18-19).   A more qualified exposition, taking into account virtually all post-1936 developments of the original manifesto theme, is provided by Barro (1993: 560-62, 564-65); but it will be a rare reader of modern work who comes away from it interpreting Keynes as anything but a (slightly old fashioned) believer in "sticky prices" as the central source of chronic dislocation in "the existing economic system."

What position Keynes actually espoused in *The General Theory* is still a source of confusion. Keynes wrote much of Chapter 2 ("Postulates of Classical Economics") on the assumption, called "not theoretically fundamental" (1936: 8), that "labour is not prepared to work for a lower money-wage"; but in the concluding pages of the same chapter he explicitly opted for the alternative contention that, even if wage rates were fully flexible, "There may exist no expedient by which labour as a whole can reduce its *real* wage to a given figure by making revised *money* bargains with the entrepreneurs. This will be our contention."

Controversy continues not so much over what Keynes said as over the question whether Keynes understood what he was saying. More shortly, had Keynes understood what he was saying, surely he would somewhere have offered stronger "proof" that even with perfect wage rate and price flexibility, the economic system would not be self-adjusting. But, to be perfectly candid (a luxury made easy by hindsight), no "proof" that Keynes could have offered in 1936 would have convinced even a weak believer in self-adjustment of the error of that belief. That was the central point made in Clower's paper on "The Keynesian Counterrevolution" (Walker, 1986: 85), though in retrospect it seems that the point was obscured by modelling doodles (e.g., the "dual decision hypothesis") that piqued the instinct to faddishness of the modal reader: Specifically it was there argued that "when income appears as an independent variable in the market excess demand functions – more generally, when transactions quantities enter into the definition of these functions – traditional price theory ceases to shed any light on the dynamic stability of a market economy." Apparently most readers did not understand that by the term "traditional price theory" Clower meant not pre-1936 "orthodox doctrine" as castigated by Keynes, but rather the whole of post-1930 neoWalrasian literature, including Hicks, Lange, Arrow-Debreu, Debreu, and Patinkin, which by 1961 had in Clower's mind become "traditional" (cf. Clower, 1995)[4]

It is one of the more curious ironies of doctrine history that 50 years before the appearance of *The General Theory* the stability question posed by Keynes in the "flex-price" argument of Chapter 19 of *The General Theory* was discussed by Mummery and Hobson in Chapter 4 of their *Physiology of Industry* (1889) and, given the same tools as were available (more accurately, familiar to) Keynes 50 years later, their answer, though denying self-adjustment and evidently persuasive to them, left Keynes unmoved. Even more ironic is the fact that, having directed attention to the self-adjustment issue in his manifesto, and having ranged himself "with the heretics," Keynes effectively ignored the self-adjustment issue in the main body of his already largely written and soon-to-be-published *General Theory of Employment Interest and Money*.

The "fatal flaw" in orthodox doctrine that was a focal point of Keynes's 1934 "manifesto," and that Keynes there linked with a supposedly mistaken orthodox "theory of the rate of interest," he identified in *The General Theory* (1936:18) with the phrase "Supply creates its own Demand," which he took to mean, "...in some significant, but not clearly defined, sense that the whole of the costs of production must necessarily be spent in the aggregate...on purchasing the product." Keynes cited no source[5] for this phrasing and interpretation, causing us to wonder how he might have "translated" Adam Smith's celebrated anticipation of Say's *Loi de Débouchés*: "It is not from the benevolence of the butcher, the brewer, or the baker, that we expect our dinner, but from their regard to their own interest" (*Wealth of Nations*, Modern Library Edition: 14). And how might Keynes have restated the modern *quid pro quo* proposition: "There's no such thing as a free lunch"? Finally, what would Keynes have made of Walras's statement: "...one cannot demand anything without making an offer. Offer is only a consequence of demand" (Jaffé, 1954: 89)?

In pondering Keynes's varied accounts of "Say's law," we conclude that Keynes was simply unable to express the analytics of the self-adjustment doctrine. More particularly, we conjecture that Keynes confused Say's commonsense notion that "products are paid for by products" with a problematic ideological proposition that we shall henceforth call *The Classical Stability Postulate*. This postulate takes for granted the coordinating efficacy of "an invisible hand," operating "behind the scenes" to ensure short-run dynamic stability of the economic system. In more technical jargon, the Classical Stability Postulate presumes that time-series representations of market economies lie "almost always" in the neighborhood of market-clearing equilibrium trajectories. As for its evidentiary base, the CSP appears to have none; it derives simply from anecdote, casual historical knowledge, and ideology (Hansen, 1953: 3-6). Thus it is hard to regard it as anything more than a metaphysical conception of "reality" or perhaps a kind of superstition, as suggested by Mummery and Hobson's casual characterization of it (1889:101) as "...confidence in...the automatic machinery of commerce." In any event, it surely is not a specific conjecture about formal properties of economic models. Keynes's apparent belief (Keynes, 1936: 21) that "Say's Law" was the Classical theory's "axiom of parallels" confused a disguised definition, called "Say's Principle" by Clower and Due (1972: 64-65), with a speculative cosmological principle (Leijonhufvud, 1985). Apparently Keynes then beguiled himself into believing that he had unearthed a logical flaw in orthodox doctrine. The rest (including Keynes's "primer" on labor economics (Ch. 2) and his more technical discussion of the dynamic stability of market economies (Ch. 19) is history (Tobin, 1980, 1988).

In our introduction we said that the question of microfoundations for macroeconomics seemed to us to have been misconceived. As portrayed by Coddington (1976: 1258), the question was how conventional methods of economic analysis should be modified to "come to terms" with the "threat" posed by Keynesian ideas. We say the question was misconceived because we can find nothing in the main body of *The General Theory* that poses a "threat" to received (Marshallian) doctrine; the fundamental issue in the 1930s and since has always been the question of self-adjustment that Keynes posed in his "manifesto" but never seriously addressed thereafter. That is still the fundamental issue, and partly because of misguided efforts (reductionist, fundamentalist, and hydraulic) to defend, amend, extend, and/or destroy the Keynes of *The General Theory*, that issue has yet to be seriously addressed.

As we see matters, the self-adjustment question cannot be meaningfully addressed at any level, micro or macro, unless we first develop analytical procedures that will permit us to make sense of the perceived performance characteristics of the world in which we live. And in our view, "to make sense" means "to devise formal models that are empirically well-confirmed," a criterion that no existing model, neoWalrasian, New Classical, new neoclassical, Keynesian, post-Keynesian, Post Keynesian, New Keynesian, Reincarnated Keynesian, *et hoc genus omne*, comes even close to satisfying. We also believe that our best (perhaps our only) hope for progress in providing a coherent foundation for economic theory lies in the systematic elaboration of empirically acceptable theories of ongoing market operation.

2.3   Firms as market makers

To the abbreviated credo just outlined, we now add our belief that the problem of making the foundations of economic theory intellectually coherent is inextricably linked with the problem of making these foundations consistent with the existence of market-making business firms. That being so, it might seem that our natural starting point would be the work that has grown from Coase (1937) on the theory of the firm, especially since Coase starts with the idea of transaction costs, whose nonexistence in neoWalrasian theory is the essential reason why money finds no place in that theory. But here there is a problem: Coase, as well as those who have more recently extended his ideas (Williamson, 1975; Hart and Moore, 1990) take it for granted that firms, instead of being an essential component of market transactions, are alternatives to markets. In Coases's words "...the distinguishing mark of the firm is the supersession of the price mechanism," as if "the price mechanism" could somehow exist independently of business firms.

If one were not interested in the large questions of economic theory concerning how a market economy coordinates economic activities within an entire society, but were concerned only with the narrower microeconomic question of the degree of integration of the typical firm, then the Coasian perspective would perhaps be appropriate. One could take it as given that other firms earlier have established market institutions to facilitate trading, and concentrate on the degree to which a single firm, regarded in isolation, chooses to organize its production activities within its own structure of control rather than assembling input by making use of markets that other firms have created. But in monetary economics we are concerned with trading relationships in markets, not with "trades" that take place *within* firms; we are concerned with the external market-making aspect of the firm that is essential to our understanding of how the overall economic system coordinates the activities of millions of independent transactors, not the internal aspects of individual decision units. Although the intellectual imperialist proclivities of some economists know no such bounds, surely it would make sense for monetary economists to take as given the internal workings of the units (e.g., kitchen and bathroom production activities of households) that engage in exchange. More generally, a theory of the firm that looks no further than internal relations and does not focus on the firm's market-making activities can never be a significant component of any theory of the economy as a whole, since the economy would not be joined together in complex trading relationships if it were not for the market-making activities of firms.

To be fair to Coase, he recognizes (1988: 7-10) that market organizations are costly to maintain, and that their organization "...is an entrepreneurial activity and has a long history." But he does not take the further step necessary for someone whose interest in the theory in the first place was motivated by the question of how an entire system is coordinated (Coase motivated his theory by reference to an ongoing debate over the feasibility of socialist planning), that is, the step of making market-making activities the focus of his analysis. Had he done so, he would surely have recognized that his central question, that of the scope of operations of a firm, is not so much a question of how production activities are conducted within the confines of the firm but how large a market it serves.

What we suggest is that the distinguishing aspect of firms is neither that they somehow "embody a technology of production" as do the ghosts of firms in neoWalrasian theory, nor that they coordinate internal activities without reference to markets, as in Coasian theory; but that they literally create and operate not just markets but also "the price system."

This concept of the nature of the firm is operationally different from the Coasian conception in at least two distinct ways that put it into conformity with everyday experience. First, it recognizes, as the Coasian theory does not, that the typical business firm in the United States economy, and also in most other industrial economies, is not a multi-owner organization employing thousands of workers, but a single-owner proprietorship, whose internal activities should concern only engineers, psychologists, anatomists, and the most introspective of intellectually imperialist economists, not someone interested in the overall working of economic systems. Except that single proprietorships typically make a much smaller market than do large corporations, which would not by itself be irrelevant in the Coasian view, single proprietorships are at least as important as (and collectively much more important than) large corporations for the effective working of the overall system. Of course, what goes on within a firm is important, at least to the extent that it determines how the firm relates to other economic transactors. But this leads us to the second fact that our conception of the firm squarely recognizes and the Coasian conception ignores: Most of the activities from which the typical firm derives the revenues that allow it to survive involve the provision of marketing services, not the transformation of commodities.

2.4   Conclusion

We conclude by returning to the theme of our introductory remarks, the difficulty of constructing an empirical science in which the relationships studied are matters of everyday experience, a difficulty that arises from the tendency to take for granted the preconditions necessary for the most familiar aspects of daily life. We have argued that recent theories of money, as also modern discussions of multiple-market stability, take for granted (more accurately, impose by arbitrary mechanical assumptions) the institutional basis of exchange, and that to deal with the economics of markets and money we must undertake a re-examination of the theory of the firm. The fact that we have been led to a conception of the firm that is diametrically opposed to that of Coase, despite the fact that we are starting from similar basic premises, is to us one more illustration of the difficulty that economic theorists face in dealing with doctrinal residues that have long outlived any usefulness outside academic classrooms. For it indicates that even someone as conscious as Coase of the need to examine the institutional basis of trading relations (see the quotation in our headnote) failed to recognize that these institutions are made up of the very business firms he proposed to study. Progress in economic theory, and especially in macroeconomics and monetary theory, depends not at all on the development of more elaborate theories of decision making, but does depend crucially on development of an empirically acceptable theoretical account of the market institutions that sustain coordinated exchange activity in the world of our everyday lives.

Endnotes

1. Tréjos and Wright (1993) have allowed a limited form of bargaining to take place, by relaxing indivisibility assumptions, but only by making the institutional framework of the model even more contrived than in the first place.

2. We refer to Keynes's (1934) as a "manifesto" because of its polemical and didactic similarities to the more famous (notorious?) Marx-Engels manifesto of 1848.
3. Dubbed "Bastard Keynesianism" by Joan Robinson in her 1962 review of a volume of essays by Harry Johnson; modernized to "Love-child Keynesianism" by Littleboy (1990: fn.113).
4. See also Howitt, 1993, on "The Neowalrasian Code," and Clower, 1975, on Hicks's role in perpetuating "The Keynesian Perplex."
5. He quotes Mill, but the passage quoted appears to have been "lifted" from Mummery & Hobson (1889) who themselves offer an interpretation of Mill that is flatly contradicted by material at the end of the quoted passage. See Davis and Casey (1977), and Kahn (1984) for further comment.

References

Abel, A. B. and B. Bernanke (1995). *Macroeconomics*, 2nd ed. Reading: Addison-Wesley.

Alchian, A. (1977). "Why Money." *Journal of Money, Credit and Banking* 9: 133-40.

Aiyagari, R. and N. Wallace (1991). "Existence of Steady States with Positive Consumption in the Kiyotaki-Wright Model." *Review of Economic Studies* 58: 901-16.

Arrow, K. J. and G. Debreu (1954). "Existence of an Equilibrium for a Competitive Economy." *Econometrica* 22: 265-90.

Barro, R. (1993). *Macroeconomics*, 4th ed. New York: McGraw Hill.

Born, M. (1962). *Einstein's Theory of Relativity*, revised ed. New York: Dover.

Chuchman, G. (1982). "A Model of the Evolution of Exchange Processes." Unpublished Ph.D. thesis, Department of Economics, University of Western Ontario.

Clower, R. (1995). *Economic Doctrine and Method*. Aldershot: Edward Elgar.

(1994). "Economics as an Inductive Science." Southern Economic Journal 60: 805-14.

(1975). "Reflections on the Keynesian Perplex." *Zeitschrift für Nationalokonomie* 35: 1-24.

(1977). "The Anatomy of Monetary Theory." *American Economic Review Proceedings* 67: 206-12.

(1971). "Theoretical Foundations of Monetary Policy." In G. Clayton, J. C. Gilbert, and R. Sedgwick, eds., *Monetary Theory and Monetary Policy in the 1970s*. London: Oxford University Press.

(1967). "A Reconsideration of the Microfoundations of Monetary Theory." *Western Economic Journal* 6: 1-8.

and J. Due (1972). *Microeconomics*. Homewood: Irwin.

and P. Howitt (1992). "Money, Markets and Coase." Paper presented at conference on Is Economics Becoming a Hard Science? Paris, 1992; published in French as "La Monnaie, les marchés et Coase." In A. d'Autumne, and J. Carelier, eds., *L'Économie Devient-elle une Science Dure?* Paris: Economica, 1995, 199-215.

Coase, R. (1937). "The Nature of the Firm." *Economica* 4: 386-405.

(1988). *The Firm, the Market, and the Law*. Chicago: University of Chicago Press.

Coddington, A. (1976). "Keynesian Economics: The Search for First Principles." *Journal of Economic Literature* 14: 1258-73.

Davis, J. R. and F. J. Casey, Jr. (1977). "Keynes' Misquotation of Mill." *Economic Journal* 87: 329-30.

Debreu, G. (1959). *The Theory of Value*. New York: Wiley.

Douglas, P. H. (1935). *Controlling Depressions*. New York: Norton.

Edgeworth, F. Y. (1888). "The Mathematical Theory of Banking." *Journal of the Royal Statistical Society* 51: 113-26.

Feenstra, R. (1986). "Functional Equivalence between Liquidity Costs and the Utility of Money." *Journal of Monetary Economics* 17: 271-91.

Feldman, A. M. (1973). "Bilateral Trading Processes, Pairwise Optimality and Pareto Optimality." *Review of Economic Studies* 40: 463-73.

Fischer, S. (1974). "Money and the Production Function." *Economic Inquiry* 12: 517-33.

Hansen, A. H. (1953). *A Guide to Keynes.* New York: McGraw-Hill.

Harris, M. (1979). "Expectations and Money in a Dynamic Exchange Economy." *Econometrica* 47: 1403-19.

Hart, O. and J. Moore. (1990). "Property Rights and the Nature of the Firm." *Journal of Political Economy* 98: 1119-58.

Heller, W. and R. Starr (1976). "Equilibrium with Non-Convex Transactions Costs: Monetary and Non-Monetary Economies." *Review of Economic Studies* 43: 195-215.

Hicks, J. R. (1989). *A Market Theory of Money.* Oxford: The Clarendon Press.

Howitt, P. W. (1993). "Cash in Advance: Foundations in Retreat." Paper presented at Montevideo conference on macroeconomics theory, September.

Jaffé, W. (1954). *Elements of Pure Economics* (translation of posthumously published 1926 'Edition Definitif' of the 4th edition of Leon Walras's *Éléments D'Économie Politique Pure*). London: Allen & Unwin.

Jevons, W. S. (1875). *Money and the Mechanism of Exchange.* London: Appleton.

Johnson, H. G. (1962). "Monetary Theory and Policy." *American Economic Review* 52: 335-84.

Jones, R. A. (1976). "The Origin and Development of Media of Exchange." *Journal of Political Economy* 84: 757-75.

Kahn, R. F. (1984). *The Making of Keynes' General Theory.* New York: Cambridge University Press.

Keynes, J. M. (1934). "Poverty in Plenty: Is the Economic System Self-Adjusting?" *Listener* 12: 850-51.

———— (1936). *The General Theory of Employment Interest and Money.* London: Harcourt.

Kiyotaki, N., and R. Wright (1989). "On Money as a Medium of Exchange." *Journal of Political Economy* 97: 927-54.

———— (1991). "A Contribution to the Pure Theory of Money." *Journal of Economic Theory* 53: 215-35.

———— (1990). "Search for a Theory of Money." Unpublished paper, University of Pennsylvania, 1990.

Kohn, M. (1991). *Money, Banking and Financial Markets.* Fort Worth: Dryden Press.

Leijonhufvud, A. (1985). "Ideology and Analysis in Macroeconomics." In P. Koslowski, ed., *Economics and Philosophy.* Tubingen: Siebeck, 182-207.

Littleboy, B. (1990). *On Interpreting Keynes.* London: Routledge.

Lucas, R. E. Jr. (1980). "Equilibrium in a Pure Currency Economy." In J. Kareken and N. Wallace, eds., *Models of Monetary Economies.* Federal Reserve Bank of Minneapolis.

Mankiw, N. G. (1992). *Macroeconomics.* New York: Worth.

Marshall, A. (1875). "Money." In *The Unpublished Writings of Alfred Marshall* 1: 164-76 (see Whitaker below).

Menger, K. (1892). "On the Origin of Money." *Economic Journal* 2: 239-55.

Mummery A. F. and J. Hobson (1889). *The Physiology of Industry.* New York: Kelley (1989 reprint).

Oh, S. (1989). "A Theory of a Generally Acceptable Mediums of Exchange and Barter." *Journal of Monetary Economics* 23: 101-19.

Okun, A. (1981). *Prices and Quantities*. Washington, D.C.: The Brookings Institution.

Ostroy, J. M. and R. M. Starr (1974). "Money and the Decentralization of Exchange." *Econometrica* 42: 1093-1113.

Patinkin, D. (1965). *Money, Interest and Prices*, 2nd ed. New York: Harper and Row.

(1949). "The Indeterminacy of Absolute Prices in Classical Economic Theory." *Econometrica* 17: 1-26.

Postan, M. M. (1944). "The Rise of a Money Economy." *Economic History Review* 14: 123-34.

Robbins, L. (1934). *The Great Depression*. London: MacMillan.

Robinson, J. (1962). "The General Theory after 25 Years." (Review of Harry Johnson's *Money, Trade, and Economic Growth*.) *The Economic Journal* 72: 690-92.

Sargent, T. (1987). *Dynamic Macroeconomic Theory*. Cambridge: Harvard University Press.

Smith, A. (1776). *An Inquiry into the Nature and Causes of The Wealth of Nations*. New York: Modern Library.

Stigler, G. (1961). "The Economics of Information." *Journal of Political Economy* 69: 213-25.

Tobin, J. (1980). "Are New Classical Models Plausible Enough to Guide Policy?" *Journal of Money, Credit and Banking* 12: 788-99.

(1988). "The Future of Keynesian Economics." *Eastern Economic Journal* 12: 347-58.

Trejos, A. and R. Wright (1993). "Search, Bargaining, Money, and Prices: Recent Resutls and Policy Implications." *Journal of Money, Credit and Banking* 25: 558-76.

Walker, D. A. (1986). *Money and Markets: Selected Essays of R. W. Clower*. Cambridge: Cambridge University Press.

Wallace, N. (1980). "The Overlapping Generations Model of Fiat Money." In J. Kareken and N. Wallace, eds., *Models of Monetary Economies*. Federal Reserve Bank of Minneapolis.

Walras, L. (1874). *Éléments D'Économie Politique Pure*. (See entry for Jaffé above.)

Williamson, O. (1975). *Markets and Hierarchies*. New York: Free Press.

Whitaker, J. (1975). *The Early Writings of Alfred Marshall – 1867-1890*, 2 Vols. New York: Free Press.

CHAPTER 3

Towards a not-too-rational macroeconomics

Axel Leijonhufvud

3.1 Computable economics

At UCLA we are establishing a Center for Computable Economics. I have been very much involved in this effort. This may surprise you. That a non-mathematical macro/monetary economist should become an enthusiast for this project is one of those things that "do not compute." But then, as I will explain, we take a special interest in things that do not compute.

One may come to computable economics by many intellectual routes. I will trace my own, not because it makes a particularly edifying story, but because it will tell you what kind of problems I hope we can make progress on by developing the field of computable economics. But before we get to that, I had better explain what I mean by computable economics.

The computer is now being used in a wide variety of fields to model and to explore the properties of complex dynamic systems. We believe that this approach has a big potential payoff also in economics.

In macroeconomics, to take an example close to my heart, the last 10 or 15 years have seen the almost total abandonment of static in favor of dynamic models. Dynamical systems, however, have to have a very simple structure if one is to obtain closed form solutions. The core of this modern macroliterature consists of representative agent (or social planner) models, where the motion of the entire system is given by the solution to a single optimization problem. It is possible to go a bit beyond the representative agent and introduce, for instance, some asymmetry of information. But analytical methods will not take us very far. The properties of more complex systems can *only* be investigated through computer simulations.

Computable economics will not only mean the study of more complex systems; it will also bring a different orientation towards the modelling of the elements of those systems, that is towards the representation of individual behavior.

My friend Daniel Heymann once remarked that practical men of affairs, if they know anything about economics, often distrust it because it seems to describe *the behavior of incredibly smart people in unbelievably simple situations*. Now, non-economists often fail to understand that standard economic theory is useful in a myriad of ways, despite its unrealistic assumptions about people's cognitive capabilities, *because* the interaction of ordinary people in markets very often does produce the incredibly smart result. When it does, it can be a convenient shortcut to model the social interaction process as if it were planned (and policed) by a representative agent or social planner possessed of rather superhuman abilities.

The defense of our craft that I have just sketched is in the best UCLA tradition, going back to Armen Alchian's classic "Uncertainty, Evolution, and Economic Theory" ([1950] 1958). But Alchian was advocating a method very much at variance with the one that dominates macrotheory today, a method "...which treats the decisions and criteria dictated by the economic *system* as more important than those made by the individuals in it. By backing away from the trees – the optimization calculus by individual units – we can better discern the forest of impersonal market forces."[1]

Efficiency, in Alchian's theory, stems less from the *ex ante* rational planning of typical economic agents than from the *ex post* elimination through competition of ill-adapted modes of behavior.[2]

We might start, then, by asking *how believably simple people cope with incredibly complex situations*. If we knew a bit about that, we could then go on to study the conditions under which market interaction will and will not configure the complex system into that incredibly smart allocational pattern – because, of course, social interaction does not always produce the perfectly rational result. Sometimes, as James Tobin once said, "the invisible hand is nowhere to be seen." Ordinary people also interact to produce booms and busts in real estate, credit crunches and bank panics, great depressions and hyperinflations – and much other misery besides.

What we should aim for is to model "systems that function pretty well most of the time but sometimes work very badly to coordinate activities" (Leijonhufvud, [1973] 1981; 1976).

The true descendants of Alchian in more recent times are Jack Hirshleifer (1978), Richard Day (1975), and Nelson and Winter (1982). But standard economic theory has not taken this tack. It proceeds instead from the foundational postulate that people are rational in the sense that they will act in the manner most appropriate to the situation. Rationality is postulated here in the service of the explanatory strategy that Latsis (1972) has termed "situational determinism." Situational determinism is so called because one seeks to explain or predict the behavior of an individual or organization from the external situation *alone*. Bounded rationality is banished in the hope that so doing will guarantee a unique prediction from the given external situation. Unbounded rationality makes "internal" questions of how decisions are reached uninteresting at best. Situational determinism, therefore, is an important fortress in the boundary defenses of economics. It has allowed the economists, most particularly, to ignore developments in the cognitive sciences. By the same token, if we give it up, the boundary defenses come down. We then have to face the frightening prospect that people in other disciplines may have something to teach us!

Situational determinism is implemented through various optimizing techniques, where the only "internal" factor is the criterion function to be optimized. Optimizing models do not allow a natural characterization either of decision-making under incomplete knowledge (ignorance) or of adaptive dynamic processes.

This research program has never lacked external critics. Now it has run into trouble on terms internal to itself. Problems have surfaced both on the level of individual behavior and on that of systemic behavior:

First, certain decisions can be shown to be uncomputable (undecideable). This means, among other things, that individual behavior in such cases cannot be predicted from a description of the external situation alone. (Of course, computable economics will not solve uncomputable problems either – but it will enable us to determine where the frontier between the computable and the uncomputable runs.)

Second, dynamic general equilibrium models have been found generally to have multiple equilibria. Thus, uniqueness is not guaranteed even in large numbers (competitive) cases. Even in principle, complete information on the "fundamentals" – on tastes, technologies, and initial resource endowments – will not uniquely determine expectations and so will not suffice to determine a unique time-path for such a system. Thus, "unbounded rationality" will not buy us "situational determinism" after all. The main attraction of this unpalatable assumption is gone, therefore. To my mind, moreover, the multiple equilibria throw doubt on the behavior assumptions that produce them.

Game theorists take to computable methods far more readily than general equilibrium and macro economists.[3] They are used to dealing with problems where the right equilibrium concept is not obvious and where rationality postulates will not buy you a convincing answer.[4] It is also in this branch of our field that the value of studying complex dynamics on the computer is being most rapidly proven. Even so, it is notable that much of the most exciting work in computable game theory is being done by non-economists.[5] Another group that should make natural allies (for much the same reasons) are the experimentalists. Computable economics is in effect a brand of experimental economics done with artificially intelligent agents.[6]

3.1.1   Bottoms up

Where do computers come in, you may ask? So far, I have been trying to persuade you that, in economics, we have gotten the relationship between the system and its elements – that is, between the economy and its individual agents – backwards.

A sideways glance at what is going on in other fields can sometimes help one's perspective. The field of Artificial Intelligence is in the grips of a controversy between those who advocate a "top down" and those who favor a "bottom up" approach. The "top down" approach relies on the sheer crunching power of a centralized processor eventually to replicate whatever human intelligence can do. The "bottom up" approach, or "distributed AI," relies on interacting networks of relatively simple processors and attempts to make neural nets evolve that, by parallel processing, will handle tasks far beyond the capacities of the components.

Neoclassical general equilibrium theory is, in these terms, quintessentially "top down." That is why, in the absence of externalities, it reduces to the optimal solution of a social planner's problem. There is little purpose to economists choosing sides and doing battle as if these two approaches were mutually exclusive across the entire discipline. But to get a handle on such ill-coordinated processes as high inflations or deep depressions, for instance, we may do better to view the system from the "bottom up." I propose the following conjecture:

> *That the economy is best conceived of as a network of interacting processors,*
> *each one with less capability to process information than would be required of*
> *a central processor set to solve the overall allocation problem for the entire*
> *system.*

Developments in computer science promise to be helpful in eventually implementing a research program along such lines. The first generation of parallel computers were programmed to rely on a central processor to "Gosplan" the allocation and scheduling of tasks to the subordinate processors. Recent work at Xerox laboratories (Waldspurger et al., 1990) has been directed towards realizing truly decentralized distributed processing. Their SPAWN program operates in effect on "market" principles, making the work flow to the processors currently showing the lowest opportunity cost.

Pursuing the parallel computing metaphor would mean that we would have to concern ourselves with the limits to the ability of agents to process information, to manage complexity, and to coordinate their activities in a complex and perhaps unstable environment. The trouble of course is that, from the standpoint of standard theory, this means venturing into rough country where the economist will have to do without many of the accustomed comforts of home.

Economic theory, the way we teach it, consists largely of a hierarchy of more or less standard decision problems, ordered from the two-dimensional blackboard illustrations up to the infinite dimensions of Arrow-Debreu. Much intuition is poured on students at the two-dimensional level to convince them that they choose bread and sausage by equating their marginal rate of substitution to the relative price. Once hooked they are taken by stages, no further intuition supplied, to infinite dimensional problems. Those that lose their faith somewhere on the way fall prey to the Darwinian laws of course grading.

Ron Heiner (1983, 1986) makes the observation that, as we ascend this hierarchy of decision-problems in economics, we always upgrade the competence of the imagined decision maker so that at each stage it is fully adequate to the added complexity. This leaves out of economic theory any and all questions of what behavior to expect when the complexity of the environment increases relative to what the agent can routinely handle. Standard theory implies, in effect, that added complexity is always matched by commensurably more sophisticated decision strategies on the part of the typical agent. This implication, Heiner maintains, is *false*.

In his own "theory of reliable interactions" (my term for it), increasing complexity will beyond some point cause agents to simplify their strategies instead. In environments that demand too much of their information gathering and processing capabilities, they will behave conservatively, "take fewer chances," and use safe thumb-rules of behavior. This may involve ignoring potentially relevant information that a more competent agent would always utilize to optimize. By not trying "to be too smart," Heiner's agent restores a *reliable* relationship between actions and their utility-relevant consequences.

The point goes beyond individuals' ability to precalculate the outcomes of their own actions. The behavioral principle that Heiner models is also his "origin of predictable behavior." We observe people's behavior in a low-dimensional space. If they were actually adapting to events at every margin in a much larger space, we might find their behavior in the observed subspace largely unpredictable, perhaps even incomprehensible. The simplified behavior patterns, the routines and rules, make our actions predictable to each other – as they have to be for complex coordinated processes to be feasible.

Heiner's work demonstrates that it is possible to theorize in a systematic manner about behavior even when agents are not able to cope "optimally" with the full complexity of the system. Leland (1990) is another persuasive example.

3.1.2   Algorithmic man[7]

Herbert Simon has long advocated turning away from the *substantive rationality* of economics to the *procedural rationality* common to the other behavioral sciences. Economists have by and large been resistant to the suggestion because it has not been clear to them how procedural rationality is to be implemented in the context of general economic theory. We propose to take the first step from substantive to procedural rationality in a particular way.

The rational economic man of standard theory is supposed to solve decision problems many of which are *not computationally feasible* ("NP hard") and some of which are *uncomputable* in principle. By insisting on computational feasibility as a criterion that economic behavior descriptions should – as far as possible – satisfy, one does not very much restrict the cognitive capabilities that agents may be assumed to possess. The departure from existing theory is not so drastic as to lose contact with well established results. It imposes a new discipline and leads one naturally to algorithmic representations of both decision rules and learning procedures (including expectations formation). The rule for computable economics modelling will be that you may assume as much "rationality" on the part of decision makers as you want – *as long as you can also specify a corresponding implementable algorithm* by which they could make their decisions.

Algorithms are, of course, procedures and the focus on decision procedures of this kind *avoids the traditional sharp distinction in economics between "given" preferences and preference formation,*[8] *between technology and technological change, between equilibrium and learning or adapting.* Historically, economics has evolved trying to generalize static models so as to cope with more or less dynamic problems. The computational approach lends itself naturally to the characterization of dynamic processes, *some* of which will converge to stationarity if not perturbed.

The paradigm of the *algorithmically rational man* forces one to face up to the irreducible limitations of *any* "logic machine" model of man, namely, Gödelian undecidability. It means that rational behavior is not always inherently predictable. When it is not, the theorist is not entitled to assume without further ado that agents can make unique inferences about each others' intentions. The uncomputability issue thus directs our attention to the institutional structures and behavioral conventions that emerge in society to make it possible for people to interact with reasonable confidence in the predictability of the results of their actions. In the recent literature, sundry institutions are seen as arrangements to control opportunistic behavior. To the need to curb such excesses of rationality, one should add the need for arrangements that provide an environment simple enough for moderate rationality to suffice.

Studying dynamical systems with the aid of the computer means doing a form of *inductive* mathematics. This is not what we are used to, and the foundations are also to be found in branches of mathematics other than those we require of our graduate students today, i.e., in computability theory, complexity theory, and algorithmic information theory (Chaitin, 1990).

The economic man that populates our models has been created in the image of his creators: he *deduces*. Since this is his nature, his creators have to supply him with all the necessary premises required for the correct deduction of the optimal course of action. Our methodological compulsion, on the one hand, to introduce often impossible knowledge assumptions and, on the other, not to admit cognitive limitations both stem from this method of generating predictions of behavior.

Now, in computable economics (the way I envisage it) we start from the recognition that we are dealing with dynamical systems too complex for our own powers of deduction. It is only natural to put the agents with which we populate our toy universes in the same position. Not only must the typical agent cope with an incredibly complex environment armed with only "bounded rationality," he must also make inferences about that environment on the basis of incomplete information.

In Daniel Heymann's and my book, *High Inflation* (1995: 40-41), we use the following illustration in a discussion about expectations formation:

> Learning what behavior to expect from the government is more akin to pattern recognition than it is to sampling from some known distribution. IQ tests often contain questions that ask the respondent to fill in the next few numbers in some numerical sequence: 1, 2, 3, 1, 2, 3, 1, x, y, ... Mathematicians often express irritation over questions of this type because they do not have uniquely correct answers to be deduced. The next number could be any number, since the simple and obvious pattern might be a component of a more complex one or be a random occurrence within a larger whole that shows no pattern at all. The psychologists have a point nonetheless: the ability to recognize patterns is an essential aspect of human intelligence. It is essential, moreover, exactly because it allows the agent to make sense of incomplete information where no uniquely correct inference is to be drawn.
>
> Agents may identify simple regularities in the behavior of the government only to see them "violated" the next time around. The knowledge that information relevant to the pattern is always incomplete means that agents always have less than complete confidence in the inferences they have drawn and recognize the limitations of their ability to predict future policy action. When an observation is drawn that does not "fit" the previously inferred pattern, the actual pattern is seen to be more complex than anticipated – how much more complex is not to be known. This in turn means that whatever the length of the "string" of past such observations happens to be, the agent comes to realize that it is less informative than he had thought....

"The search for simplicity in the growth of complexity is the exercise of reason."[9] Rissanen's theory of stochastic complexity (1988, 1992) offers a rational approach to IQ tests of the type just referred to. His minimum description length (MDL) principle is a criterion for the most economical description of the regularities to be found in "strings" of data. We should not look at Rissanen's work as "only" providing a new statistical foundation to the econometricians; it also offers theorists a way to populate their models with agents that learn by *induction*.

Many economic decisions are obviously based on induction from incomplete data. Recent work in artificial intelligence on problems of pattern recognition shows how such behavior patterns can be captured. Neural net models are capable of representing decisions based on incomplete data (and on fuzzy logic as well). Neural networks and other artificial intelligence algorithms are opening up new approaches to the crucial problem of expectations formation in economics. John McCall's recent work (1990) maps out a program for developing a new dynamic economics that would draw on recent advances in neuroscience and artificial intelligence in the analysis both of individual behavior and of the complex system.

3.2   Why computable? a personal view

My own path to an interest in Computable Economics starts in the mid-sixties with two interwoven problems, namely (i) the relationship between Keynesian and "Classical" economics and (ii) the problem of the "microfoundations of macroeconomics." Let me take the second one first.

The phrase is now dated. It refers to a set of problems much debated in the years around 1970, but not today. If they are now taken as settled – the settlement bearing the label of New Classical Economics – it is in large part because the frame of reference has shifted and the questions are differently understood today.

The central question that was given that label was *How to unify economic theory?* In the 1960s, microtheory showed us a well-ordered universe where competitive markets coordinated optimal individual decisions quite perfectly. Macroeconomics showed us all manner of things going wrong: persistent involuntary unemployment, thrift-paradoxes, accelerator-multiplier systems forever oscillating and incapable of homing in on their equilibrium time paths – and sometimes even the vision of social betterment that could be had by the simple expedient of printing paper money. Microeconomics was superbly rational; macro was not.

Some of that 1960s macro was nonsense – dangerous nonsense in so far as people sought to make public policy on that basis. (Today, we can proudly say, our nonsense is very different from what it was back then!) At that same time, however, my generation took it for granted, I think, that aggregate outcomes of social interaction could easily be "bad." The tension between individual purposive rationality and episodic purposeless irrationality at the level of the system was something that social theory had somehow to resolve. It could not be ignored or defined away.

The tension was to be resolved, I thought, by modelling systems where individual agents "did the best they could" but where things could and sometimes did "go wrong" in the coordination of their activities. (To resolve it by postulating that the system behaved as a single optimizing agent would have seemed nonsensical to us then – and to show you how little I have learned, I am pretty much of the same opinion today.)

The task could not be to "rationalize" all of received macrotheory along such lines. Much of it could not be trusted. The talk about "microfoundations" began, I believe, with the simple idea to use the simplest and empirically robust elements of ordinary price theory – "demand curves slope downward" – to sort through macrotheory and see what pieces could be relied on.

The image from price theory was of a complex system where, as I said, agents did the best they could and "market mechanisms" forced them to obey "the law of supply and demand" and thus coordinate activities. Keynesian macroeconomics as of 1960 had various ways of wreaking havoc with this by proposing, for instance, that people did not respond to price incentives in all dimensions of commodity space or that certain prices did not obey the law of supply and demand.

In a book of more than 25 years ago, I tried to challenge all that and I did so by trying to enlist Keynes on my side, arguing that "Keynesian economics" had taken the wrong track away from where it had begun. So I gave an interpretation of the economics of Keynes where (i) agents do their best to maximize utility or profit, (ii) price incentives are always effective; (iii) all prices do respond to market forces, (iv) and, in principle, a coordinated equilibrium exists.

We should think, I suggested, of a system that differed from the general equilibrium model only in that agents do not know the equilibrium price vector to start with but have to find it. *The economy should be looked at as a machine that has to "compute" the equilibrium.*

Now, there existed a "story," sketched by Walras, of how an economic system could solve the system of interdependent demand and supply equations by iteration in prices. I personified this *algorithm* as "Walras' auctioneer" in an attempt to make it concrete to readers and make them realize that *it would not in general work as presupposed.* Following up on the original insight of Robert Clower (1965), I argued that Keynes's theory implied that this procedure for finding the equilibrium price vector could fail – and that this was his "revolutionary" contribution.

In the late 1960s, of course, no one had heard of "parallel" or "distributed" as opposed to centralized processing. But today we can look at the matter in those terms. Then, the argument that "there is no Walrasian auctioneer" says, in effect, that there is no central processor programmed to solve the problem. The computations to determine the allocation of resources are made in parallel at two hierarchically separate levels: by individual agents and by markets. The array of markets runs algorithms that iterate on the basis of *effective excess demands,* not "notional" excess demands. The elements of the vector of effective excess market demands do not always have the same sign throughout as the corresponding "notional" elements. When the signs differ on some elements, the "parallel computer" will end up with a different answer – a *Keynesian* answer – from that of the hypothetical "centralized computer."

3.2.1   What kind of theory?

Rather soon thereafter, I came to realize (Leijonhufvud, 1973) that by my interpretation of Keynes, the system would fail much too easily and too often to find a reasonably coordinated state – and that a system that bad at self-regulation was not a very plausible product of Darwinian evolution. The income-constrained process had spending too tightly geared to current income. Reconsidering the Keynesian model with buffer stocks of liquid assets added yields a more plausible picture: The system now has a "corridor" of stability and it is only for displacements that take it outside the corridor that it will exhibit serious effective demand failures.

This system will *work quite well under most conditions but will work badly under some (extreme) conditions*. Qualitatively, this is as it should be, I think. All other self-regulating systems that we know in nature or from engineering have *bounded homeostatic capabilities*. Macroeconomists ought to wed themselves to models that work "for richer, for poorer, in sickness or in health." What we have inherited, however, are models of just two types of systems – those that work without fail, and those that always fail to work.[10]

Since that time, I have been particularly interested in "out-of bounds" behavior, i.e., in what happens in economies under extreme conditions: hyperinflations, great depressions, transformation from socialism. In a non-experimental field, one should pay particular attention to observational "outliers" and economics is still very largely a non-experimental field. But such extreme episodes can teach us better than anything else *how crucial are the things we take for granted*.

3.2.2   The Theory of Markets – and Marshall

My book on Keynes (1968) ended with a long section, influenced by reading W. Ross Ashby and Norbert Wiener at the time, advocating a "cybernetic" approach to macro. By this I meant systems built up from components governed by negative feedback controls. The components, of course, would be the system's markets.

A little-known paper by Richard Goodwin (1951) contains the suggestion that we are now pursuing: *"... it seems entirely permissible to regard the motion of an economy as a process of computing answers to the problems posed to it."* In this paper, Goodwin models a market as a single servomechanism regulating price by an iterative procedure.

I built a little model of a single product market with separate controls for output rate and price (1970, 1974). Masanao Aoki (1976) later investigated it in some detail. The Walrasian story iterated only in the price. But the market for a produced good has to have two servomechanisms – one regulating price, the other output. Such a Marshallian market might be represented by two differential equations: (1) the rate of change of prices as a function of excess demand, and (2) the rate of change of output as a function of excess supply price. It is obvious that this little system of two *coupled oscillators* may very easily generate complex dynamics. Marshall tamed the potential chaos, which he did not have the mathematical tools to handle, with the assumptions about relative adjustment speeds underlying his market-day, short-run and long-run period analysis. Those assumptions constrained his market process to go to a stationary attractor. But I do not think he trusted those assumptions. When I realized what the dynamics of that model were like, I thought I understood Marshall's (in)famous distrust of the mathematics of comparative statics.

In the early 1970s I was quite fascinated by my (subjective) discovery that while Marshall's economics may be neoclassical – indeed, it has the best claim to that label if we take it very literally – *it is not based on choice theory* and that, therefore, it might offer an escape from the teleological statics of general equilibrium theory into a brand of process analysis that macroeconomics could utilize. Marshall's agents do not pick optimal points ex ante from given opportunity sets. Instead, they obey simple feedback-based *decision rules* in less than completely known environments. His producers increase output if their supply price is below market price; his consumers increase consumption if their demand price exceeds the market price.

Recently, I have come back to my (1974) treatment of Marshall's consumer in connection with Heymann's and my work on high inflations. I want to use it here because Marshall's theory of demand makes a perfect illustration of computable economic theory with boundedly rational agents.

In standard neoclassical economics, an agent's activity vector is the result of just one single choice. The Slutzky consumer chooses a basket of n consumer goods; if the economist puts him in a temporal context, he will obediently choose an nT-dimensional timepath; if faced with the uncertainty of c possible states of nature per time period, he will unerringly precalculate his contingent paths through this nTc-dimensional jungle, unfazed by the multiplication of margins at which first- and second-order conditions have to be checked. In each instance, there is just a single decision.[11]

If Slutsky demand theory were more concerned with actual consumer behavior, it might be considered a weakness that it has trouble explaining "shopping." Alfred Marshall's demand theory may have other weaknesses, but his *computable consumer* can go shopping – making up her mind on what to buy as she goes along. Marshall's consumer is able to break down her Slutsky cousin's horrendous decision problem into a sequence of manageable pieces. Her main trick is knowing the marginal utility of money, but it helps a lot that she has a cardinal, additive utility function.

The conceptual experiment goes as follows. The consumer receives her income as periodic money payments. Into the present period she carries with her the memory of the "final" utility of the last shilling spent in the latest pay period. This historical magnitude she treats as a constant. She has a marginal utility function for each separate consumer good. This marginal utility, however, is a subjective magnitude that cannot be meaningfully communicated to others. To express demand for the good it has to be made subject to the "measuring rod of money." The number of utils anticipated from consuming the third package of tea divided by the constant number of utils attached to a shilling equals the number of shillings she is willing to pay for a third package of tea. The consumer's decision rule is: If the demand-price for a good, calculated thusly, exceeds the market price: Buy! Knowing "the value of money" (to herself, in utils), she will thus be able to weigh it against market prices of goods in simple pairwise comparisons, make consecutive "shopping" decisions, and still end up at the optimal point on her n-dimensional budget constraint.

A rule of thumb decision strategy of this sort spares one's mental health from contemplating all marginal rates of substitution in n-space before buying a cup of coffee. It is in the nature of rules of thumb, however, that they may introduce error. Using the rule, a Marshallian consumer can set out to spend her money without knowing beforehand all the goods that may be offered for sale, or all the prices, or even her own tastes in all dimensions of the commodity space. Each area of ignorance, naturally, becomes a potential source of allocational error.

Suppose, in particular, that the consumer spends a major portion of her income on commodities whose prices have not changed before discovering – too late – that other goods, which she had been used to consuming, have become significantly more expensive. This will mean that, when the budget is exhausted, various marginal rates of substitution are out of line with relative prices. Such a discovery teaches her in effect that she has been calculating her demand prices with the help of a measuring rod that has "stretched" – i.e., on the basis of a subjective evaluation of what money is worth that, though learned in the past, no longer applies. She must then "recalibrate" the marginal utility of money, as best she can, before setting out to spend next month's wages, and so on. In times of rapid inflation, therefore, this behavior pattern relies on learning of a type subject to higher than average depreciation – and this depreciation is one of the social costs of inflation.

Marshall's "biological vision" was of a complex system in real time consisting of innumerable agents, all subject to birth and death processes, constantly adapting by gradient procedures towards equilibria that keep shifting. His mode of theory construction has its own limitations and deficiencies of which I would single out two: (i) His basic supply and demand apparatus operates totally by feedback, i.e., by adapting based on evaluating the results of behavior in the immediate *past*. It is completely backward looking. If modern theory has gone off the teleological deep end, Marshallian theory is entirely too evasive about expectations. It isn't much use if the subject is asset markets, for instance. With the help of Masanao Aoki, I worked out a Marshallian model of investment in which forward-looking expectations are revised on the basis of feedback (1988). If the lag in feedback is minimal and Darwinian pressures strong, the expectations of the "surviving fittest" will converge on rational expectations. (ii) Simple "cellular automata" agents constantly crawling up their profit- or utility-mountains will not do well if their habitat is full of non-convexities. Increasing returns in production means indivisibilities are present and gradient rules will not help you cope with integer constraints. Marshall did not succeed in providing a simple, convincing description of the behavior of firms operating under increasing returns matching the behavior rule followed by his increasing marginal cost producers. His theory of producers' behavior, Sir John Hicks used to maintain, dealt with a world that was already disappearing around the turn of the century. Manufacturing in the 20th century has been predominantly a story of decreasing cost firms operating as price setters rather than price takers.

Of course, a hundred years later, we are doing no better. We are if anything more addicted to models where people only choose quantities and no one decides prices. I can offer myself as a warning example, having dealt with increasing returns and the division of labor in a couple of papers (1986; 1989) – in which the representative firm's short-run decision problem is not formalized or solved. It is a problem requiring combinatorial optimization methods, and finding an effective algorithm that has a plausible behavioral interpretation will be a great challenge for computable economics.[12]

3.2.3   Optimal choice versus adaptive behavior

As I have explained, I find Marshall interesting as a neoclassical economist who does *not* put his theory on choice-theoretical foundations. At the risk of some exaggeration – a risk I have bravely decided to take – let me suggest that choice theory has been "a snare and a delusion" for us all.

Perhaps, I ought to explain that a bit(?). When the context is social, the choice paradigm needs to be supplemented with a competitive equilibrium or other coordinating assumption so that opportunity sets are clearly defined. When you then extend the application of the paradigm to intertemporal planning, the result is a view of the world as a Clockwork – a machine whose future path is predetermined once wound up at the origin of time. This is a profoundly unsatisfactory image of an economic system and there is no real escape from it. (Many economists do, of course, regard stochastic clockworks as providing an escape, but I do not so regard them.) My disenchantment with this brand of microfoundations

– spelled out in my Marshall Lectures in 1974 but never published – was such that, to be frank, I drifted out of the professional mainstream from the mid 1970s onwards, as intertemporal optimization became all the rage.

As a final illustration of the difference between the two approaches, let me take a problem from my recent work with Heymann on high inflations. To my mind, the core of the literature on inflation theory portrays a system that remains "much too rational" no matter how high the inflation rate; the main if not the only consequences of inflation are the sundry distortions due to the so-called "inflation tax." Basically, this view of the matter is in the clockwork tradition.

Now, one of the things that happen in inflations is that *markets disappear*. In the quite moderate U.S. inflation of the 1970s, the 30-year bond market disappeared and the 30-year fixed rate mortgage market just about disappeared. In high inflations – by which we mean those where people quote inflation rates per month rather than *per annum* – the longest maturities for nominal contracts that survive are often shorter than 12 months and sometimes no longer than 6 weeks. The questions are: Why do these intertemporal markets disappear? and What difference does it make?

If inflationary policies introduce new uncertainties, clockwork theory would make us expect new markets to emerge to cope with the added contingencies. But if they disappear instead of multiplying, it is not clear that the clockwork is impaired thereby. Our standard *incredibly smart agents will most likely find the situation unbelievably simple*: they will just replace equilibrium prices in the missing markets with the rational expectations of the same prices and proceed to draw up the their intertemporal consumption plans exactly as if the markets were really there. The question then becomes whether it really matters to them that some of the planned trades cannot be executed already at $t = 0$. I am not suggesting that the answer to that one is a simple No. There is by now a sizeable technical literature on missing markets, investigating the conditions under which people can or cannot get around imposed constraints not to transact in parts of the commodity space. What is less clear is why such clever people choose to labor under these constraints.

To understand what is actually going on, I strongly believe, one must abandon this entire mode of theory construction and rethink the matter from Alchian's evolutionary perspective. Here *believably simple people face incredible complications* and, finding themselves unable to precalculate the consequences, give up trading in most future markets. New externalities[13] appear where price interaction has withered away. As coordinating mechanisms disappear, imperfect decision makers no longer face the same Darwinian pressures to adapt. Potential gains from trade are left unexploited. Various inefficient practices survive. Resources fail to find their highest valued uses.[14]

The difference between the two approaches matters. The rationally expectant optimizers of today's standard theory do not need market interaction to teach them how to attain the efficient social outcome. Alchian's imperfect decision-makers do. But an Alchian market process is not an aggregate of mutually consistent optimal decisions. So, it cannot be modelled in the standard way. But I believe we can do it in the computable way.

Endnotes

Distinguished Guest Lecture, 1992 Annual Meeting of the Southern Economic Association and first published in the *Southern Economic Journal* (1993; Vol. 60, No. 1: 1-13) and used with permission. An earlier version of this lecture was given at the 1992 Aalborg University-UCLA Summer School in Computable Economics. My borrowings below from my book with Daniel Heymann (1995) are evidence of my debt to him. I am particularly grateful to my colleague, Kumaraswamy Velupillai, who has taught me all I know about computability, complexity, and related matters. That I do not know more than I do is not his fault!

1. Alchian (1958:209). To the passage quoted, Alchian appends a note advocating "...reverting to a Marshallian type of analysis combined with the essentials of Darwinian evolutionary natural selection." Compare the notes on Marshall later in my paper.
2. Recent work by Gode and Sunder (1993), following Gary Becker (1962) rather than Alchian, does away with the "trees" altogether to get a clearer picture of the "forest": They demonstrate that "zero intelligence traders" disciplined by simple budget constraints and interacting under double auction rules will succeed in extracting a very high proportion of the maximum attainable surplus. It is particularly noteworthy that Darwinian evolutionary mechanisms play no part in generating this result.
3. See, however, Sargent (1993).
4. See, e.g., Binmore (1987; 1988) and Friedman (1991).
5. Some recent examples are the papers by Glance and Huberman (1994), Lomborg (1992), and Novak and May (1992).
6. Compare the views of Holland and Miller (1991).
7. .. a few millennia later than Neolithic Man.
8. A more radical computable formulation asserts "the irrelevance of primitive assumptions of preference structures for the analysis of predictable behaviour." Rustem and Velupillai (1990: 420).
9. Quoting Rustem and Velupillai (1990: 432).
10. The most recent multiple equilibria models are adopting a somewhat similar perspective. Now, however, the context is growth rather than coordination and the contrasts drawn are between rapid growth and poverty traps rather than between equilibrium and far-from-equilibrium states.
11. This modern conception of rational choice may be contrasted, for instance, to that of Pareto who was willing to postulate a rationality in the economic realm that he did not expect elsewhere because he conceived of economic behavior as consisting largely of *frequently repeated actions* the outcomes of which could be checked against intentions in a direct and reliable manner. Pareto's agents *learn to be rational* through trial and error. They will fit perfectly into Alchian's evolving world. The modern Slutskyite's consumption choice is not such a repeated action – it is a once-in-a-lifetime choice.
12. For an attack on it, see Scarf (1989).
13. Actually, some addition to our terminology may be needed here. A "missing market" gives rise to a "true" externality (I think we can agree) when the reason for its absence is that property rights have not been created in the relevant good. This, however, does not fit the "disappearing" intertemporal markets. In this case price interaction is currently not taking place (and

misallocations can occur due to this lack of communication) but it is known that it will take place in the future. People will do their best to *anticipate* what that price will be once a market makes its appearance. "Quasi-externality" is hardly euphonius – but some such term is needed.

14. In a sense, of course, survival still goes to the fittest – but it is a tautological sense because inflation changes the definition of "fitness" (1986).

References

Alchian, A. A. (1950). "Uncertainty, Evolution, and Economic Theory." *Journal of Political Economy*, 50. Reprinted in R. B. Heflebower and G. W. Stocking, ed., *Readings in Industrial Organization and Public Policy*. Homewood, Ill.: Richard D. Irwin, Inc., 1958.

Aoki, M. (1976). *Optimal Control and System Theory in Dynamic Economic Analysis*. Amsterdam: North-Holland.

Aoki, M. and A. Leijonhufvud (1988). "The Stock-Flow Analysis of Investment." In M. Kohn and S.C. Tsiang, eds., *Finance Constraints, Expectations, and Macroeconomics*. Oxford: Clarendon Press.

Becker, G. S. (1962). "Irrational Behavior and Economic Theory." *Journal of Political Economy*, 70: 1-13.

Binmore, K. (1987). "Modelling Rational Players." Part I. *Economics and Philosophy*: 179-214.

(1988). "Modelling Rational Players." Part II. *Economics and Philosophy*: 9-55.

Chaitin, G. J. (1990). *Algorithmic Information Theory*. Cambridge: Cambridge University Press.

Clower, R. W. (1965). "The Keynesian Counter-Revolution." In F. H. Hahn and F. Brechling, eds., *The Theory of Interest Rates*. London: Macmillan, 103-125.

Day, R. H. (1975). "Adaptive Processes and Economic Theory." In R. H. Day and T. Groves, *Adaptive Economic Models*. New York: Academic Press, 1-38.

Friedman, D. (1991). "Evolutionary Games in Economics." *Econometrica*, 59: 637-666.

Glance, N. S. and B. A. Huberman (1994). "Dynamics of Social Dilemmas." *Scientific American* 270: 76-81.

Gode, D. K. and S. Sunder (1993). "Allocative Efficiency of Markets with Zero Intelligence Traders: Market as a Partial Substitute for Individual Rationality." *Journal of Political Economy* 10: 119-37.

Goodwin, R. (1951). "Iteration, Automatic Computers, and Economic Dynamics." *Metroeconomica*, 3: 1-7.

Heiner, R. A. (1983). "The Origin of Predictable Behavior." *American Economic Review*, 83: 560-95.

(1986). "Uncertainty, Signal-Detection Experiments, and Modelling Behavior." In R. N. Langlois, ed., *Economics as Process: Essays in the New Institutional Economics*. Cambridge: Cambridge University Press.

Heymann, D. and A. Leijonhufvud (1995). *High Inflation*. Oxford: Oxford University Press.

Hirshleifer, J. (1978). "Natural Economy versus Political Economy." *Journal of Social and Biological Structures* 1: 319-37.

Holland, J. H. and J. H. Miller (1991). "Artificial Adaptive Agents in Economic Theory." *American Economic Review*: 365-70.

Latsis, Spiro J. (1972). "Situational Determinism in Economics." *British Journal for the Philosophy of Science* 27: 51-60.

Leijonhufvud, A. (1968). *On Keynesian Economics and the Economics of Keynes*. New York: Oxford University Press.

(1970). "Notes on the Theory of Markets." *Intermountain Economic Review* Fall: 1-13.

(1973). "Effective Demand Failures." *Swedish Journal of Economics* 75: 27-58, Reprinted (1981) in *idem, Information and Coordination*. New York: Oxford University Press.

(1974). "Maximization and Marshall." Unpublished 1974 Marshall Lectures, Cambridge University.

(1976). "Schools, 'Revolutions,' and Research Programmes in Economic Theory." In S. J. Latsis, ed., *Method and Appraisal in Economics*. Cambridge: Cambridge University Press. Reprinted in *Infomation and Coordination, op. cit.*

(1984). "Inflation and Economic Performance." In B. Siegel, ed., *Money in Crisis*. San Fransisco: Pacific Institute.

(1986). "Capitalism and the Factory System." In R. N. Langlois, ed., *Economics as Process: Essays in the New Institutional Economics*. Cambridge: Cambridge University Press.

(1989). "Information Costs and the Division of Labor." *International Social Science Journal* 120:165-76.

Leland, J. W. (1990). "A Theory of Approximate Expected Utility Maximization." Forthcoming.

Lomborg, B. (1992). "The Structure of Solutions in the Iterated Prisoner's Dilemma." University of Copenhagen, Institute of Political Science Working Paper.

McCall, J. (1990). "The 'Smithian' Self and Its 'Bayesian' Brain." UCLA Working Paper No. 596.

Nelson, R. R. and S. G. Winter (1982). *An Evolutionary Theory of Economic Change*. Cambridge, Mass.: Harvard University Press.

Novak, M. A. and R. M. May (1992). "Evolutionary Games and Spatial Chaos." *Nature* October 29: 359

Rissanen, J. (1988). "Understanding the 'Go' of It." *IBM Research Magazine*. Winter.

(1992). "Stochastic Complexity, Information, and Learning." Working Paper, IBM Almaden Research Center.

Rustem, B. and K. Velupillai (1990). "Rationality, Computability, and Complexity." *Journal of Economic Dynamics and Control* 14:419-32.

Sargent, T. (1993). *Bounded Rationality in Macroeconomics*. Oxford: Oxford University Press.

Scarf, H. E. (1989). "Mathematical Programming and Economic Theory." Cowles Foundation Discussion Paper No. 930.

Velupillai, K. (1992). "The Computable Approach to Economics." Lecture at the Aalborg University-UCLA Summer School in Computable Economics.

Waldspurger, C. A., T. Hogg, B. Huberman, J. O. Kephart, and S. Stornetta (1990). "SPAWN: A Distributed Computational Economy." Xerox System Sciences Laboratory Working Paper SSL-89-18.

CHAPTER 4

The macrofoundations of micro

David Colander

In the opening chapter of his pathbreaking textbook, Paul Samuelson reproduced a picture from N. R. Hanson's *Patterns of Discovery* (1961).[1] From one perspective, it looked like a picture of antelopes; from another perspective, it looked like a picture of birds. The point of the example was that the same reality can look fundamentally different depending on one's perspective and that revolutions in a discipline occur through these changes in perspective.

Perspective is fundamental to understanding theories, because, ultimately, any theory is built on a vision – a way of putting reality together. That vision guides one in choosing assumptions and in interpreting results. Vision allows one to make the leap of faith necessary to believe that one's "theory" is more than a jumble of meaningless tautological equations. It was Keynes's vision that made Keynesian economics "spread like a disease among South Sea Islanders" (Samuelson, 1964), and it was Lucas's vision that made New Classical economics spread like the flu virus in a university. (In both cases economists over 50 were immune.)

This paper argues that such a change in perspective is currently underway in macro and that a new Post Walrasian perspective which requires a "macrofoundations of micro" is emerging. This new perspective changes the nature of the macroeconomic debate and provides a theoretical foundation for a non self-adjusting macroeconomic revival, in which the Walrasian unique equilibrium model is seen as a special case of the more general Post Walrasian multiple equilibria model. It argues that the Post Walrasian perspective encompasses the Keynesian perspective and, thus, rather than the Keynesian model being a special case of the Classical model in which nominal wage inflexibility is assumed (the way things are currently), the Classical model is seen as a special case of the more general Keynesian model.

This perspective is arrived at by carrying Lucas's critique of macro models to its logical conclusion. Not only does policy change the structural characteristics of the model, so do individuals' expectations; without making *ad hoc* assumptions, it is impossible to distinguish structural and non-structural changes.

The first Keynesian revolution set off by the publication of *The General Theory* initially involved such a change in perspective, and it is not surprising that Samuelson's book, which translated the Keynesian revolution into a textbook model that students could follow, should have included the bird/antelope picture. The change in perspective that the first Keynesian revolution brought about completely separated macro from micro. They were different approaches: macroeconomics looked at the aggregate economy from one perspective, micro from another. The new macro perspective allowed one to talk about interrelationships among aggregates without specifying the underlying individual choice theoretic framework, while the micro perspective retained the traditional individual choice theoretic perspective in which individuals maximized utility over the entire set of choices.[2]

4.1   The neoKeynesian evolution and the microfoundatons of macro

This dual perspective was problematic, since most individuals agreed that micro and macro are related and should be unified. Much work in what came to be called neoKeynesian economics involved relating the macro analysis to microeconomic choice theoretic notions. That work began a shift in perspective away from a macro- and toward a micro-perspective, a shift in perspective that would ultimately lead to the New Classical revolution. The reason is that the neoKeynesian integration of micro and macro was done from a micro perspective. As the work became known, a slow and subtle change from a macro- to a micro-perspective took place in researchers' minds. The evolving neoKeynesian perspective differed from the old Keynesian perspective, and as the evolution proceeded, those antelopes kept looking more and more like birds.

The neoKeynesian work was not the only work being done that focused on microfoundations. As the neoKeynesian developments were occurring, simultaneously much work in micro was relating individual choice to aggregate general equilibrium results over infinite horizons. These two sets of work started to come together in the late 1960s and early 1970s as the microfoundations-of-macro literature developed. That microfoundations-of-macro work attempted to connect macro results with microfoundations directly, in a much more fundamental way than previous neoKeynesian attempts. The basic premise of the microfoundations-of-macro literature was that if an aggregate model were to assume any individual behavior, such as is implied by wage or price inflexibility, that behavior had to come out of a microeconomic choice theoretic framework. This work extended the shift in perspective that the neoKeynesian evolution had begun; the picture was looking more like birds all the time. All those old Keynesians who insisted that they kept seeing antelopes were having illusions (money or otherwise).

This microfoundations-of-macro work was soon incorporated with work on rational expectations that originated with Muth (1961), but that did not become well known until it was picked up by Robert Lucas (1972) and other New Classical macroeconomists. What New Classical macroeconomics did was to bring macro expectations into the microeconomic choice theoretic framework and complete the change in perspective. In a New Classical perspective there was no question that the picture was one of birds. From an analytic viewpoint, the result was impressive because the rational expectations assumption allowed a broader integration of microeconomic individual choice theory with macro than had hitherto existed.

That combination was fruitful in the sense that it generated significant research by both Classicals and Keynesians. New Classicals, such as Robert Lucas (1975) and Thomas Sargent and Neil Wallace (1976), showed that, assuming competitive markets and a unique equilibrium, the macroeconomic problem disappeared when individuals had rational expectations.

This New Classical work led to Keynesian responses that offered a number of justifications for the Keynesian approach. Elsewhere, I have divided those responses into two categories: New Keynesian and New neoKeynesian (Colander, 1992a; 1992b). The New neoKeynesian response, which includes the work of economists such as Gregory Mankiw and David Romer (1991), took a micro perspective and attempted to explain why individuals would rationally choose to override the Walrasian market. This New neoKeynesian work showed that with fixed money contracts, menu costs, or various types of imperfect information, Keynesian results could be coaxed out of the traditional microeconomic choice theoretic foundations.

This was not an easy thing to do; since this work was using a micro perspective, it was the equivalent of convincing people that Classical birds were really Keynesian antelopes, even though they looked, felt, and chirped like birds. If the people you were convincing were nearsighted enough, and wanted to believe, they could be convinced, but, from a micro perspective, with clear eyesight, a New neoKeynesian antelope looks like what it is, a Classical bird in antelope clothing.

A key element of this New neoKeynesian work is the representative agent approach. New neoKeynesian formal analysis is done at the partial equilibrium level, and then the results are intuitively extended to the aggregate economy using a representative agent analogy. No explicit consideration is given to the problems of that aggregate extension of the partial equilibrium analysis, and the resulting analysis is meshed into a unique-equilibrium Walrasian framework.

I initially classified that coaxing of Keynesian results out of a traditional choice theoretic framework as New neoKeynesian rather than simply New Keynesian to separate that work from another set of work, which I now call Post Walrasian, that makes a much more substantive shift in response to the New Classical challenge. Post Walrasian work involves a fundamental change in perspective, and from that new perspective, the macro picture is clearly one of antelopes, and one can see birds in it only by the reverse mental gymnastics used by the New neoKeynesians.

This work starts from the premise that one cannot analyze the aggregate using a representative agent analogy because any analysis that does not deal with those interdependencies is conceptually flawed.

4.2   The importance of interdependencies and multiple equilibria

Post Walrasian work changes the perspective; it gives up the unique-equilibrium Walrasian competitive framework, replacing it with a multiple equilibrium framework. In a Post Walrasian framework disequilibrium adjustment paths can affect equilibrium outcomes and there is no unique connection between individual decisions and equilibrium outcomes. All decisions are conceived as fully interdependent with other decisions.

Any resulting formal macroeconomic model that follows from this vision is hopelessly complex from an analytic standpoint, but the problems it describes are intuitively obvious. Depending on the nature of the interdependencies assumed among individual decision makers, any aggregate outcome is possible. The resulting equilibria are sometimes called sunspot equilibria – because an equilibrium can be caused by seemingly irrelevant aspects of the economy; in other models they are called path-dependent equilibria, because the equilibria arrived at are dependent on the disequilibrium adjustment paths that led to those equilibria. But the key element of these models is that almost any result is possible, depending on where one begins.

The existing formal Post Walrasian models and discussion are embryonic. No Post Walrasian claims that their models are any more than suggestive of the dynamic interdependencies that exist. What distinguishes Post Walrasians is their unwillingness to make the leap of faith that allows them to brush aside the problems of interdependencies and to assume a unique aggregate equilibrium.

Giving up that micro framework changes the perspective and the nature of the questions asked. From this multiple-equilibria perspective the New neoKeynesian response, which tries to justify the Keynesian view within a unique-equilibrium framework, is viewed as a slight modification to Classical economics. It is tangential to the main Keynesian analysis since from a multiple-equilibria macro perspective there is no need to justify fixed nominal wages and prices as a reason for output fluctuation. An output fluctuation is simply a movement from one equilibrium to another and is to be expected. It does not need explanation. What needs explanation is why the real-world aggregate economy is as stable as it is – why output does not fluctuate more than it does.

The stability of output in the real-world economy is often used as implicit justification for the unique-equilibrium assumption. Post Walrasians do not accept that; they believe the stability is caused by conventions and institutional constraints on individual behavior and that to understand the general stability and periods of instability in the economy requires a far more complicated analysis than can be captured in a model assuming a unique aggregate equilibrium.

The absence of a unique equilibrium poses serious questions for the New Classical resolution to the macro/micro integration, since many alternative choices may be individually rational, each consistent with a different aggregate equilibrium. Even using all information available to them through the market, individuals, acting alone, will have no way of knowing which equilibrium to expect. One arrives at a unique equilibrium only by making strong *ad hoc* assumptions. From a Post Walrasian perspective, it is Classical, not Keynesian, economics that is guilty of "adhocery" in its assumption of a unique equlibrium. (This is not to say that Keynesian work doesn't exhibit adhocery elsewhere.)

From the Post Walrasian multiple-equilibria perspective, talking about a microfoundation of macro, independent of institutional context, is meaningless. In specific, traditional individual choice theory, in which aggregate results correspond to non-contextually determined representative agent decisions, is irrelevant to the microfoundations to macro. The Post Walrasian perspective maintains that before there is any hope of undertaking meaningful micro analysis, *one must first determine the macro context within which that micro decision is made*. It is that macro context that lets individuals choose among likely multiple equilibria and makes the choice theoretic foundation contextually relevant. In doing so, however, the macro context imposes institutional constraints on individual decision makers, and these constraints must be considered in deriving any microfoundations to macro. Thus establishing appropriate macrofoundations of micro must logically be done before one establishes any microfoundations of macro, and any micro analysis independent of a macrofoundation is irrelevant game-playing.[3]

Now one could argue that Walrasian perfectly competitive markets provide an appropriate macrofoundation. Elsewhere I have argued that they do not for three reasons. The first is that they are institutionally unstable (Colander, 1994), by which I mean that some individuals will have an incentive to monopolize and change the perfectly competitive institutions to monopolistic ones and that at the margin no one will have an incentive to oppose them. Thus, Walrasian markets do not meet the minimum logical requirement of local stability. Any institutional structure used as a macrofoundation should be, at least, locally stable.

The second reason is that the traditional Walrasian general equilibrium structure requires more rationality than individuals have. It requires them to make billions of rational calculations every moment of every day. Doing so is the equivalent of assuming that because a person can jump off the ground – can make a contextual rational decision – that the person can fly like a bird – can make non-contextual rational decisions. It is far more reasonable to picture individuals, like ourselves, with limited brainpower, able to exhibit some rationality, but relying on inertia and rules of thumb to make many decisions. If individuals are rational, their rationality is a bounded rationality within an institutional and expectational context. The macrofoundations of micro must specify that context.

The third reason is related to the second and concerns the absence of money in the Walrasian general equilibrium system. Money is a social convention that makes the aggregate economy operate more efficiently. It affects the coordination of the entire system and reduces the number of calculations an individual must make. Money has *no role* if individuals are super-rational and there is a perfectly competitive system. But it does have a role in our real-world economy and hence in any real-world relevant macrofoundations of micro. But money enters the economy not as a component of individual utility, or even aggregate production functions; instead, it is part of the macrofoundational structure of the economic system, and must be modeled as such.[4] Questions about money illusion and whether there is a dichotomy between the real and nominal sectors are non-questions since, in the macro institutional structure, the real and nominal decisions are so entwined that illusion and reality blend into one. Thus, in the Post Walrasian literature, the entire attempt to integrate money into the Walrasian general equilibrium system is a needless waste of time. It must be integrated in the macrofoundations of micro, and its integration is incompatible with a Walrasian general equilibrium system.

The analytic basis of this macrofoundations-of-micro approach goes back to Herbert Simon's work on bounded rationality (1959). Simon argues that deciding over an entire range of possible choices exceeds the processing capacity of economic decision making units. Because it does, the decision making process has meaning only with a macro context. There is no one-to-one mapping between aggregate results and individual decisions. Put another way, the aggregate economy acquires a life of its own.

This view of the aggregate economy suggested by the Post Walrasian approach is, in many ways, Austrian, since the information processing achieved by the economic system is not directly related to the information processing of individuals. Many Austrians, however, make an additional normative assumption that the existing institutional structure should be seen within a broader evolutionary context that makes the existing institutional structure efficient, or at least beyond the society's ability to improve upon it. In Simon's approach, that assumption is inappropriate. All one can say is that the existing institutional structure exists. That difference is important because it opens up the possibility of studying alternative institutional structures and potentially finding a preferable one.

Ironically, it was a project extending Simon's research program examining how to integrate process into microeconomic analysis, in which Muth (1961) was a participant, that led to rational expectations. Struggling with the problem, Muth proposed to cut the Gordian Knot and eliminate process entirely (Simon, 1978, 1979). Forget process: assume in the model expectations consistent with the equilibrium of that model. He called those model-consistent expectations "rational expectations." The Post Walrasian approach is a reversion back to Simon's work. It assumes that process is fundamentally important and that Muth's solution presumed far too much information processing capability of individuals.

In the Post Walrasian perspective one cannot escape process, and one cannot meaningfully relate non-contextual individual choice theory with macro analysis until one has first determined the relevant macro context within which a micro decision is made. Thus, whereas the microfoundations-of-macro work forged an integration of micro and macro from a unique Walrasian general equilibrium perspective, the Post Walrasian perspective is attempting to forge an integration from a macro perspective and to devise a micro perspective to fit into macro simultaneously as one finds a micro to fit the macro. Put simply, the model cannot assume markets exist without explaining the incentives people have for creating markets.

4.3   How can one determine an appropriate macrofoundation?

To say that before one starts developing a microfoundation to macro one needs a macrofoundation to micro is not to argue that what we currently view as Keynesian macrofoundations is the right approach. The mechanistic multiplier and the modified IS/LM model are naive and misleading. They involve as much a denial of the importance of institutional structure as does the microfoundations literature.

Exactly how to go about determining an appropriate analytic macrofoundation for micro is not clear. The work of Barkley Rosser (1991), Michael Woodford (1986, 1990), Andrei Schleifer (1986), John Bryant (1983), and others is attempting to arrive at an analytic solution to the problem. While these researchers have been successful in demonstrating analytically the possibility of multiple equilibria and in showing how, once one takes seriously the possibility of nonlinear dynamics, jumps from one equilibrium to another can occur, they have not been very successful in providing much assistance in determining a meaningful macrofoundation. The main value of their analytic work has been to demonstrate the need for, and the difficulty of determining, a macrofoundation.

I suspect that if an analytic approach is going to provide a macrofoundation of micro, a multistep analytic approach must replace the one-step analytic approach currently being used. The first step would be what might be called a "deductive institutional approach" in which one analyzes the rational choice of economic institutions along the lines suggested by Buchanan's constitutional analysis (Colander, 1994). Those deductively-derived institutions then become the macrofoundation for microeconomic theorizing. This means that the constraints those institutions impose on individuals must be built into the micro theorizing. Thus, Post Walrasian economics might have a representative agent but it would be a fundamentally different representative agent than used by New neoKeynesians or New Classicals. In its conception the Post Walrasian representative-agent would incorporate macro-institutional constraints on its behavior. More likely, it will have a number of representative agents interacting along the lines described by Allan Kirman (1992).

An analytic approach is not the only way to arrive at a macrofoundation. Two alternative approaches are a simulation approach proposed by Axel Leijonhufvud in the previous paper and the institutional or Post Keynesian approach. In this institutional approach, as opposed to computer simulation, one uses the real-world economy to simulate the reduced-form relationships. Since these aggregate real-world individual decisions are made contingent on the existing institutional structure, empirical observation is the only way to determine a reasonable macro-constrained micro choice. The work on wage contours and price ratchets falls within this framework. (A modification of this approach is to supplement empirical observation with institutionally-constrained micro-analytics in which the perceived reality determines the institutional constraints, but one still conducts analytic choice theoretic exercises within that observationally-determined environment.)

4.4   The Post Walrasian approach and the canonical model

Once one views the macroeconomic problem from a Post Walrasian perspective, many of the issues that had previously been in debate are simply non-issues. Price inflexibility does not need a unique-equilibrium Walrasian microfoundation; the search for reasons for price inflexibility as a justification for fluctuations in aggregate output is a group of irrelevant exercises, at least at this stage of inquiry. Menu cost analysis and implicit contract theorizing become, perhaps, fun analytic exercises, but unnecessary for establishing a basis for non self-equilibrating macroeconomics.

Since these issues become so clear in the Post Walrasian perspective, I have been perplexed to explain why they have received so little attention in the literature. Keynes made it quite clear that he believed that his was the general theory and the Classical theory was the special case, assuming full employment. From a Post Walrasian perspective, Keynes is correct; from a Walrasian perspective it is the Classical theory that is the general theory and the neoKeynesian model that is the special case, the Classical model modified by fixed wages and prices.

I have come to the conclusion that one of the prime reasons why Keynesian, or non self-equilibrating macro, insights have been lost is that a unique Walrasian general-equilibrium perspective has been embedded in the canonical aggregate model used by both neoKeynesians and Classicals. The micro perspective inherent in that model directed all formal analysis to a micro perspective.

Specifically, the canonical model's use of an aggregate production function that assumes a one-to-one mapping between inputs and aggregate output eliminated the analytic possibility of multiple equilibria, and the assumption of a linear dynamics eliminates the possibility both of sudden jumps from one equilibrium to another and of path dependency. Since all previous attempts to provide a microfoundation for macro have been based on that unique-equilibrium aggregate production function with linear dynamics, it is not surprising that any time a microfoundation was formalized, the logical outcome was a micro perspective. Formal modeling of the macrofoundations-of-micro perspective must start with the proposition that the standard aggregate production function is inconsistent with multiple aggregate-equilibria and hence with a perspective that identical inputs of capital and labor can be associated with different levels of output. Garretsen (1991) and van Ees (1991) make arguments along these lines.

To incorporate the macro perspective into the model, one must specify an aggregate production function that can have different properties than the individual firm production function. It must be a function that has no one marginal productivity of inputs, but, instead, has many, depending on at which of the multiple equilibria the economy arrives. In the macrofoundations-of-micro perspective, the individual decisions can only be specified given one of those macro equilibria.

4.5 A more limited realm for theory

To point out that this alternative Post Walrasian perspective exists is only a very limited first step in the analysis. It is also the easiest one. It disparages much of the existing work without replacing it and suggests that the understanding of macro questions lies in taking seriously the complexity of those questions, not assuming away complexity for analytic convenience. It is a step that, once taken, is nihilistic: much existing macro theory and even the possibility of doing tractable macro theory is obliterated.

It is, I suspect, these nihilistic implications of the Post Walrasian approach that have led macro theorists to avoid them. If the macro economy is almost infinitely complex, any tractable model will at best be suggestive. At best, what we might hope to achieve from macro theorizing are suggestive results of directional implications of observed shocks. Global normative statements fall by the wayside and are replaced by statements about potential tendencies to deviate from a dynamic path.

The Post Walrasian perspective will also fundamentally change the way we do macroeconometrics. Macroeconometric models built up from micro relationships specified independently of institutional context will also fall by the wayside and will be replaced with models with far fewer theoretically-imposed structural limitations on the models. Robert Basmann's (1972) and Christopher Sims's (1980) attacks on macroeconometrics fit in nicely with the Post Walrasian perspective. Once one accepts that macro theory can lead to almost any result, forecasters will have to turn elsewhere — to pure statisticians who can extract maximum information from statistics independent of theory.

4.6   Conclusion

The fact that the perspective one takes determines the conclusion one arrives at is not surprising. What is surprising is that the importance of perspective has been so little discussed in the literature. Recent developments in the Post Walrasian macroeconomics bring the debate back to a debate about perspective and for that reason are a welcome advance – one likely to bring significant gains to our understanding of the aggregate economy, or at least to our understanding of what we do not know about that macro economy. Ultimately, any research program will be based on a leap of faith. Developing meaningful dialogue about faith is difficult; justifying faith with analytics is impossible. Ultimately, any researcher must answer the question: What simplifications will my faith allow me to make in the name of analytic tractability? Those simplifications define the perspective, and are what ultimately will differentiate macro models.

The change in perspective that an alternative leap of faith involves is not only for macro. Ironically, the changes will be more major for micro than for macro, since from a Post Walrasian perspective much of what we currently teach as micro is out if its macro context and hence inappropriate. Exactly where the Post Walrasian approach might lead is unclear. Changes in perspectives are the most difficult to predict and – who knows? – maybe when the work is complete, Hanson's picture described at the beginning of this article will be of neither birds nor antelopes. Some economist may well pull a rabbit out of it.

Endnotes

This paper is reprinted from the *Eastern Economic Journal* (Vol. 18, No. 4) with permission. It has been editd here for stylistic consistency. I would like to thank Robert Clower, Kenneth Koford, Paul Samuelson, Paul Davidson, Kevin Hoover, Barkley Rosser, Christof Rühl, and Harold Hochman for helpful comments on early drafts of this paper.

1.   The earliest edition to which I had access, the 6th edition, had this diagram in it. I do not know whether it was in earlier editions.

2. There are, of course, different branches of microeconomics, and, as discussed in Landreth and Colander (1994), it was the neoWalrasian tradition that dominated the profession. Thus, when I refer to a micro perspective, I refer to the neoWalrasian perspective. This neoWalrasian perspective saw macro issues from a micro perspective. The Marshallian tradition was somewhat different; it did not accept that one could build up from individual to general. The Marshallian approach was not followed up, except for the work of Post Keynesians, Leijonhufvud and Clower. The Post Walrasian approach follows in this Marshallian tradition, and could be called Marshallian Macro.

3. The term macrofoundations, I suspect, has been around for a long time. Tracing the term is a paper in itself. Axel Leijonhufvud remembered using it in Leijonhufvud (1981). I was told that Roman Frydman and Edmund Phelps (1983) used the term and that Hyman Minsky had an unpublished paper from the 1970s with that title; Minsky remembered it, but doubted he could find it and told me that he used the term in a slightly different context. I was also told by Christof Rühl that a German economist, Karl Zinn, wrote a paper with that title for a *Festschrift* in 1988, but that it has not been translated into English. I suspect the term has been used many more times because it is such an obvious counterpoint to the microfoundations of macro, and hence to the New Classical call for microfoundations. While he does not use the term explicitly, Bruce Littleboy (1990), in work that relates fundamentalist Keynesian ideas with Clower and Leijonhufvud's ideas, discusses many of the important issues raised here.

4. See Clower and Howitt's paper is this volume

References

Basmann, R. L. (1972). "The Brookings Quarterly Econometric Model: Science or Number Mysticism?" and "Argument and Evidence in the Brookings-S. S. R. C. Philosophy of Econometrics," respectively, Chapters 1 and 3. In K. Brunner, ed., *Problems and Issues in Current Econometric Practice*. Columbus, Ohio: College of Administrative Science, Ohio State University.

Bryant, J. A. (1983). "A Simple Rational-Expectations Keynes-Type Model." *Quarterly Journal of Economics* 97: 525-28.

Clower, R. and P. Howitt (1992). "Money, Markets and Coase." Paper presented at conference on Is Economics Becoming a Hard Science? Paris, 1992; published in French as "La Monnaie, les marchés et Coase." In A. d'Autumne and J. Carelier, eds., *L'Économie Devient-elle une Science Dure?* Paris: Economica, 1995, 199-215.

Colander, D. (1992a). "The New, the Neo and the New neo." *Methodus: Bulletin of the International Network for Economic Method* 4: 166-70..

——— (1992b). "Is New Keynesian Economics New?" Unpublished manuscript.

——— (1992c). "New Keynesian Economics in Perspective." *Eastern Economic Journal* 18: 438-48.

——— (1994). "Economists, Institutions and Change." In M. Rizzo, ed., *Advances in Austrian Economics*. Greenwich, Conn.: JAI Press.

Diamond, P. A. (1982). "Aggregate Demand Management in Search Equilibrium." *Journal of Political Economy* 51: 88-94.

Frydman, R. and E. Phelps (1983). *Individual Forecasting and Aggregate Outcomes: "Rational Expectations" Examined*. Cambridge: Cambridge University Press.

Garretsen, H. (1991). *Keynes, Coordination and Beyond*. U. K.: Edward Elgar.

Hanson, N. R. (1961). *Patterns of Discovery*. New York: Cambridge University Press.

Howitt, P. (1985). "Transaction Costs and the Theory of Unemployment." *American Economic Review*: 88-100.

Kirman, A. (1992). "Whom or What Does the Representative Individual Represent?" *Journal of Economic Perspectives* 6: 117-34.

Landreth, H. and D. Colander (1994). *History of Economic Thought,* 3rd ed. Boston: Houghton Mifflin.

Leijonhufvud, A. (1968). *On Keynesian Economics and the Economics of Keynes.* New York: Oxford University Press.

(1981). *Information and Coordination: Essays in Macroeconomic Theory.* New York: Oxford University Press.

(1993). "Towards a Not-Too-Rational Macroeconomics." *Southern Economic Journal* 60: 1-13.

Lerner, A. and D. Colander (1981). *MAP: A Market Anti Inflation Plan.* New York: Harcourt Brace Jovanovich.

Littleboy, B. (1990). *On Interpreting Keynes: A Study in Reconciliation.* London: Routledge.

Lucas, R. (1972). "Expectations and the Neutrality of Money." *Journal of Economic Theory* 4: 103-24.

(1975). "An Equilibrium Model of Business Cycles." *Journal of Political Economy*: 83: 1113-44.

Mankiw, G. and D. Romer (1991). *New Keynesian Economics*, 2 Vols. Cambridge, Mass.: MIT Press.

Muth, J. (1961). "Rational Expectations and the Theory of Price Movements." *Econometrica* 29: 315-35.

Phelps, E. (1969). *Microfoundations of Macroeconomics*. New York: Norton.

Rosser, B. (1991). *From Catastrophe to Chaos: A General Theory of Economic Discontinuities.* Boston: Kluwer Academic Publishers.

Samuelson, P. (1961). *Economics.* New York: McGraw Hill.

(1964). "The General Theory in 1936." In R. Lekachman, ed., *Keynes's General Theory.* New York: St. Martin's Press.

Sargent, T. and N. Wallace (1976). "Rational Expectations and the Theory of Economic Policy." *Journal of Monetary Economics* 2: 169-83.

Schleifer, A. (1986). "Implementation Cycles." *Journal of Political Economy* 94: 1163-90.

Shackle, G. L. S. (1974). *Keynesian Kaleidics.* Edinburgh: Edinburgh University Press.

Simon, H. (1959). "Models of Man." New York: Wiley.

(1978). "On How to Decide What to Do." *Bell Journal of Economics* 9: 494-507.

(1979). "Rational Decision Making in Business Organizations." *American Economic Review* 69: 493-513.

Sims, C. A. (1980). "Macroeconomics and Reality." *Econometrica* 48: 1-48.

van Ees, H. (1991). *Macroeconomic Fluctuations and Individual Behavior.* U.K.: Edward Elgar.

Woodford, M. (1986). "Stationary Sunspot Equilibria in a Finance Constrained Economy." *Journal of Economic Theory* 40: 128-37.

(1990). "Self-Fulfilling Expectation and Fluctuation in Aggregate Demand." In G. Mankiw and D. Romer (1991), *New Keynesian Economics.* Cambridge, Mass.: MIT Press.

PART II

THE UNDERPINNINGS OF POST WALRASIAN
MACROECONOMICS

CHAPTER 5

The evolution of macroeconomics: the origins of Post Walrasian macroeconomics

Perry Mehrling

Hysteresis and path-dependence are properties not just of real-world economies, but also of our theories about those economies. Ways of talking and thinking live long beyond the time when anyone remembers why (or even that) we once decided this was a good way to talk and think. The daily business of normal science, at least in economics, is largely about local improvement, refinement, and reformulation. Consequently, starting points matter a great deal. No full understanding of the evolution of macroeconomics since World War II is possible without understanding where we started, and why we started there.

We started of course with the neoClassical Synthesis. Every economist knows that the Synthesis was an historical compromise (some would say an unholy marriage) between the Classical and Keynesian views of the world. The Hicksian IS/LM model became the ground on which the postwar intellectual battles were fought. Because the model seemed to suggest that the difference between the Classical and Keynesian views was about slopes of curves and speeds of adjustment, the battles were fought with statistics, and as a consequence macroeconomics became much more empirical than it had been previously.

It is less often remembered that the Synthesis was also a bridge between the old institutionalist economics and the new more formal styles that soon came to dominate. The formulation of the Synthesis as a set of simultaneous equations was seen by some as the mathematical object most appropriate for the institutionalist vision of the economy. The discipline of converting qualitative institutional knowledge into mathematical equations with statistically estimated quantitative parameters felt to its practitioners like a progressive research program. The payoff from the program was the opportunity afforded by the simultaneous equations framework for studying the interaction of diverse institutions, or so it was hoped. The first large-scale econometric models were not intended as forecasting instruments but rather as scientific research tools for understanding the structure of the American economy.[1]

The Synthesis was also a bridge between professional academic economists and their new client, the government. Prewar economics had engaged largely with the most progressive and thoughtful elements of the business world, and that engagement had deeply influenced the style and content of economic research. Depression and war shifted the focus of the profession toward the concerns of a newly enlarged and ambitious government. The point of the new economics was not to interpret the world but to change it. In macroeconomics that meant using fiscal and monetary policy to stabilize aggregate fluctuations and the IS/LM model, with one curve for fiscal and one for monetary, offered a simple and graphic way to engage that policy discussion.

Finally, the Synthesis was a bridge between professional economists and the burgeoning student population of the postwar educational expansion. The pressures of large-scale teaching put a premium on teachability and testability, and the IS/LM model scored in both categories. As any teacher knows, a theory that can be summarized by curves in a two-dimensional diagram can be taught and tested much more easily than one that cannot. Flexible enough to capture the range of academic viewpoints, pointed enough to capture the changed role of government, simple enough for the average student to master, the IS/LM model rapidly became the core of economic pedagogy.

In all these respects, in the beginning, the neoClassical Synthesis was more a way of talking than a way of thinking, a common language that allowed the diverse groups interested in economic issues to converse with one another. As after the Flood "the whole earth had one language and few words" (Genesis 11:1), so after the confusion of Depression and War came order and system. And along with order came intellectual vitality, as the translation of diverse insights into a common tongue brought cross-fertilization and new insights. Soon hardly anyone used the old languages any more, but rather devoted their common energies to building the new economics.

As more and more economists came to speak the new language, it became not just a way of talking but also a way of thinking. What could not be said in the new language could not be understood, and hence must be nonsense. The price paid for the unification of economics discourse was therefore a certain flattening of that discourse. Arguments about whether money was a prime cause or a consequence of aggregate output became arguments about the elasticity of money demand. Arguments about whether the market system was able to coordinate economic adjustment became arguments about the speed of price adjustment. Large and somewhat ill-formed ideas got transformed into smaller but sharper ideas. Something was gained, but something was also lost.

As the neoClassical Synthesis evolved, so too did the IS/LM model, from a way of illustrating the key features of a larger theory into a way of theorizing about the economy. The model became the theory, and the theory became the model. As a consequence, the theory/model began to come under a new kind of scrutiny. Of a model it could be asked, leaving aside the question of whether it was consistent with observed phenomena, is it *internally* consistent? And if not, how could it be made internally consistent? Thus, in addition to the intellectual vitality that came from the translation of diverse insights into the new language, there came a new source of internally generated vitality. Refinements of the model came to be understood as refinements of the theory, and vice versa.

5.1   The unraveling of the Synthesis

As usually told, the story of the unraveling of the neoClassical Synthesis in the 1970s revolves around the failure of the Synthesis to account for the observed phenomenon of stagflation. It may be admitted that in the hands of some of its more enthusiastic practitioners, the new economics did promise more than it was able to deliver, and policy failures did undermine the status of economics in the larger society. More important however as a factor determining the future evolution of macroeconomics was the status of the new economics among economists themselves, and for them the apparent internal inconsistency of the Synthesis was more decisive. Suspicion that the model did not hang together logically undermined the confidence of those who sought incremental theoretical change to account for new phenomena. Meanwhile, attempts to pare the model down to a consistent core pointed the direction toward a new model, and a new theory, to replace the so-recently hegemonic Synthesis. Thus was born the New Classical school.

To understand why the Synthesis unraveled as it did, it is helpful to view it as a "completion" of a Walrasian competitive equilibrium model with two missing components: a theory of disequilibrium adjustment and a theory of money. Originally, these completions were understood as "placeholders," filling in the gaps in high theory until the time when a definitive completion would be developed. In principle of course there was and is nothing wrong with the placeholder strategy. The idea that the theory of value, the theory of business fluctuation, and the theory of money are relatively independent of one another, to be mixed and matched as the need arises, dates to Classical economics. Because Classical economists adopted a theory of value in which (so-called "natural") price is determined by long-run costs, their theories of fluctuations and money could be developed independently. They were free to build a theory of fluctuations that took relative prices as fixed at their long-run equilibrium levels. And they were free to build a theory of money that took the level of prices as fixed by the cost of producing gold.[2]

With the neoClassical shift in the theory of value, the "completion strategy" for macroeconomics became more problematic. In the neoClassical theory of value, the focus shifts to market prices which are determined by supply and demand, and it becomes impossible to separate out the theory of value and the theory of business fluctuations. Any explanation of business fluctuations seems to require some explanation of why prices do not adjust to make supply equal to demand. Yet a theory of value that understands price as determined by market clearing has no room for price stickiness. Thus, the theory of value and the theory of business fluctuations come inherently into conflict. This conflict turned out to be the main source of the instability of the neoClassical Synthesis.

The neoClassical revolution in value theory raised problems of a different kind for monetary theory. Value theory says that prices are determined by supply and demand, which suggests that it is necessary to develop a theory of money demand in order to explain the price level. But at the same time, value theory is developed without an intrinsic role for money, so as a matter of logic there may be no demand for money, and the price of money may be zero in equilibrium (Hahn, 1965:126-35). In this way, the theory of value and the theory of money come into conflict. This conflict was the second source of the instability of the neoClassical Synthesis.

In the original neoClassical Synthesis, these two conflicts were managed, but not resolved, by making a distinction between the short run and the long run. Consider the disequilibrium adjustment story. In the short run prices were not supposed to clear markets while in the long run they were. In this way, short run prices were left without any clear analytical foundation – for if they don't clear markets then what do they do? Consider also monetary theory. In the short-run the nominal quantity of money was supposed to determine the rate of interest, while in the long run it was supposed to determine the level of prices. This meant that monetary theory essentially turned out to be the quantity equation with short-run price stickiness, a theory without any clear analytical foundation even in the long run, given a theory of value constructed with no intrinsic role for money.

The *ad hoc* story of disequilibrium price adjustment came under criticism first. Lacking any analytical foundation, the short-run story of price adjustment depended on empirical studies of pricing arrangements in particular markets. The results of this research were summarized in a series of dynamical equations that were estimated and simulated to study the interaction of different sectors of the economy.[3] The claim that these equations captured the fundamental dynamics of the U.S. economy was undermined by the experience of the 1970s and opened the door for the theoretical critique of Lucas and others (Lucas, 1976:19-46).[4] What Lucas pointed out was that the analytical foundations of the dynamical equations in macroeconometric models were not consistent with the analytical foundations of the competitive equilibrium toward which the dynamics were supposed to be leading. Following the Lucas critique, New Classical economists set out to develop a theory of business fluctuation that would be completely consistent with the theory of value. They did so by emphasizing exogenous shocks as the source of fluctuation, shocks that had lasting effects because of intertemporal substitution in technology or preferences. Because the first models relied on shocks to technology and tastes, and did not include a role for money, the new class of models came to be known as Real Business Cycle theory (Long and Plosser, 1983: 39-69; King and Plosser, 1984: 363-80; Barro and King, 1984: 817-39).

A complete challenge to the neoClassical Synthesis required the New Classicals to find a place in their construct for money, but this they could not easily do. As Hahn had earlier pointed out, the Walrasian equilibrium framework within which the New Classicals were determined to work simply has no place for money. The methodological high ground, which had been so effective in critiquing *ad hoc* disequilibrium price adjustment stories, had to be abandoned if the New Classicals were to include money in their models.

The strategy the New Classicals adopted was much like that of the neoClassical Synthesis – they simply tacked a simplistic quantity theory of money onto the competitive equilibrium model. They suggested that the competitive equilibrium model could be interpreted as a monetary economy with an infinite velocity of money, so that an infinitesimal quantity of money is adequate for all transactions. The analytical problem was how to slow down velocity enough that the implicit money could be seen and analyzed. The answer was found by imposing a cash-in-advance constraint.[5] In a typical formulation, cash holdings turn over once every period so the velocity of money is fixed at unity. There is no Hahn problem of money demand falling to zero since agents are constrained to hold money in order to trade. And since it is real balances that agents care about, the nominal quantity of money determines the level of prices.

The cash-in-advance constraint enabled New Classical economists to manage the inherent conflict between money and the theory of value, but not to resolve it.[6] As monetary theory, the cash-in-advance models were hardly less *ad hoc* than the discarded price adjustment stories. Indeed, given the strong Walrasian predilections of the New Classicals, the *ad hoc* character of the construction was even more glaring than it had been in the Synthesis. That this most vulnerable chink in the New Classical armor has yet to come under sustained attack must be put down to the fact that no one as yet has a better idea of how to resolve the conflict. In recognition of the fact that the New Classical way of managing the conflict is no worse than their own, the New Keynesians who seek to defend and even reestablish the neoClassical Synthesis have largely left the monetary side of the New Classical models alone.[7]

5.2   The New Keynesian response

The New Keynesian response to the New Classical critique was structured as research into the foundations of Patinkin's 1956 Walrasian model of the neoClassical Synthesis (Patinkin, 1956). His *Money, Interest, and Prices* purported to show how monetary and value theory could be integrated within a model of price flexibility and full employment. In the framework of that model, the essence of the Keynesian message seemed to be that price rigidity stymied (or at least slowed) the natural tendency toward full employment. Fatefully, in Patinkin's formulation it was difficult to see either of the two conceptual difficulties that drove later developments. For Patinkin, equilibrium was the solution to a set of simultaneous equations, one of which concerned the demand and supply of money. If prices for some reason were not in their equilibrium configuration then markets would not clear and disequilibrium would reign for as long as it took prices to adjust.

When the Synthesis came under attack, it was Patinkin's simultaneous equation version of Walrasian equilibrium that defenders felt compelled to bolster. The first step in providing support was the development of fixed-price models by Barro and Grossman (1976), Malinvaud (1977), Benassy (1982), and others. After these models, in turn, came under criticism on the grounds that there was no reason for prices to be fixed, the second step involved developing stories for price stickiness in particular markets. The final step, showing how particular market imperfections interact in the aggregate, is the topic of current research (Bertola and Caballero, 1990: 237-87).

Strong claims are currently being made for this line of research. A manifesto for the New Keynesians is the essay of Mankiw and Romer introducing their two-volume edited collection of articles titled *New Keynesian Economics* (1991). The collection is unified largely by disbelief in real business cycles,[8] but also by a common positive framework that can be summarized as follows. Business fluctuations arise in large part because of fluctuations in demand. Fluctuations in demand affect output in the short run because prices do not adjust. Both real and nominal prices are slow to adjust because of market imperfections at the microeconomic level, imperfections that arise from imperfect information. In the long run prices do adjust, but since the underlying information problems may still be present, the long-run equilibrium may be inefficient and thus there is a possible role for government policy.

For those who sign on to the Mankiw-Romer manifesto, the New Keynesian goal is to reestablish the neoClassical Synthesis. Within the general framework they propose, there is room for debate about the "relative potency of monetary and fiscal policy," and about whether or not government intervention is desirable (Mankiw and Romer, 1991: 3), i.e., exactly the debates that occupied monetarists and Keynesians in the 1960s. Mankiw and Romer conclude:

> After two decades of ferment, macroeconomics may be in the process of returning to a state similar to that of the 1960s. The new classical argument that the Keynesian assumption of nominal rigidities was incapable of being given theoretical foundations has been refuted. More importantly, the broad outlines of an account of macroeconomic fluctuations based on nominal rigidity are

becoming clear. The key ingredients are small barriers to full and immediate nominal adjustment and the real rigidities in the markets for labor, goods, and credit that cause these small barriers to generate large amounts of price stickiness. (1991: 15)

It is instructive to compare today's New Keynesians with their forebears who built the first econometric models. Old Keynesians believed that detailed study of individual sectors of the economy would uncover regularities that could be summarized in a system of simultaneous equations to reveal the complex workings of the modern economy. Their modern counterparts believe that detailed study of the microeconomics of information as applied to individual sectors of the economy will uncover similar regularities which they can put to a similar use. The New Keynesians emphasize deduction from *a priori* theory, while their forebears emphasized induction from empirical facts, but the logic of their research programs is quite the same. Ultimately the truth claim boils down to one of greater realism and practicability.

The New Keynesians propose a new historical compromise much like the one adopted by their forebears. Their message is: New Classicals may have the theoretical high ground, but New Keynesians have the empirical high ground, so why not capitalize on both strengths and work together to build a model that is both clean and relevant? Surely there are gains from trade to be achieved by building a bridge between our two hilltop civilizations, gains which could be used to rebuild other bridges sadly in disrepair, such as that between the economics profession and its two main clients, government and students. What underlies the New Keynesian proposal is the dream of an economics unified once again around a common language. "Come, let us build ourselves a city, and a tower with its top in the heavens, and let us make a name for ourselves, lest we be scattered abroad upon the face of the whole earth" (Genesis 11: 4).

Nostalgia for a former golden age is human, but it is hardly a realistic program for scientific progress. From the perspective of general equilibrium theory, the New Keynesian program looks not much less *ad hoc* than the old Synthesis. It is to be expected that we will soon see an updated version of the Lucas critique focused now on the question of whether a coherent macroeconomic model can actually be constructed from the varied collection of New Keynesian stories.[9] In a sense the key event that undermined the old neoClassical Synthesis was the clarification of the nature of Walrasian equilibrium through the work of Arrow, Debreu, and others. The old Keynesians had already accepted as a basic principle that in the long run the economy was Walrasian, back when they thought Walrasian meant Patinkin and simultaneous equations. The Arrow-Debreu model revealed the conflict between the long-run theory of value and the short-run theory of business fluctuation, and it remained only for Lucas and the New Classicals to mount a sustained attack on the conflict in order to undermine the Synthesis for good. The key fact preventing a restaging of the neoClassical

Synthesis in new microfoundational costumes is that now everyone understands what you can do with Walrasian equilibrium and what you can't. The lesson should have been learned by now that the middle ground the New Keynesians seek to occupy does not exist.

5.3   The end of the Walrasian age

Recent developments in general equilibrium theory suggest that the hills occupied by current schools of macroeconomics, both New Classical and New Keynesian, are in fact dunes of shifting sand. Confidence in the Walrasian equilibrium model was a source of strength for the original Synthesis, and confidence in the Arrow-Debreu version of that model was a source of strength for the New Classical view. Now it has become clear that rational choice-theoretic foundations have very few aggregative consequences, that the Walrasian model is more open-ended – it is consistent with a wider range of phenomena – than we had previously thought. The future of macroeconomics depends on what we make of this new fact.

The theory of general competitive equilibrium achieved its mature expression almost 20 years ago.[10] In a general equilibrium with no externalities or information imperfections, two main results were demonstrated. First, although typically there are many equilibria, generically each one is locally unique. This result is important because it provides the foundation, albeit a limited one, for the method of comparative statics. Second, competitive equilibrium is efficient (First Welfare Theorem). This result is important because it suggests a sense in which markets do a good job in allocating resources. Both these results were first demonstrated in a framework with a fixed number of commodities, but both hold also in infinite commodity models (e.g., models with an infinite time horizon) provided the equilibrium path is saddle-point stable.

It was never clear that this model had much to say about real-world economies. The problem is not just that the assumptions required for existence are unlikely to be satisfied by any real-world economy, but that the model lacks both a satisfactory dynamical analysis and an intrinsic role for money. Without a dynamical analysis there is no reason to think that the economy tends toward equilibrium. Without a role for money there is no room in the model for aggregate demand effects. Hence the "placeholder" strategy of the original neoClassical Synthesis.

Both problems have been well-known for more than 20 years, and subsequent research has provided no reason to suppose that these troubles can be rectified within the competitive equilibrium framework (Ingrao and Israel, 1990:10-12). This disappointment has caused a fracturing of the high theory research program and a proliferation of equilibrium concepts – sequence equilibrium, temporary equilibrium, fix-price equilibrium, etc. (Weintraub, 1979;

Gale, 1982, 1983). Yet none of these models has attracted any significant following as a possible framework for macroeconomic analysis. Despite its problems, the competitive equilibrium model still remains the benchmark for most economic analysis.

Continuing work to refine understanding of that benchmark by studying equilibrium with an infinite number of commodities has suggested however that the trouble is even worse than previously suspected. In infinite economies, there typically exist many equilibrium paths that are not saddle-point stable – limit cycles, chaotic paths, and "sunspot" equilibria are all possible.[11] In these cases the welfare theorems may not hold, a result that undermines the principal justification of markets as a means of allocation. Even more damning, in the view of some, local uniqueness may also fail, and there may be a continuum of equilibria. Thus equilibrium is in a sense indeterminate, and the method of comparative statics cannot be applied.

It is therefore surprising, to say the least, to find the New Classical school of macroeconomic thought basing its analysis of real-world economies on the assumption that these economies behave as though they were in competitive equilibrium. We have seen how New Classicals sidestep the difficult issue of disequilibrium adjustment by analyzing the economy as though it were in equilibrium at all times, and how they manage the problem of money by means of an *ad hoc* cash-in-advance constraint. The New Classical response to the new discoveries about general equilibrium theory has been to confine attention to saddle-point stable paths, thus sidestepping the possibility of inefficient equilibria and indeterminacy that typically arise in infinite economies. With inefficient equilibria ruled out by assumption, equilibrium is efficient and there is no role for government intervention, but the result is hardly as compelling as it once was.

Some New Keynesians, by contrast, have embraced the new exotic equilibria and in so doing have sought to take possession of the theoretical high ground so recently occupied by the New Classicals. In contrast to the New Classical view of the business cycle as driven by exogenous shocks, the existence of exotic equilibrium paths in infinite economies suggests the possibility of explaining business fluctuations as endogenous phenomena even within the framework of competitive equilibrium. Since these exotic equilibria may be inefficient, there is a potential role for government in the model. The indeterminacy of equilibrium however suggests that it will not be possible to construct a theory of policy around the selection of a preferred equilibrium. Rather, the theory of policy consists in identifying policies that change the *set* of equilibria and rule out the worst ones (Woodford, 1990).

In this debate New Keynesians hold the high ground but it is not clear that it will do them any good. The discovery that there may exist multiple exotic equilibria is perhaps more useful as a critique of New Classical models than as a foundation for an alternative model. No one has yet succeeded in bringing data to bear on any of the exotic models, nor is it clear that success is possible given their indeterminacy. How is one to ascertain which equilibrium pertains to the real world? Refinement of the equilibrium concept is one possible road, but then the debate will revolve around whether the proposed New Keynesian refinement is better or worse than the New Classical refinement. Because it is hard to imagine any decisive criteria for concluding such a debate, it is likely that debate will continue for some time without doing much to lead macroeconomics forward.

Deeper problems also exist with this new literature, problems which it is not clear that any refinement can resolve. In a world of multiple equilibria there is a real question how multiple agents all come to expect the same equilibrium outcome. Even more troubling, there is a real question how to conceptualize rational choice. If many things can happen, but only one thing will happen, a rational agent should surely take that indeterminacy into account, but the models typically assume that the agent assigns unit probability to the one thing that does happen. Unfortunately rational choice theory gives little guidance on what else the agent might do, because there are no natural probabilities associated with the different equilibria. And even if we had such a behavioral model, it would surely suggest different behavior and hence different equilibrium outcomes. Not only is the model of behavior at odds with the multiplicity of equilibria, but a more satisfactory model of behavior seems likely to require a different equilibrium concept.[12]

Finally, it must be noted that there is nothing in the new general equilibrium theory that helps us move closer to a proper theory of money.[13] There is no more intrinsic role for money in the new exotic equilibria than before. Money is an old and tough problem that was put to one side by both New Classicals and New Keynesians because it appeared that the Walrasian road held out hope of progress on another old and tough problem, that of integrating the theory of business fluctuation with the theory of value. Given our current understanding of the Walrasian road, further travel on it seems to offer diminishing returns even on the latter problem. Perhaps it is time to focus attention instead on making progress on the problem of money.

5.4   The road ahead

The story of the evolution of macroeconomics has in large part been driven by the fateful decision long ago to adopt Walrasian equilibrium as the long-run model. Because of this decision, disequilibrium dynamics and monetary theory could not thrive and were eventually pruned off. Because of this decision, developments in Walrasian equilibrium theory have been (and continue to be) decisive for the evolution of macroeconomics. We originally chose the Walrasian road because it seemed to hold out promise that we could talk to one another, a *sine qua non* for the future vitality of economics. And for a while we *were* able to talk to one another; we felt that nothing was impossible for us, that we could build a tower with its top in the heavens. But the tower we built turned out to be a Tower of Babel.

The language of the neoClassical Synthesis was a collage of incongruous parts that broke into pieces once it came under scrutiny. With each pruning, the range of possible conversation was narrowed further, and conversation that had once been conducted inside macroeconomics came to be conducted only on the fringe, if at all. Finally even the ostensible payoff of the paring down – a solid and reliable benchmark for future theorizing – slipped through our grasp. To-day macroeconomics has no core, only fringe. But that doesn't mean we can't talk to one another. It only means that we must learn a number of languages in order to do so. Tomorrow's macroeconomics can emerge only from today's difficult conversations, not from nostalgia for the easy conversations of the past.

The history of macroeconomics sketched above suggests that one of the most important conversations for the future will concern the articulation of the theory of value with the theory of fluctuation and the theory of money. We have learned that the Walrasian theory of value has no room for either economic dynamics or money. One consequence of this lesson is that macroeconomists have begun to explore non-Walrasian theories of value in the hope that such theories might have more room for macroeconomics. Another consequence is that macroeconomists have begun to develop theories of economic dynamics and money independent of the constraint of any particular theory of value. Most of the essays in this volume follow the latter tack but, if the history of macroeconomics is any indication, macroeconomists will eventually have to consider how their theories articulate with the theory of value. In this respect it is perhaps not premature, even at this early stage, to consider briefly certain complementarities between the Post Walrasian research program and the ongoing revolution in the theory of value that marches under the banner of the new information economics.

The new information economics has as a major theme that prices do not just clear markets but fulfill other functions as well. In particular they convey information. The significance for macroeconomics of the new information economics is that a theory of value built on the new information economics may well have more room for a theory of business fluctuation, and even a theory of money, than did the old Walrasian theory. Consider the theory of business fluctuation. In the new information economics, there is no need to invoke price stickiness to explain why markets do not clear, since they need not clear even when markets are in equilibrium. A macroeconomics rooted in the economics of information therefore goes beyond the economics of sticky prices because informational asymmetries have consequences more fundamental and widespread than sticky prices. Consider also the theory of money. Since economies with informational asymmetries have room for money, the new information economics offers the possibility of developing a monetary theory that is fully consistent with the theory of value. Informational asymmetries give rise to missing markets and a precautionary motive for holding money. A monetary theory built around the precautionary motive can therefore be consistent with value theory in a way that one built around the transactions motive cannot.[14]

Some economists who march under the New Keynesian banner have begun to embrace the possibilities of the new information economics. Greenwald and Stiglitz, for example, define New Keynesian Economics as "the study of imperfect information and incomplete markets" (Greenwald and Stiglitz, 1987: 119-33; see also Phelps, 1994). What distinguishes their general approach from that of other New Keynesians is that they seek not merely to provide microfoundations for price stickiness but to promote a more thoroughgoing revolution in macroeconomic theory. In their view, the Keynesian revolution is incomplete. "The New Keynesian Economics begins with Keynes's basic insights. But it recognizes the need for a more radical departure from the neoclassical framework, and for a much deeper study of the consequences of imperfections in capital markets, imperfections which can be explained by the costs of information." The central theme of Keynes's *General Theory* was that involuntary unemployment is a consequence of the phenomenon of liquidity preference, a phenomenon that systematically distorts consumption, investment, and portfolio behavior. With the new information economics, so the argument goes, it is now possible to go beyond Keynes by understanding liquidity preference as a rational response to incomplete information and imperfect markets.

Obviously the new information economics opens up much more space for macroeconomics than was allowed by the older Walrasian approach. The other essays in this volume however demonstrate the size of the gap that still exists between even this new theory of value and a satisfactory theory of fluctuation and money. The new information economics bears few of the distinguishing characteristics of the Post Walrasian approach – multiple equilibria and complexity, bounded rationality, and institutions and non-price coordinating mechanisms. The roots of information economics lie very much in the theory of rational choice, a theory that is questioned (at the very least) by most of the essays in this volume, including this one, since it is not at all clear how to formulate the choice problem of an agent inhabiting a Post Walrasian world.

Nevertheless, notwithstanding the size of the gap between information economics and the Post Walrasian approach, the history of macroeconomics suggests that much of the future effort of macroeconomists will be devoted to erecting a span across the gap. The feasibility of such a construction project may be doubted, but that it will be undertaken seems a certainty. Given the width of the gap, it is inevitable that construction will have to proceed from both sides at the same time. Indeed, the new information economics and the Post Walrasian economics of the present volume might be considered the abutments on each shore of a future spanning bridge. As each side builds out farther, it would be wise to keep its eyes on the opposite shore. If the spans are to meet, it is just as important for the Post Walrasian approach to keep its eyes on what is happening with the new information economics as vice versa.

In sum, the demise of the neoClassical Synthesis presents us with an historic opportunity that it would tragic to waste. Instead of the false unity of a reconstructed neoClassical Synthesis, instead of the Babel of the fractured pieces of the old neoClassical Synthesis, we have the opportunity to construct a genuine conversation between the different languages of economics. The conversation between the different essays of this volume makes a modest start. The history of macroeconomics suggests that the next step will be to widen the conversation to include the new information economics.

Endnotes

1. See Kuh (1965: 362-69).
2. For an excellent account of Classical monetary theory see Glasner (1989:201-29).
3. See, e.g., Duesenberry et al. (1965). The original idea was to include equations describing disequilibrium dynamics in the financial sector as well (Brainard and Tobin, 1968). For an example of the flow approach see Bosworth and Duesenberry (1973).
4. For a collection of the papers that served as the New Classical manifesto, see Lucas and Sargent (1981).
5. There is an interesting story to be told here about how an idea that originated with Clower as a way of formalizing the idea of coordination failure was appropriated and popularized by Lucas and others as a way of restoring the quantity theory of money (Clower, 1967; Lucas and Stokey, 1987). A survey of the cash-in-advance literature is provided by Svensson (1985).
6. Other attempts to manage the tension between value theory and monetary theory were even less successful. There were some attempts to develop a theory in which money is a produced commodity. In one model, "monetary services are privately produced intermediate goods whose quantities rise and fall with real economic developments" (King and Plosser, 1984). The problem with this approach is that the price of monetary services is just a relative price like other relative prices, so the price level is left hanging. King and Plosser manage this difficulty by completing the model with a quantity equation.

   More interesting were the attempts to develop a modern version of the Classical analysis of a convertible currency. The problem is that convertibility into fiat money leaves the price level hanging in the following sense. Changes in the quantity of fiat money might cause proportionate changes in the amount of bank money and so drive up the price level. But they also might just substitute for an equal quantity of bank money, leaving the nominal quantity of money and the price level unchanged. To resolve this indeterminacy, various attempts were made to drive an analytical wedge between the fixed fiat money base and the flexible quantity of bank money. The idea was to argue that the money base, *not* the convertible currency, determines the price level, e.g., the "legal restrictions" theory of Wallace (1988), and Lucas's (1987) distinction between goods purchased with money and goods purchased with credit.
7. An important exception is the recent paper of Christiano and Eichenbaum (1992).
8. According to Mankiw, "If there is a single theme that unites Keynesian economics, it is the

belief that economic fluctuations reflect not the Pareto efficient response of the economy to changes in tastes and technology, but rather some sort of market failure on a grand scale" (Mankiw, 1990). Thus he defines New Keynesian economics by what it excludes, namely Real Business Cycle theory.

See also Robert Gordon (1990). Blanchard and Fischer (1989) promote much the same view in their *Lectures on Macroeconomics*. They summarize: "At this stage we cannot discern which model or combination of models will 20 years hence be regarded as absolutely essential to serious macroeconomic theory.... However, we can give educated guesses. In the labor markets, notions of efficiency wages have a definite ring of truth. So does monopolistic competition, as a stand-in for imperfect competition, in the goods markets. We believe that the recent work attempting to account for certain features of the financial markets from the viewpoint of asymmetric information is extremely important and that it will be increasingly integrated into complete macroeconomic models. Finally, we are quite sure that nominal rigidities are an important part of any account of macroeconomic fluctuations and that staggering of price and wage decisions is an important element in any complete story" (ibid., 489).

9. The most ambitious attempt to construct such a model is that of Phelps (1994). Phelps contrasts his "structuralist" approach with the "monetary" approach pursued by most other macroeconomists, New Keynesian and New Classical alike. Unlike most New Keynesians, he wants to build an equilibrium theory; unlike most New Classicals he wants that theory to explain involuntary unemployment. Most important, he seeks to break out of the Walrasian straitjacket by emphasizing the far-reaching consequences of imperfect information. In this respect his work looks forward to a new Post Walrasian macroeconomics, rather than backward to the old neoClassical Synthesis.

10. The argument that follows owes much to Foley (1990).

11. For an account that focuses on the overlapping generations model, see Blanchard and Fischer (1989: Ch. 5).

12. These deep problems with Walrasian equilibrium and the rational choice model of behavior have opened up new space for alternative approaches, examples of which abound in this volume. Clower and Howitt, for example, use the new space to insert a role for economic institutions, in particular the business firm as an organizing agent acting on its economic environment. Leijonhufvud uses the new space to investigate the emergence of macroeconomic order (not equilibrium) in a system of interacting "algorithmic" (not rational) agents.

13. For a recent review of the state of monetary theory, see Hellwig (1993).

14. In the author's view, the beginnings of such a theory are suggested by the work of Bewley (1983). See also Mehrling (1995).

References

Barro, R. J. and H. Grossman (1976). *Money, Employment and Inflation*. Cambridge: Cambridge University Press.

Barro, R. J. and R. G. King (1984). "Time-Separable Preferences and Intertemporal-Substitution Models of Business Cycles." *Quarterly Journal of Economics* 99: 817-39.

Benassy, J.-P. (1982). *The Economics of Market Disequilibrium*. New York: Academic Press.

Bertola, G. and R. Caballero (1990). "Kinked Adjustment Costs and Aggregate Dynamics." In *NBER Macroeconomics Annual 1990*. Cambridge, Mass.: MIT Press, 237-87.

Bewley, Truman (1983). "A Difficulty with the Optimum Quantity of Money." *Econometrica* 51:1485-1504.

Blanchard, O. J. and S. Fischer (1989). *Lectures on Macroeconomics*. Cambridge, Mass.: MIT Press.

Bosworth, B. and J. S. Duesenberry (1973). "A Flow of Funds Model and its Implications." In *Issues in Federal Debt Management* Conference Series No. 10. Boston: Federal Reserve Bank of Boston.

Brainard, W. C. and J. Tobin (1968). "Pitfalls in Financial Model Building." *American Economic Review* Papers and Proceedings 58: 99-122.

Christiano, L. and M. Eichenbaum (1992). "Liquidity Effects, Monetary Policy, and the Business Cycle." *NBER Working Paper* No. 4129.

Clower, R. (1967). "A Reconsideration of the Microeconomic Foundations of Monetary Theory." *Western Economic Journal* 6: 1-8.

Duesenberry, J. S., G. Fromm, L. Klein, and E. Kuh (1965). *The Brookings Quarterly Econometric Model of the United States*. Chicago: Rand-McNally.

Foley, D. K. (1990). "Recent Developments in Economic Theory." *Social Research* 57: 665-87.

Gale, D. (1982). *Money: in Equilibrium*. Cambridge: Cambridge University Press.
    (1983). *Money: in Disequilibrium*. Cambridge: Cambridge University Press.

Glasner, D. (1989). "On Some Classical Monetary Controversies." *History of Political Economy* 21: 201-29.

Gordon, R. (1990). "What is New-Keynesian Economics?" *Journal of Economic Literature* 28: 1115-71.

Grandmont, J.-M. (1989). "Keynesian Issues and Economic Theory." *Scandinavian Journal of Economics* 91: 265-93.

Greenwald, B. and J. E. Stiglitz (1987). "Keynesian, New Keynesian, and New Classical Economics." *Oxford Economic Papers* 39: 119-33.

Hahn, F. H. (1965). "On Some Problems of Proving the Existence of Equilibrium in a Monetary Economy." In F. H. Hahn and F. P. R. Brechling, *The Theory of Interest Rates*. London: Macmillan, 126-35.

Hellwig, M. F. (1993). "The Challenge of Monetary Theory." *European Economic Review* 37: 215-42.

Ingrao, B. and G. Israel (1990). *The Invisible Hand, Economic Equilibrium in the History of Science*. Cambridge, Mass.: MIT Press.

King, R. G. and C. I. Plosser (1984). "Money, Credit, and Prices in a Real Business Cycle." *American Economic Review* 74: 363-80.

Kuh, E. (1965). "Econometric Models: Is a New Age Dawning?" *American Economic Review* 55: 362-69.

Long, J. B., Jr. and C. I. Plosser (1983). "Real Business Cycles." *Journal of Political Economy* 91: 39-69.

Lucas, R. E., Jr. (1976). "Econometric Policy Evaluation: A Critique." *Journal of Monetary Economics* 1: 19-46.

Lucas, R. E., Jr. and T. J. Sargent, eds. (1981). *Rational Expectations and Econometric Practice*. Minneapolis: University of Minnesota Press.

Lucas, R. E., Jr. and N. L. Stokey (1987). "Money and Interest in a Cash-in-Advance Economy." *Econometrica* 55: 491-514.

Malinvaud, E. (1977). *The Theory of Unemployment Reconsidered*. Oxford: Blackwell.

Mankiw, N. G. (1990). "A Quick Refresher Course in Macroeconomics." *Journal of Economic Literature* 28:1645-60.

Mankiw, N. G. and D. Romer, eds. (1991). *New Keynesian Economics,* 2 Vols. Cambridge, Mass.: MIT Press.

Mehrling, P. (1995). "A Note on the Optimum Quantity of Money." *Journal of Mathematical Economics* 24: 249-58.

Patinkin, D. (1956). *Money, Interest, and Prices; An Integration of Monetary and Value Theory.* White Plains, N.Y.: Row, Peterson and Co.

Phelps, E. S. (1994). *Structural Slumps, The Modern Equilibrium Theory of Unemployment, Interest, and Assets.* Cambridge, Mass.: Harvard University Press.

Svensson, L. E. O. (1985). "Money and Asset Prices in a Cash-in-Advance Economy." *Journal of Political Economy* 93: 919-44.

Wallace, N. (1988). "A Suggestion for Oversimplifying the Theory of Money." *Economic Journal* 98: 25-36.

Weintraub, E. R. (1979). *Microfoundations, The Compatibility of Microeconomics and Macroeconomics.* Cambridge: Cambridge University Press.

Woodford, M. (1990). "Equilibrium Models of Endogenous Fluctuations: An Introduction." *NBER Working Paper* No. 3360.

CHAPTER 6

Chaos theory and Post Walrasian macroeconomics

J. Barkley Rosser, Jr.

6.1   Introduction

In Chapter 4, David Colander conceptualizes the problem of multiple equilibria and coordination failure[1] as constituting the problem of the "macrofoundations of micro."[2]   Whereas New Classical economists argue that the rational expectations hypothesis (REH) provides a rigorous "microeconomic foundation of macro," Colander argues Post Walrasian theory has stood the earlier problem on its head in that the apparent ubiquity of coordination failure problems in a world of REH multiple equilibria destroys the alleged microfoundations that were to determine macro.   Micro decision making is seen to be contingent on solving the macro coordination problem.

In this paper I spell out some of the analytic foundations for positions such as Colander's. In doing so I show that the problems for the REH microfoundations approach become even more severely exacerbated when it is recognized that such models not only can generate multiple equilibria, but that many of these equilibria may well be chaotic or complex in other ways. This fact profoundly impacts both the complexity of the coordination problem and the likelihood that failures will arise in a decentralized decision making economy. Combined with indeterminacy of equilibria, the possibility of such dynamics makes it extremely unlikely that economic agents can form rational expectations (Rosser, 1995). In effect the new approach presented by the authors in this book uses the rational expectations hypothesis to show how if one takes it seriously, it undermines not only much of the Keynesian macroeconomic theory of the past, but also the New Classical theory.[3] This paper provides a discussion of some of the mathematics underlying this new approach.

Section 6.2 of this paper briefly defines chaotic dynamics. Section 6.3 reviews several models in which chaotic macrodynamics can be deduced assuming rational expectations. Section 6.4 reviews models of chaotic macrodynamics that do not rely on the REH. Section 6.5 considers extended concepts of complexity and chaos, including non-chaotic strange attractors and transient chaos, fractal basin boundaries and multiple attractors, and interacting particle systems, with some macro applications. Section 6.6 considers some responses to all of this. Section 6.7 presents the conclusions that such dynamics make it very difficult to actually form rational expectations in a complex economic environment, and that coordination problems are likely to be ubiquitous and serious.

6.2   Defining chaos

Chaos theory originated in late nineteenth studies of celestial mechanics.[4] However it was not recognized as such until the 1960s and especially the 1970s when the term "chaos" in this context first began to be used. A seminal event in the eyes of many observers was the dramatically serendipitous discovery of the characteristic of sensitive dependence on initial conditions (SDIC) in a climatology model by Edward Lorenz (1963). Lorenz labeled this the "butterfly effect" because it implied that under the right circumstances a butterfly flapping its wings in Brazil could cause a hurricane in the U.S. Although other aspects of complex dynamics are often associated with chaos, SDIC is now widely regarded as the defining characteristic of chaotic dynamics *per se*.

SDIC is more precisely a local instability characteristic in which adjacent initial parameter values lead to sharply divergent trajectories. Despite their local explosiveness, chaotic dynamics are globally bounded and, while highly irregular, may oscillate around some discoverable long-run mean, thus allowing the possibility for rational expectations to operate in the long run, although shorter-term forecastability may be difficult to impossible. If one is dealing with a perfectly deterministic system, very short-run forecasting may be possible.[5] The rate of decay of such forecastibility turns out to be closely related to the measure which shows the presence of SDIC, namely the value of the maximum Lyapunov exponent.

If F is a dynamical system, $Ft(x)$ is the t-th iterate of F starting at initial condition x, D is the derivative, and $\vec{v}$ is a direction vector, then Lyapunov exponents are solutions to

$$L = \lim_{t \to \infty} ln(\|DFt(x)\vec{v}\|)/t \tag{6.1}$$

If the maximum real part of any of these exceeds zero then F exhibits SDIC and thus chaotic dynamics. The greater the value of such a positive real part of a maximum Lyapunov exponent, the more rapidly will the forecastibility of a deterministic chaotic system decay.[6] If more than one Lyapunov exponent has a positive real part, the system is called "hyperchaotic" (Thomsen, Mosekilde, and Sterman, 1991).

A well-known theorem for the presence of chaotic dynamics is that of Li and Yorke (1975). It shows that if a system exhibits a three-period cycle then it is chaotic. Closely related to this is the phenomenon of period-doubling (Feigenbaum, 1978) that many chaotic systems exhibit. As a crucial "tuning parameter" is varied in value, the system goes from a unique point equilibrium to a two-period cycle to a four-period cycle to an eight-period cycle and so forth, as it passes through a sequence of critical bifurcation values. This "transition to chaos" culminates with the appearance of a three-period cycle and thus of full-blown chaotic dynamics.

The problem for macroeconomic theory of the possibility of chaotic dynamics is for the formation of rational expectations. In the presence of SDIC even the slightest error quickly leads to a collapse of forecastability. Thus unless one already has rational expectations, the ability to form them is nearly impossible.

6.3   Rational expectations models of chaotic macrodynamics

6.3.1   Overlapping generations models

Overlapping generations (OLG) models (Allais, 1947; Samuelson, 1958) were the first to be used for generating chaotic macrodynamics models with REH, indeed with perfect foresight. Gale (1973) initially showed that they could be used to generate endogenous cycles[7] and Benhabib and Day (1980, 1982) first used them to show perfect foresight chaotic dynamics.

In each time period t let there be two generations with the young possessing endowments of w_y and the old possessing endowments of w_o. At $t = 0$ the old possess fiat money $= M$. $P(t)$, $c_y(t)$, and $c_o(t)$ are respectively prices, consumption by the young, and consumption by the old in time t. The young maximize utility

$$\max U[c_y(t), c_o(t + 1)], \tag{6.2}$$

subject to their intertemporal budget constraint

$$p(t)c_y(t) + p(t + 1)c_o(t + 1) = p(t + 1)w_o. \tag{6.3}$$

(6.2) and (6.3) generate an inter-generational offer curve by the young, O, as $p(t)$ and $p(t + 1)$ vary. In time $= 1$ the old face the constraint

$$p(1)c_o(1) = p(1)w_o + M. \tag{6.4}$$

(6.2), (6.3), and (6.4) combine with a Ricardian intertemporal production possibilities frontier

$$R = [(c_y, c_o): c_y + c_o = w_y + w_o] \tag{6.5}$$

to solve for a sequence of efficient perfect foresight price and consumption equilibria levels. This implies a multiplicity of equilibria as the initial conditions vary.

The degree of nonlinearity of the offer curve, O, determines the nature of the dynamics. Benhabib and Day (1982) show sufficient conditions on the constrained intertemporal marginal rate of substitution, levels of endowments, and rates of population growth for chaotic dynamics to occur.[8] Such a case is shown in Figure 6.1.

An even more influential model based on this OLG model and deriving more directly from the sunspot-self-fulfilling-prophetic tradition of multiple equilibria outcomes is that of Grandmont (1985). He focuses on how interest rate changes drive conflicts between intertemporal wealth and substitution effects. Chaotic dynamics can emerge if older agents have a sufficiently greater marginal propensity to consume leisure than do younger ones. If a is real wealth and V is the indirect utility function of either generation, then the Arrow-Pratt relative degree of risk aversion which gives the curvature of V is

$$R(a) = -V''(a)a/V'(a). \qquad (6.6)$$

If $R_o(a_o) > R_y(a_y)$, then chaotic cycles will occur.

Figure 6.2 shows such a perfect foresight case for the Grandmont model with the axes being real money balances, μ, in time t on the horizontal and $t + 1$ on the vertical. Nonlinearity of $x(\mu)$ increases with $R_o(a_o)$, holding $R_y(a_y)$ constant. Grandmont sees this causing an "expectations coordination problem." He argues that government fiscal policy regarding intergenerational transfers can pin down expectations of the interest rate and eliminate these cycles, an argument we shall return to in section 6.6.[9]

6.3.2   Infinite horizon models

OLG models are not infinite horizon optimization models because of the finite horizon of the agents. This opens them and related incomplete financial markets models (Woodford, 1989) to criticism by strict New Classicals whose models generally involve infinitely-lived agents optimizing over their lifetimes with complete markets in a full Walrasian intertemporal general equilibrium. However, a number of models have appeared in which chaotic dynamics can arise even under these circumstances.[10]

It has been known since Sutherland (1970) that very high discount rates can lead to non-convergence to a unique steady-state equilibrium in optimal, multisector, infinite horizon models. Boldrin and Montrucchio (1986) show that chaotic dynamics can occur in such a situation. Although their initial model only generates such a result for wildly unrealistic discount rates of 10,000% and above, this number can be lowered by alterations such as increasing the number of

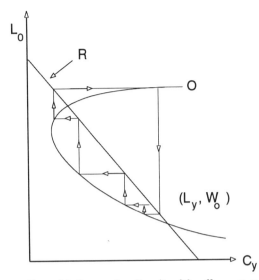

Figure 6.1 Degree of nonlinearity of the offer curve and the nature of dynamics.

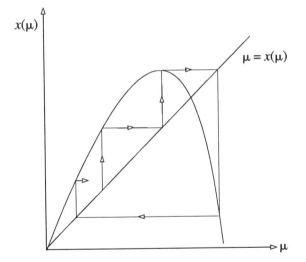

Figure 6.2 A perfect foresight case for the Grandmont model.

substitutable factors and their ranges of substitutability (Neuman, O'Brien, Hoag, and Kim, 1988; Boldrin, 1989).

Deneckere and Pelikan (1986) show that strongly decreasing returns to scale and sectoral capital-intensity reversals can generate perfect foresight, infinite horizon chaotic dynamics.

Matsuyama (1991) develops a model of optimal infinite horizon optimization with complete markets in which real money balances directly enter the utility function of agents in a manner non-separable from consumption goods. The crucial factors in his model turn out to be the rate of growth of real money balances compared to the discount rate and the elasticity of intertemporal substitution of the real balances. He derives a sufficient condition for chaotic dynamics based on these variables that is positively related to the growth rate of real money balances relative to the other variables.

This demonstration of the possibility of chaotic dynamics even in models with complete rational expectations and intertemporal optimization means that the forecastability issues associated with SDIC are not artifacts simply of some "Keynesian market incompleteness" or other alleged non-Walrasian deficiency. They can occur in fully specified Walrasian and New Classical models. If there are multiple equilibria and any noise at all, short-run errors can explode into larger scale coordination failures.

6.4   Chaotic macrodynamics without rational expectations

A large and growing set of models have been adduced in which chaotic macrodynamics can arise in contexts in which neither perfect foresight nor REH hold. The earliest of these were derived from an ecological model of May (1976), who provided the earliest discussion of the possibility of deriving economics models that might exhibit chaotic dynamics. Thus it is not surprising that many of these models either depend on Malthusian demoeconomics, analogies to predator-prey models, or pollution-generated constraints on aggregate growth that become the source of the nonlinearities underlying chaotic dynamics.

One model directly influenced by May's work is due to Stutzer (1980). This is an updated version of an earlier "evolutionary" model of Haavelmo (1954) with a population density limit producing nonlinearity. As the natural population growth rate increases so does the degree of nonlinearity and the tendency to chaotic dynamics.

Day (1983) presents an overtly Malthusian model which depends on a maximum population level. Sufficiency conditions depend on the natural population growth rate, the average product of labor at the maximum population, and the level of subsistence.

Bhaduri and Harris (1987) develop a Ricardian model with fixed land and a maximum marginal product of labor. Chaotic dynamics can emerge with a sufficiently high ratio of the maximum marginal product of labor to the wage rate ("the rate of exploitation at primitive accumulation" or "maximum rate of exploitation").

Pohjola (1981) shows possible chaotic dynamics in a model using Lotka-Volterra predator-prey dynamics derived from a class-conflict model due to Goodwin (1967). Nonlinearity arises from the interaction of the natural rate of growth of employment interacting with a wage markup parameter. A sufficiently high rate of employment growth triggers chaotic dynamics.

Day (1982) derives chaotic dynamics from a modified Solow-type neoclassical growth model. It operates in discrete time with capital stock a lagged function of savings and output. Most crucially there is an upper limit to the capital-labor ratio and a productivity-inhibiting factor related to the capital stock, presumed by Day to be due to negative pollution feedbacks or possibly a variable savings function.

Various nonlinear investment function models exist. One by Day and Shafer (1985) is essentially a fix-price-IS/LM neoKeynesian type with investment as a nonlinear and non-monotonic function of income. Chaos emerges with sufficient nonlinearity of that latter function. Other nonlinear investment function models derive from the Kaldor (1940) trade cycle model (Dana and Malgrange, 1984), and the Hicks (1950) trade cycle model (Blatt, 1983).

There have been a number of models taking off from nonlinear multiplier-accelerator models. One class derives from Samuelson's (1939) recognition that the consumption function might be nonlinear, especially at higher income levels. These include Blatt (1983) and Gabisch (1984). Another category follows the nonlinear accelerator approach of Goodwin (1951) and is exemplified by Puu (1993).

Yet another category looks at chaotic long wave dynamics. A traditional emphasis on innovations clustering and absorption is Goodwin (1986). Another model focusing on a long wave cycle of socialist investment and related systemic transformation is Rosser and Rosser (1994).

Finally, we have a group of models that focus on financial constraint issues (Foley, 1987; Woodford, 1989; Semmler and Sieveking, 1993). A version of this approach that emphasizes Minsky-like properties and also self-fulfilling multiple equilibria aspects is due to Delli Gatti, Gallegati, and Gardini (1993).[11]

In these models the issue is no longer the breakdown of the ability to form rational expectations or even the breakdown of forecastability assuming rational expectations. Chaotic dynamics and thus SDIC are seen to be possible in a variety of models for a variety of reasons. The implication is that forecasting breakdowns can occur even if other forms of expectations are being used, such as adaptive. Explosive forecast errors can arise from small initial mistakes. This totally complicates coordination efforts in multiple equilibria situations, thus increasing the likelihood of general coordination failure.

6.5   Complexity beyond formal chaos

6.5.1   Non-chaotic strange attractors and transient chaos

Let $G(x)$ be a dynamical system in n-dimensional real number space. A is an *attractor* (or attracting set) if it is closed and if there exists a neighborhood U of A such that if $G(x)$ in U for $t > 0$, then $G(x) \rightarrow A$ as $t \rightarrow \infty$. A *repellor* (or repelling set) is defined equivalently except by replacing t with $-t$. A *basin of attraction of* A is the set of all points from which $G(x)$ will converge on A. A fixed point that is neither an attractor nor a repellor is a *saddle*.

In economic systems attractors correspond with our concept of stable long-run equilibria, the simplest case being a point attractor for an entire system. However, attractors may take the form of limit cycles and more complex sets. From an early time the association was made between systems exhibiting highly complex or irregular dynamics and the presence of an attractor set of a sufficient degree of topological complexity.

This was formalized in the concept of the *strange attractor*. We shall not provide a formal definition here of such an attractor (Rosser, 1991: Ch. 2). However we note that it is not a finite set of points, is not a closed curve, is not smooth, and is not bounded by a piecewise smooth closed surface (Brindley and Kapitaniak, 1991). A very important characteristic of such a set, and the key to its econometric detection, is that it possesses non-integer dimensionality, labeled *fractal dimensionality* by Mandelbrot (1983). The canonical example of such a set is the Cantor set, which is the residual in the unit interval left after an infinite process whereby one removes the open middle third, then the open middle thirds of what remains, and so forth.

There is more than one way to define such fractal dimensionality. A popular one for the purposes of seeking "strange hidden structure" in economic data has been the *correlation dimension* of Grassberger and Procaccia (1983). This involves examining the number of pairs of points in a trajectory that are less than distance r apart, that is $N(r)$. In particular this dimension is given by

$$\lim_{r \to 0} \ln N(r)/\ln r. \tag{6.7}$$

This measure enters into the construction of the BDS statistic (Brock, Dechert, and Scheinkman, 1987) which has been widely used as a general test for nonlinear dependence in economic data.

For quite a long time it was thought that chaotic dynamics as defined by SDIC and the presence of a strange attractor were equivalent concepts, and indeed there are many dynamical systems which exhibit both simultaneously.[12] But it is now known that they are merely overlapping. This has led to the study of non-chaotic strange attractors (Grebogi, Ott, Pelikan, and Yorke, 1984). Such systems may exhibit *transient chaos*, that is they may exhibit SDIC for an arbitrarily long period of time, but will eventually lose that characteristic in the long run. They may look chaotic but are not really.

Such systems have been studied within macroeconomics by Lorenz (1992; 1993b). In the earlier of those papers he considers a modified version of the Kaldor (1940) trade cycle model in which there is a long-run non-chaotic strange attractor but short-term dynamics are chaotic.[13]

Letting $Y = GDP$, K = capital stock, and C = consumption, the specific model studied by Lorenz is one modified by Hermann (1986) and is given by

$$\Delta Y_{t+1} = \alpha(\beta(\gamma Y_t - K_t) + \delta K_t + C(Y_t) - Y_t), \tag{6.8}$$

$$\Delta K_{t+1} = (\Delta Y_{t+1}/\alpha) + Y_t - \delta K_t - C(Y_t), \tag{6.9}$$

with $\alpha > 0$, $\beta > 0$, $\gamma > 0$. The solution to this set of differential equations includes numerous ranges of transient chaos within the range of the larger non-chaotic strange attractor dominating long-run dynamics.

This suggests that chaotic dynamics can appear and disappear in systems without any warning and without any changing of structural parameters or coefficients. Thus forecastability can break down without warning and coordination failure can spontaneously erupt with little warning in a multiple equilibria world.

6.5.2 Fractal basin boundaries and multiple attractors

Lorenz (1992, 1993b) also examines a complication that can arise in such models, namely that of multiple attractors, a question of obvious interest to students of multiple equilibria and coordination failures. Now offhand this would not seem to be an issue. Once a trajectory is in a basin of attraction it should stay there even if the attractor itself is strange. However, it turns out that the dynamics depend on the nature of the boundaries of the basins of attraction – are they regular or strange (fractal)?

Basins of attraction possess boundaries and those boundaries can be categorized according to their topological character. Those which are smooth and connected and possess integer dimensionality are regular. But it is possible for basin boundaries to fail to be any of the above – to be fractal (McDonald, Grebogi, Ott, and Yorke, 1985).

In such a case a trajectory can spend a long time in a saddle zone without actually being in a basin. Because of the tangled nature of the basin boundaries, a trajectory can in effect track one attractor for quite a long time without actually being in its basin of attraction, and then can quite suddenly jump to following another attractor definitively. The first may be strange with the second being regular (an m-period orbit),[14] the fact that basin boundaries are fractal not implying necessarily that the attractors themselves are fractal. Also the long-run attractor of a system may be infinity, but it may remain in a finite orbit, strange or otherwise, for an arbitrarily long time. Lorenz (1993b) notes that what is likely to happen in such cases is that the system itself will evolve and become something different, thus leading to a sequence of truncated trajectories wherein the short-term dynamics may have nothing to do with the long-run attractors.

Allowing parameter variation simply makes all of this worse. Although not directly presented in economics models, a variety of bifurcations that can happen under different systems with fractal basin boundaries have been categorized by Thompson (1992). Among those that can occur are catastrophic exploding bifurcations where an attracting set is suddenly enlarged and catastrophic dangerous bifurcations wherein there can be the "blue-sky disappearance" of an attractor with a sudden distant jump to another attractor of any form.

6.5.3   Interacting particle systems models

Yet another approach to both chaotic and more general complex dynamics has come from considering the internal interactions of agents within macroeconomies. This can be done by using the interacting particle systems (IPS) or random mean-field theory approach followed by Brock (1993) and Durlauf (1993). This approach posits optimizing agents whose coordinating behavior is explicitly modeled according to certain interaction parameters.[15]

Following Brock (1993) we let there be an underlying probability structure facing welfare-maximizing decision makers. Let $u(\omega_i)$ be the utility for agent i of choice ω_i, J denote the sum of utilities of the n "neighbors of i," m be the average own-utility to other agents, h be a discrete-choice parameter for own-behavior over the expectation of errors, β represent "intensity of choice," x be actual values, N be the number of agents, and $M = nm$. The component of social utility generated by agent i is

$$V(\omega_i;m) = u(\omega_i) + Jm\omega_i + h\omega_i + \mu\varepsilon(\omega_i),   \qquad (6.10)$$

with $\varepsilon(\omega_i)$ independent and identically distributed extreme value (IIDEV). Given the overall probability distribution, m is an order parameter which can be solved assuming stochastic maximization as m^* for $N \rightarrow \infty$. Drawing on a parallelism between the welfare measure of discrete choice theory (Manski and McFadden, 1981) and the free energy function of statistical mechanics, let

$$y = x(\beta J/N)^{1/2},   \qquad (6.11)$$

from which we get

$$y^* = \text{Argmax}[M(\beta h + y)\exp(-y^2/2\beta J),   \qquad (6.12)$$

which solves for a Nash social welfare optimum m^* as

$$m^* = M'(\beta h + y^*)/M(\beta h + y^*). \tag{6.13}$$

For the special discrete case of (-1, 1) outcomes, this becomes

$$m = \tanh(\beta Jm + \beta h), \tag{6.14}$$

which bifurcates at $J = 1$ with two nonzero solutions $m(-) = -m(+)$, arising for $\beta J > 1$. This is the phase transition which in a particle system could represent the shift from one state of matter to another (liquid to solid, unmagnetized to magnetized).

In the discrete choice framework this indicates a suddenly heightened, or lowered, degree of interaction between the agents. In a financial market this could generate the emergence of a speculative bubble or the collapse of one. In a multiple equilibria, coordination-of-real-investment model this could represent a discrete change in the degree of coordination and hence a jump to a discretely different macroeconomic equilibrium. Or it could indicate a discrete change in the level of externalities in a search model (Howitt, 1985) with an associated discontinuous jump in the equilibrium outcome.

This model, which does not necessarily generate chaotic dynamics, may be more useful for characterizing economic time series in which there are long periods of apparent stability followed by some discontinuous shift in behavior with a new equilibrium arising. In this case it must be remembered that this shift is endogenously generated.

6.5.4   Self-organized criticality

A competing approach to that of the IPS model is that of self-organized criticality or "sandpile" models. It can achieve somewhat similar apparent outcomes as the IPS approach but with some fundamental differences. Bak, Chen, Scheinkman, and Woodford (1993) have developed such a model with a detailed lattice structure of production in stages. Exogenous shock demands ("sand") for goods arrive at one end and are transmitted through the lattice to the stage of actual production. The nature of the internal relationships allows for bunching of production orders to occur through the stages of the lattice, "avalanches" which can be identified as surges of production increases or decreases.

Ultimately Bak, Chen, Scheinkman, and Woodford show that while the distribution of exogenous shocks may be Gaussian normal, the bunching process through the stages of production leads to a distribution of outcomes that is non-normal. There is a "tail" of "avalanches," dramatic increases or decreases of output. At any point the system is poised in what could be called a temporary equilibrium that is not a long-run equilibrium. This temporary equilibrium is described as reflecting "self-organized criticality" but the fact that it is constantly out of long-run equilibrium is key to the tendency for "avalanches" from time to time as shocks occasionally trigger the influence of the longer-run equilibrium (no sandpile) on the temporary equilibrium (flattening a sandpile to where it stabilizes at a new level of self-organized criticality).

This model can be viewed as one of motion from one equilibrium to another in a multiple equilibria world, driven by coordination failures within the production lattice. On the other hand it can be argued that this is simply a New Classical model where all macroeconomic motion arises from exogenous shocks, even if these shocks are reinforced by internal mechanisms from time to time.

6.5.5   Other approaches to complex self-organization

Self-organized criticality is just one of several approaches to self-organization in complex economic systems. The full development of these is beyond the scope of this paper, but we note a few strands and their relation to discussions of Post Walrasian macroeconomics. In particular we focus upon those that use notions of strategic complementarity or external economy, ideas influential in post Walrasian macroeconomics more generally because of their role in generating multiple equilibria.

Prominent in this regard is the work of W. B. Arthur (1988). Although generally focusing more on questions of technological innovation and diffusion rather than on macroeconomic models, his work has implications for the latter as in Arthur, Ermoliev, and Kaniovski (1987). In these models of technological innovation and diffusion, the existence of either returns to learning or scale or strategic complementarities bring about not only multiple equilibria but also the phenomenon of "path-dependence." This suggests that at an early stage in the process many outcomes may be possible, but that beyond some point where movement in one direction reaches a "critical mass" it dominates all other outcomes and the system "locks-in" on that particular attractor toward which it then moves.

A very important point is that there is no guarantee that this outcome will be optimal. Random events may influence the early stages and bring about the lock-in – in the case of technology, possibly to an "inferior" technology such as the infamous case of the "QWERTY" keyboard in near virtually universal use (David, 1985). In macroeconomics there is the clear possibility of lock-in to a low growth path with various other undesirable features.

It is noteworthy here that such models can involve either intermittent or transient chaos at the beginning stage prior to the lock-in. Although the initial processes may be purely random, they might also be deterministic to some extent and subject to SDIC. Such ideas have been associated with views of evolutionary processes in which ordered structures emerge out of chaotic transition zones. Such ideas have been prominent in the "Brussels School" associated with Ilya

Prigogine (Prigogine and Stengers, 1984). Applications in economics of this approach have generally been for urban and regional economics (Allen and Sanglier, 1981) or for the technology innovation and diffusion issue (Allen, 1994), but the same basic ideas of strategic complementarities and multiple equilibria underlying endogenous self-organization are there.[16]

Finally, we cannot leave the topic of self-organizing economies without noting the Austrian view on this subject. That free markets spontaneously self-organize is a deeply rooted idea in Austrian economics dating clear back to Carl Menger and his analysis of the spontaneous emergence of commodity monies. Hayek (1967) updated such discussion in a non-mathematical form, but eventually would be influenced by chaos and complexity theory in his ideas (Lavoie, 1989). Of course the Austrians have faith that if an economy is sufficiently laissez-faire, what will evolutionarily emerge is probably "the best of all possible worlds." Generally the possibility of multiple equilibria or of path-dependent lock-in to an undesirable path is ruled out by them, but not by others considering complex self-organization.

6.6   Overcoming chaos

In a world where full rationality leads to chaotic or other complex dynamics, what will rational individuals do? In the face of computational complexity the response is likely to be to adopt simple rules of thumb and adaptive learning schemes (Heiner, 1983; Leijonhuvfud, 1993). Rationality involves abandoning rational expectations, at least in the short run. This overthrows New Classical economics except as a possible long-run, asymptotic outcome, thus re-signifying the old Keynesian charge that "in the long run we are all dead."

One school of thought argues that appropriately structured learning processes will converge on the rational expectations steady-state golden rule path, least-squares learning having this property under the right conditions (Marcet and Sargent, 1989). Several problems arise here. One is that such learning processes may converge on cycles (Grandmont, 1985), on sunspot equilibria (Woodford, 1990),[17] or even possess chaotic dynamics (Evans, 1985). More fundamentally, such models presume a unique real outcome with the multiplicity of equilibria ultimately being unstable bubbles. Guesnerie (1993) shows that this strategy will fundamentally fail if there are multiple real equilibria, which is exactly what occurs in the world of coordination failures and complex dynamics.

Basically in a world of multiple self-fulfilling prophetic equilibria there are both an "expectations coordination" problem and a related "learning coordination" problem. How do we get different people to adopt learning processes that converge on the same equilibrium, preferably a full-employment Pareto optimal one? Drawing on Woodford (1990), Evans and Honkapohja (1993) argue that even with multiple sunspot equilibria, fiscal policy can be used to generate path-dependence on a learning track to an optimal outcome in a model with external increasing returns to scale and coordination failures in an OLG framework. The fiscal policy is a subsidy to output financed by a lump-sum tax. Clearly this nice result may not hold in a fundamentally chaotic environment where the government may also not be able to make a proper forecast of the various equilibrium outcomes.

It may be, as Grandmont (1985) argues, that even with potential chaos, government fiscal (and perhaps monetary) policy can pin down expectations or generate an appropriate learning process. But there may be some further level of coordination that can play a role. One such, suggested by Guesnerie (1993), is the "concerted" indicative planning process used by the French with great success in the 1950s and 1960s. In that system major actors discuss together possible scenarios, thus jointly forming a macroeconomic plan that, while strictly voluntary, may succeed in coordinating expectations and in the best outcome bringing about a favorable self-fulfilling prophetic outcome. In the case of French planning, this broke down from unexpected shocks (student riots and oil prices especially) that undid the carefully laid plans and ultimately destroyed the credibility of the planning process.

More broadly, even if governments lack the knowledge or the ability to forecast sufficiently so as to implement optimal policies within a chaotic or complex dynamics environment, just as individuals lack this ability, nevertheless they can create a stabilizing force simply through establishing inertial tendencies within an economy. Fundamental to this is the existence of an institutional framework that bounds economic behavior. In effect, the existence of such a framework "rules out" many potential equilibria. Expectations are formed and operate within the existing institutional framework which then provides a degree of stability for individual decision makers, the macrofoundation of micro. However, even though institutions frequently perform such a function, they themselves are subject to complex evolutionary dynamics and processes. Thus there will be times when decision makers face ultimate indeterminacy and multiplicity.

6.7   Conclusions

The problem of finding a macrofoundation for micro decision making is profoundly complicated by the possible existence of complex and chaotic nonlinear dynamics interacting with the possible existence of coordination failure associated with multiple equilibria. Chaotic dynamics imply sensitive dependence on initial conditions and thus, when combined with exogenous noise, great difficulty in making predictions even in situations of rational expectations.

Indeed the implication of such dynamics is that rational expectations will be impossible to form because the appropriate learning will be impossible. This result generalizes to a large degree to broader categories of complex dynamics processes that may not be strictly chaotic, such as non-chaotic strange attractors, fractal basin boundaries, interacting particle systems models, self-organized criticality, and models exhibiting path-dependence arising from network externalities and strategic complementarities.

This leads many to argue for intervention by government to generate an appropriate macrofoundation for microeconomic decision making through fiscal, monetary, or even concerted indicative planning policy which can eliminate chaotic or complex dynamics. However we must be cautious even here as the possibility of such interventions actually generating more noise and creating chaotic dynamics where none were occurring must be taken into account as well. Thus what may be most important of all is the bounding of decisions that occurs due to the existence of an institutional framework, even if it is "nonoptimal," reducing to some degree the difficulty of the Post Walrasian decision making environment. But it should be remembered that even such bounding is no guarantee against the endogenously generated "unexpected" in a potentially chaotic and dynamically complex economy

Endnotes

The author wishes to acknowledge the receipt of useful materials or comments from William A. Brock, David Colander, Paul Davidson, Richard H. Day, Steven Durlauf, Harry Garretsen, Roger Guesnerie, Hans van Ees, Peter Howitt, Ted Jaditz, Hans-Walter Lorenz, Benoit B. Mandelbrot, Rob McClelland, John D. Sterman, Tonu Puu, Mark White, and several anonymous reviewers.

1. The concept of coordination failure is due to Clower (1969) and Leijonhufvud (1973). More recent development is due to Bryant (1987), Cooper and John (1988), and Guesnerie (1993).

2. Colander (1992) distinguished New Keynesianism based on multiple equilibria from that based on information problems or menu costs (Mankiw and Romer, 1991) which he labeled "New neoKeynesian" economics. This author (1990) made a similar distinction calling, the former "Strong New Keynesianism" and the latter "Weak New Keynesianism." Van Ees and Garretsen (1992, 1993) provide extended discussions comparing the approaches. Colander has now shifted the terminology to Post Walrasian, and I follow his new terminology in this paper.

3. Many observers, including this one, argue that this result is consistent with the emphasis on Keynesian uncertainty that undergirds much of U.S. Post Keynesian theory. However, this is disputed by one of that theory's major developers, Paul Davidson (1992: 449) who asks, "Where's the Keynesian beef in New Keynesian economics?"

4. See Rosser (1991, Ch. 2) for a detailed account of the history of chaos theory. Gleick (1987) provides a popular account.

5. The presence of noise sharply reduces this forecastability under SDIC (Casdagli, Eubank, Farmer, and Gibson, 1991).

6. The term "deterministic chaos" implies a basic conflict in that chaotic dynamics look random on the surface. This is the source of many of the numerous econometric difficulties in estimating such systems (Brock, Hsieh, and LeBaron, 1991). No definitive econometric demonstra-

tion of deterministic chaos in an economic system has been made yet. Part of the problem is that none of the existing methods for estimating Lyapunov exponents (such as Nychka, Ellner, Gallant, and McCaffrey, 1992) possess known distributions of reliability statistics.

7. Such models have been the workhorse of the "sunspot equilibria" approach (Cass and Shell, 1983; Azariadis and Guesnerie, 1986) which depends on the concept of self-fulfilling prophetic outcomes driven by "extrinsic" variables. This approach has been important in studying the general problem of multiple equilibria and of coordination problems, even in the absence of chaotic dynamics.

8. The efficiency of these chaotic trajectories has led some observers (Mirowski, 1990; Carrier, 1993) to criticize these models as merely more sophisticated justifications of the basic neoclassical approach that fail to address the true severity of fundamental uncertainty, an argument that echoes the complaint of Davidson: "Although a rose by any other name is still a (sweet smelling) rose, it does not follow that calling the foul smelling fruit of the gingko tree a rose will make it smell any better for policy making purposes" (1992: 456) .

9. Many argue that the government will be no better than individuals at forecasting under such circumstances. Dwyer (1992) and DeCoster and Mitchell (1992) go further to argue that attempted government stabilization policies can actually induce chaotic dynamics where none would exist under laissez-faire. See also Bullard and Butler (1993) for further policy discussion.

10. See Boldrin and Woodford (1990) for a survey of these.

11. This review only scratches the surface of these models. See Rosser (1991) and Lorenz (1993a) for more extended discussions.

12. In fact there continues to be disagreement about the meaning of "chaos" with a holdout faction favoring the strange attractor concept, notably Mandelbrot.

13. This must be contrasted with the concept of "intermittency" of chaos. Intermittency involves changing parameter values of a system and observing that as a parameter is monotonically changed, a region of chaotic dynamics can appear, disappear, and then reappear. In the case of transiency the parameter values are held constant and chaotic dynamics are appearing and disappearing.

14. It should be noted that if an attractor is a cycle of very long period, it may look irregular in shorter time horizons.

15. A related model is that of Glance and Huberman (1993) which takes a game theoretic approach to critical points for cooperation or non-cooperation within groups.

16. Closely related to the Brussels School is the Stuttgart School of synergetics. See Haken (1977), Weidlich and Haag (1983), and Zhang (1991).

17. Guesnerie and Woodford (1992) present learning process cases where sunspot equilibria will be expectationally stable but the Classical steady state is not.

References

Allais, M. (1947). *Économie et Interêt*. Paris: Imprimerie National.

Allen, P. M. (1994). "Evolutionary Complex Systems: Models of Technology Change." In L. Leydesdorff and P. Van den Besselaar, eds., *Evolutionary Economics and Chaos Theory: New Directions in Technology Studies*. New York: St. Martin's Press, 1-17.

Allen, P. M. and M. Sanglier (1981). "Urban Evolution, Self-Organization and Decision Making." *Environment and Planning A* 13: 167-83.

Arthur, W. B. (1988). "Self-Reinforcing Mechanisms in Economics." In P.W. Anderson, K.J. Arrow, and D. Pines, eds., *The Economy as an Evolving Complex System*. Redwood City, Calif.: Addison-Wesley, 9-32.

Arthur, W. B., Y. M. Ermoliev, and Y. M. Kaniovski (1987). "Path-Dependent Processes and the Emergence of Macro-Structure." *European Journal of Operational Research* 30: 294-303.

Azariadis, C. and R. Guesnerie (1986). "Sunspots and Cycles." *Review of Economic Studies* 53: 725-36.

Bak, P., K. Chen, J. Scheinkman, and M. Woodford (1993). "Aggregate Fluctuations from Independent Sectoral Shocks: Self-organized Criticality in a Model of Production and Inventory Dynamics." *Ricerche Economiche* 47: 3-30.

Benhabib, J. and R. H. Day (1980). "Rational Choice and Erratic Accumulation." *Economics Letters* 6: 113-7.

  (1982). "A Characterization of Erratic Dynamics in the Overlapping Generations Model." *Journal of Economic Dynamics and Control* 4: 37-55.

Bhaduri, A. and D. J. Harris (1987). "The Complex Dynamics of the Simple Ricardian System." *Quarterly Journal of Economics* 102: 893-901.

Blatt, J. M. (1983). *Dynamic Economic Systems: A Post-Keynesian Approach*. Armonk, N.Y.: M.E. Sharpe.

Boldrin, M. (1989). "Paths of Optimal Accumulation in Two-Sector Models." In W.A. Barnett, J. Geweke, and K. Shell, eds., *Economic Complexity: Chaos, Sunspots, Bubbles, and Nonlinearity*. Cambridge: Cambridge University Press, 231-52.

Boldrin, M. and L. Montrucchio (1986). "On the Indeterminacy of Capital Accumulation Paths." *Journal of Economic Theory* 40: 26-39.

Boldrin, M. and M. Woodford (1990). "Equilibrium Models Displaying Endogenous Fluctuations and Chaos: A Survey." *Journal of Monetary Economics* 25: 189-222.

Brindley, J. and T. Kapitaniak (1991). "Existence and Characterization of Strange Nonchaotic Attractors in Nonlinear Systems." *Chaos, Solitons & Fractals* 1: 323-37.

Brock, W. A. (1993). "Pathways to Randomness in the Economy: Emergent Nonlinearity and Chaos in Economics and Finance." *Estudios Economicos* 8: 3-55.

Brock, W. A., W. D. Dechert, and J. Scheinkman (1987). "A Test for Independence Based on the Correlation Dimension." SSRI Paper No. 8702, University of Wisconsin-Madison.

Brock, W. A., D. Hsieh, and B. LeBaron (1991). *Nonlinear Economic Dynamics, Chaos, and Instability*. Cambridge, Mass.: MIT Press.

Bryant, J. (1987). "The Paradox of Thrift, Liquidity Preferences and Animal Spirits." *Econometrica* 55: 1231-37.

Bullard, J. and A. Butler (1993). "Nonlinearity and Chaos in Economic Models: Implications for Policy Decisions." *Economic Journal* 103: 849-67.

Carrier, D. (1993). "Will Chaos Kill the Auctioneer?" *Review of Political Economy* 5: 299-320.

Casdagli, M., S. Eubank, J. Doyne Farmer, and J. Gibson (1991). "State Space Reconstruction in the Presence of Noise." *Physica D* 51: 52-98.

Cass, D. and K. Shell (1983) "Do Sunspots Matter?" *Journal of Political Economy* 91: 193-227.

Clower, R. W. (1969). "The Keynesian Revolution: A Theoretical Appraisal." In R. W. Clower, ed., *Monetary Theory: Selected Readings*. Harmondsworth: Penguin, 270-97.

Colander, D. (1993). "The Macrofoundations of Micro." *Eastern Economic Journal* 19: 447-58.

  (1992). "The New, the Neo, and the New Neo." *Methodus: Bulletin of the International Network for Economic Method* 4: 166-70.

104   J. Barkley Rosser, Jr.

Cooper, R. and A. John (1988). "Coordinating Coordination Failures." *Quarterly Journal of Economics* 103: 441-65.

Dana, R.-A. and P. Malgrange (1984). "The Dynamics of a Discrete Version of a Growth Model." In J. P. Ancot, ed., *Analysing the Structure of Econometric Models.* Boston: Martinus Nijhoff, 115-42.

David, P. (1985). "CLIO and the Economics of QWERTY." *American Economic Review Papers and Proceedings* 75: 332-37.

Davidson, P. (1992). "Would Keynes be a New Keynesian?" *Eastern Economic Journal* 18: 449-64.

Day, R. H. (1982). "Irregular Growth Cycles." *American Economic Review* 72:406-414.
    (1983). "The Emergence of Chaos from Classical Economic Growth." *Quarterly Journal of Economics* 98: 201-13.

Day, R. H. and W. Shafer (1985). "Keynesian Chaos." *Journal of Macroeconomics* 7: 277-95.

DeCoster, G. P. and D. W. Mitchell (1992). "Dynamic Implications of Chaotic Monetary Policy." *Journal of Macroeconomics* 14: 267-87.

Delli Gatti, D., M. Gallegati, and L. Gardini (1993). "Investment Confidence, Corporate Debt and Income Fluctuations." *Journal of Economic Behavior and Organization* 22: 161-88.

Deneckere, R. and S. Pelikan (1986). "Competitive Chaos." *Journal of Economic Theory* 40: 13-25.

Durlauf, S. N. (1993). "Nonergodic Economic Growth." *Review of Economic Studies* 60: 349-66.

Dwyer, G. P., Jr. (1992). "Stabilization Policy Can Lead to Chaos." *Economic Inquiry* 30: 40-46.

Evans, G. W. (1985). "Expectational Stability and the Multiple Equilibria Problem in Linear Rational Expectations Models." *Quarterly Journal of Economics* 100: 1217-33.

Evans, G. W. and S. Honkapohja (1993). "Learning and Economic Fluctuations: Using Fiscal Policy to Steer Expectations." *European Economic Review* 37: 595-602.

Feigenbaum, M. J. (1978). "Quantitative Universality for a Class of Nonlinear Transformations." *Journal of Statistical Physics* 19: 25-52.

Foley, D. (1987). "Liquidity-Profit Rate Cycles in a Capitalist Economy." *Journal of Economic Behavior and Organization* 8: 363-77.

Gabisch, G. (1984). "Nonlinear Models of Business Cycle Theory." In G. Hammer and D. Pallaschke, eds., *Selected Topics in Operations Research and Mathematical Economics.* Berlin: Springer-Verlag, 205-22.

Gale, D. (1973). "Pure Exchange Equilibrium of Dynamic Economic Models." *Journal of Economic Theory* 6: 12-36.

Glance, N. S. and B. A. Huberman (1993). "The Outbreak of Cooperation." *Journal of Mathematical Sociology* 17: 281-302.

Gleick, J. (1987). *Chaos: The Making of a New Science.* New York: Viking.

Goodwin, R. M. (1951). "The Nonlinear Accelerator and the Persistence of Business Cycles." *Econometrica* 19: 1-17.
    (1967). "A Growth Cycle." In C. H. Feinstein, ed., *Socialism, Capitalism, and Economic Growth.* Cambridge: Cambridge University Press, 54-58.
    (1986). "The Economy as an Evolutionary Pulsator." *Journal of Economic Behavior and Organization* 7: 341-9.

Grandmont, J.-M. (1985). "On Endogenous Competitive Business Cycles." *Econometrica* 53: 995-1045.

Grassberger, P. and I. Procaccia (1983). "Measuring the Strangeness of Strange Attractors." *Physica D* 9: 189-208.

Grebogi, C., E. Ott, S. Pelikan, and J. A. Yorke (1984). "Strange Attractors that Are Not Chaotic." *Physica D* 13: 261-68.

Guesnerie, R. (1993). "Successes and Failures in Coordinating Expectations." *European Economic Review* 37: 243-68.

Guesnerie, R. and M. Woodford (1992). "Endogenous Fluctuations." In J.-J. Laffont, ed., *Advances in Economic Theory: Sixth World Congress*, Vol. II. Cambridge: Cambridge University Press, 289-412.

Haavelmo, T. (1954). *A Study in the Theory of Economic Evolution*. Amsterdam: North-Holland.

Haken, H. (1977). *"Synergetics" Nonequilibrium Phase Transitions and Social Measurement*. Berlin: Springer-Verlag.

Hayek, F. A. (1967). "The Theory of Complex Phenomena." In *Studies in Philosophy, Politics, and Economics*. London: Routledge & Kegan Paul, 22-42.

Heiner, R. A. (1983). "The Origins of Predictable Behavior." *American Economic Review* 33: 137-58.

Hermann, R. (1986). "Stability and Chaos in a Kaldor-type Model." DP 22, Department of Economics, University of Groningen.

Hicks, J. R. (1950). *A Contribution to the Theory of the Trade Cycle*. Oxford: Oxford University Press.

Howitt, P. (1985). "Transactions Costs and the Theory of Unemployment." *American Economic Review* 35: 88-100.

Kaldor, N. (1940). "A Model of the Trade Cycle." *Economic Journal* 50: 78-92.

Lavoie, D. (1989). "Economic Chaos or Spontaneous Order? Implications for Political Economy of the New View of Science." *Cato Journal* 8: 613-35.

Leijonhufvud, A. (1973). "Effective Demand Failures." *Swedish Journal of Economics* 75: 27-58.

(1993). "Towards a Not-Too-Rational Macroeconomics." *Southern Economic Journal* 60: 1-13.

Li, T.-Y. and J. A. Yorke (1975). "Period 3 Implies Chaos." *American Mathematical Monthly* 82: 985-92.

Lorenz, E. N. (1963). "Deterministic Non-Periodic Flow." *Journal of Atmospheric Science* 20: 130-41.

Lorenz, H.-W. (1992). "Multiple Attractors, Complex Basin Boundaries, and Transient Motion in Deterministic Economic Systems." In G. Feichtinger, ed., *Dynamic Economic Models and Optimal Control*. Amsterdam: North-Holland, 411-30.

(1993a). *Nonlinear Dynamical Economics and Chaotic Motion*, 2nd ed. Berlin: Springer-Verlag.

(1993b). "Complex Transient Motion in Continuous-Time Economic Models." In Peter Nijkamp and Aura Reggiani, eds., *Nonlinear Evolution of Spatial Economic Systems*. Berlin: Springer-Verlag, 112-37.

Mandelbrot, B. B. (1983). *The Fractal Geometry of Nature*, 2nd ed. New York: W. H. Freeman.

Mankiw, N. G. and D. Romer, eds. (1991). *New Keynesian Economics*. Cambridge, Mass.: MIT Press.

Manski, C. and D. McFadden. (1981). *Structural Analysis of Discrete Data*. Cambridge, Mass.: MIT Press.

Marcet, A. and T. J. Sargent (1989). "Convergence of Least Squares Learning Mechanisms in Self-Referential Linear Stochastic Models." *Journal of Economic Theory* 48: 337-68.

Matsuyama, K. (1991). "Endogenous Price Fluctuations in an Optimizing Model of a Monetary Economy." *Econometrica* 59: 1617-31.

May, R. M. (1976). "Simple Mathematical Models with Very Complicated Dynamics." *Nature* 261: 459-67.

McDonald, S. W., C. Grebogi, E. Ott, and J. A. Yorke (1985). "Structure and Crisis of Fractal Basin Boundaries." *Physics Letters A* 107: 51-4.

Mirowski, P. (1990). "From Mandelbrot to Chaos in Economic Theory." *Southern Economic Journal* 57: 289-307.

Neuman, D., T. O'Brien, J. Hoag, and H. Kim (1988). "Policy Functions for Capital Accumulation Paths." *Journal of Economic Theory* 46: 205-14.

Nychka, D., S. Ellner, R. Gallant, and D. McCaffrey (1992). "Finding Chaos in Noisy Systems." *Journal of the Royal Statistical Society B* 54: 399-426.

Pohjola, M. T. (1981). "Stable, Cyclic and Chaotic Growth: The Dynamics of a Discrete Time Version of Goodwin's Growth Cycle." *Zeitschrift für Nationalokonomie* 41: 27-38.

Prigogine, I. and I. Stengers (1984). *Order out of Chaos*. New York: Bantam.

Puu, Tonu (1993). *Nonlinear Economic Dynamics*, 3rd ed. Berlin: Springer-Verlag.

Rosser, J. Barkley, Jr. (1990). "Chaos Theory and the New Keynesian Economics." *Manchester School of Economic and Social Studies* 58: 265-91.

(1991). *From Catastrophe to Chaos: A General Theory of Economic Discontinuities*. Boston: Kluwer Academic Publishers.

(1995). "Chaos Theory and Rationality in Economics." In E. Elliott and J. D. Kiel, eds., *Chaos Theory in the Social Sciences*. Ann Arbor: University of Michigan Press.

Rosser, J. Barkley, Jr. and M. V. Rosser (1994). "Long Wave Chaos and Systemic Economic Transformation." *World Futures: The Journal of General Evolution* 39: 197-207.

(1995). "Macroeconomic Collapse During Systemic Change." In. M. Knell, ed., *From Stabilization to Growth in Central and Eastern Europe*. Aldershot: Edward Elgar.

Samuelson, Paul A. (1939). "A Synthesis of the Principle of Acceleration and the Multiplier." *Journal of Political Economy* 47: 786-97.

(1958). "An Exact Consumption-Loan Model of Interest with or without the Social Contrivance of Money." *Journal of Political Economy* 66: 467-82.

Semmler, W. and M. Sieveking (1993). "Nonlinear Liquidity-Growth Dynamics with Corridor-Stability." *Journal of Econmic Behavior and Organization* 22: 189-208.

Stutzer, M. J. (1980). "Chaotic Dynamics and Bifurcation in a Macro Model." *Journal of Economic Dynamics and Control* 2: 353-76.

Sutherland, W. (1970). "On Optimal Development in a Multi-Sectoral Economy: The Discounted Case." *Review of Economic Studies* 37: 585-89.

Thomsen, J. S., E. Mosekilde, and J. D. Sterman (1991). "Hyperchaotic Phenomena in Dynamic Decision Making." In M. G. Singh and L. Trave-Massuyes, eds., *Decision Support Systems and Qualitative Reasoning*. Amsterdam: North-Holland, 149-54.

Thompson, J. M. T. (1992). "Global Unpredictability in Nonlinear Dynamics: Capture, Dispersal and the Indeterminate Bifurcations." *Physica D* 58: 260-72.

van Ees, H. and H. Garretsen (1992). "On the Contribution of New Keynesian Economics." *Eastern Economic Journal* 18: 465-77.

(1993). "How to Derive Keynesian Results from First Principles: A Survey of New-Keynesian Economics." *De Economist* 141: 323-52.

Weidlich, W. and G. Haag (1983). *Concepts and Models of a Quantitative Sociology: The Dynamics of Interaction Populations*. Berlin: Springer-Verlag.

Woodford, M. (1989). "Imperfect Financial Intermediation and Complex Dynamics." In W. A. Barnett, J. Geweke, and K. Shell, eds., *Economic Complexity: Chaos, Sunspots, Bubbles, and Nonlinearity*. Cambridge: Cambridge University Press, 309-334.

(1990). "Learning to Believe in Sunspots." *Econometrica* 58: 277-307.

Zhang, W-B. (1991). *Synergetic Economics: Time and Change in Nonlinear Economics*. Berlin: Springer-Verlag.

CHAPTER 7

Marshallian general equilibrium analysis

David Colander

In an assessment of Alfred Marshall, Paul Samuelson (1967) writes that "The ambiguities of Alfred Marshall paralyzed the best brains in the Anglo-Saxon branch of our profession for three decades." In making this assessment he carried on a tradition of Marshall-bashing that has a long history in economics, dating back to Stanley Jevons and F. Y. Edgeworth, who accused Marshallian economists of being seduced by "zig zag windings of the flowery path of literature" (Edgeworth, 1925).

These harsh assessments of Marshall and his approach to economics have influenced the modern profession and, other than historians of economic thought, few young economists know much about him. Fewer still see themselves as Marshallians.[1]

Today, Marshall is best remembered for his contribution to partial equilibrium supply and demand analysis.[2] For the true economic theorists of the 1990s, however, this contribution is *de minimus*; the partial equilibrium approach is for novice economists with no stomach for real economic theory – general equilibrium. The profession's collective view of Marshall in the 1990s is that Marshall is passé – at most a pedagogical stepping stone for undergraduate students, but otherwise quite irrelevant to modern economics. The motto of recent 20th century economics has been:

> Marshall is for kids and liberal arts professors; real economists (professors at universities) do Walras.

Since Marshall's name is synonymous with partial equilibrium analysis, the title of this paper will seem strange to many. (One well-known economist, upon hearing it, labeled the title an oxymoron.) Most economists think of general equilibrium analysis as synonymous with Walrasian general equilibrium analysis. In this paper I argue that this is not true. *Marshall was centrally concerned with general equilibrium analysis*; he was, after all, a Classical economist and drew on, and saw his work as extending, the work of Adam Smith, David Ricardo, and John Stuart Mill, all of whom were concerned with general equilibrium, not partial equilibrium, issues.

I also argue that the profession's negative assessment of Marshall is wrong. Specifically, I argue that conceptually Marshallian general equilibrium analysis is at a much higher level than Walrasian general equilibrium analysis, and, therefore, is far more compatible with modern developments in economics than is Walrasian general equilibrium. Thus, Marshall's work is not a stepping stone *to* Walras, but instead is a stepping stone *beyond* Walras. It is consistent with a fundamentally different conception of general equilibrium, one that recognizes that the mathematical formulation of a meaningful general equilibrium model is much more intractable than those with which Walras and later Walrasians dealt.

7.1   Marshall's interest in general equilibrium analysis

Marshall's interest in general equilibrium is more than simply a personal conjecture. In Note 20 (Note 21 of 2nd-9th editions) of *Principles of Economics,* Alfred Marshall discusses the issues of general equilibrium in his "bird's eye view of joint demand, composite demand, joint and composite supply when all arise together." In discussing this note in a letter to J.B. Clarke, Marshall comments that "my whole life has been and will be given to presenting in realistic form as much as I can of my Note 21. If I live to complete my scheme fairly well, people will, I think, realize that it has unity and individuality" (1908).

Consistent with this view we can find discussions of interrelationships among markets in his *Principles*. (See, e.g., 711.) But what those discussions present are observations of realities, not analytics. As I argue below, Marshall used real-world observations as a guide to the interrelationships among markets because he believed that an analytic understanding of these interrelationships was beyond the mathematical specifications of the time. Given that belief, it is not surprising that Marshall's discussions were not about abstract mathematical interrelationships, but were about observed interdependencies that acknowledged institutional realities. In a sense Marshall used the actual economy as an analog for the analytic model. If, in the short run, observed prices were relatively fixed and quantities were variable, then one solution to the complicated general equilibrium model underlying the economy must be relatively fixed nominal prices and fluctuating quantities. Observations served as the basis for his discussions of the interrelationships among markets.

7.2   Why Marshall shied away from developing a formal general equilibrium model

Why did Marshall focus his analysis on partial equilibrium and not formally develop his conception of general equilibrium? One possible explanation is that he was not the mathematician or conceptualizer that Walras was, and that he knew he was incapable of formally specifying a general equilibrium system. I think it is correct that he felt incapable of specifying a meaningful formal general equilibrium system, but not because he was unable to formulate a system such as Walras's. Marshall was a trained mathematician, and by most accounts a good one. He understood simultaneous equations and had the ability to solve systems of simultaneous equations. His Note 21 summarizes the essence of a broad conception of general equilibrium better than any other one page written on the subject.

Marshall didn't formally analyze general equilibrium issues because he demanded intuitive correspondence between math and his understanding of the economy. Without that correspondence, the math was irrelevant; such irrelevant math was to be discarded.[3]

Marshall's recognition of the analytic intractability of the general equilibrium problem, given the math available to him and his desire for concreteness in his economics, led him to shy away from abstract specifications of general equilibrium. Léon Walras, meanwhile, had less aversion to abstraction devoid of intuitive correspondence with reality, and trod where others would not go. Unfortunately, it was a path that others followed, and Walras's version of the general equilibrium system has become the foundation of modern 20th century economics, leaving Marshallian general equilibrium economics undeveloped.[4] Thus, when Paul Samuelson developed the mathematical foundations of modern economics (Samuelson, 1967), he developed them around Walrasian economics. Similarly, when the microfoundations to macro were developed, they were developed along Walrasian general equilibrium lines.

To Marshall, once one mastered the intuition of the general equilibrium reasoning, going through formal specification in the way Walras did was laborious but trivial. Such an exercise was worth one page in an appendix in the *Principles*. Anyone with reasonable training in math could work out a system of general interrelated equations. Marshall did not do so because it would not have added much to our understanding and would have violated the law of significant digits, since such a specification would have been incomplete. The problem was the interrelation between dynamic and static issues; such interrelationships clearly existed and, in Marshall's mind, invalidated any static analytic conclusion at which one could arrive. Marshall followed the maxim: Better to be ambiguous and relevant than precise and irrelevant.

Marshall was not the only economist of the time who did not make the jump to Walrasian-style general equilibrium. Auguste Cournot and F. Y. Edgeworth were also superb mathematicians, and they too shied away from developing a formal general equilibrium system. Only Walras made the jump to a formal specification of the general equilibrium system. One possible explanation for why Walras trod where others did not is that Walras was the better mathematician. But that isn't true. Walras, if anything, was less of a mathematician than Marshall and therefore did not recognize the mathematical complications of specifying a meaningful general equilibrium system. Supporting this view is his failure to gain admittance to the Ecole Polytechnique. Moreover, as Landreth and I argue (Landreth and Colander, 1994), Walras relied on others to clear up mathematical problems. For example, his development of marginal productivity followed Wicksteed's superior treatment. Similarly, his knowledge of multivariate calculus was limited, and his early editions demonstrated confusion about interdependent derivatives where cross partials were required. Thus my conclusion on this question of comparative mathematical ability is that Marshall was lost in the "zig zag windings of the flowery path of literature" by choice, not by relative lack of understanding or mathematical ability.

What I am arguing is that Marshall understood the intricacies of general equilibrium far better than did Walras and knew that the formal mathematical specification of those intricacies necessary to meet his demand for correspondence between the math and the intuition was beyond him. Consider his description of the stability of a supply demand equilibrium. He writes:

> When demand and supply are in stable equilibrium, if any accident should move the scale of production from its equilibrium position, there will be instantly brought into play forces tending to push it back to that position; just as, if a stone hanging by a string is displaced from its equilibrium position, the force of gravity will at once tend to bring it back to its equilibrium position....
>
> But in real life such oscillations are seldom as rhythmical as those of a stone hanging freely from a string; the comparison would be more exact if the string were supposed to hang in the troubled waters of a millrace, whose stream was at one time allowed to flow freely, and at another partially cut off. Nor are these complexities sufficient to illustrate all the disturbances with which the economists and the merchants alike are forced to concern themselves. If the person holding the string swings his hand with movements partly rhythmical and partly arbitrary, the illustration will not outrun the difficulties of some very real and practical problems of value. For indeed the demand and supply schedules do not in practice remain unchanged for a long time together, but are constantly being changed; and every change in them alters the equilibrium amount and the equilibrium price, and thus gives new positions to the centres about which the amount and the price tend to oscillate. (Marshall, 1920: 346-47)

As Barkley Rosser (1991) points out, the metaphor in this passage is a system that exhibits chaotic, or at least partially chaotic, dynamics. To analyze such a system meaningfully requires an interdependent system of equations involving, at a minimum, complex second- and third-order differential equations. The solutions to such systems are anything but simple; they exhibit path dependency and sensitive dependence on initial conditions.

Marshall recognized this complexity and did not try to fly before the airplane had been invented. He knew he could not deal with the issues formally, so he did the best he could to deal with them informally. In Walras, observed reality is forced to be consistent with available mathematical techniques. In Marshall what is, is what we observe, and if what we observe doesn't fit the available math, then we will simply have to write about the ambiguities in words and wait for the mathematical techniques to develop.

Marshall introduced his period analysis with a market period, a short period, and a long period as his method of dealing with this complexity. As Axel Leijonhufvud (1995) points out, this period approach to studying the adjustment of potentially complex nonlinear systems was the type of approach physicists were using in studying problems involving nonlinear dynamics. It was known as *adiabatic transformations* in the older thermodynamics literature.

My point is not that Marshall's treatment of such issues was satisfactory; it had serious problems, and Marshall knew it. For example, he wrote that his treatment of time and the various runs was the weakest element of his analysis (Marshall, 1908). My point is that Marshall recognized that these issues were of fundamental importance and that the then-available mathematics was insufficient even to begin to handle those problems. Since such complicated issues were central to understanding the workings of the aggregate economy, why formulate formal models that deviated so much from observations? Only now, in the 1990s, are economists becoming sufficiently familiar with the math relevant to such situations – nonlinear dynamics, chaotics, and complexity – to start to apply them in their models.

Another reason Marshall did not formally specify his general equilibrium system was that he was a cautious man; for example, although he had worked out the central elements of partial equilibrium supply and demand analysis, and his foundations of neoclassical economics, in the 1870s when Menger and Jevons were espousing their claims, he did not publish them until the 1890s – 20 years later. Keynes, reflecting on Marshall's cautious nature, writes: "Jevons saw the kettle boil and cried out with the delighted voice of a child; Marshall too had seen the kettle boil and sat down silently to build an engine" (Keynes, 1956: 56). Marshall recognized that the jump to general equilibrium was, in contrast to the jump to partial equilibrium, a gigantic leap worthy of at least a 100-year wait, if partial equilibrium took a 20-year wait.

7.3   The Marshallian general equilibrium system

I admire Marshall, but do not share his cautiousness. I have more the personality, and the mathematical ability, of Walras. Moreover, mathematics has developed enormously since the late 1800s; work in complexity theory, nonlinear dynamics, chaos theory, and the developments in computers have given us tools needed to gain more understanding of complex systems – tools Marshall did not have. In short, our formal tools have begun to catch up with Marshall's intuition. This new work and Marshall's approach to general equilibrium are very similar.

These developments in math, combined with an inherent incautiousness, place me in an ideal position to do what Marshall would not do – to spell out a possible vision of his conception of general equilibrium, and to show how it contrasts with Walras's.[5] It is a broad vision, one that will likely raise as many questions as it answers. But, I believe, that while I do not adequately specify a Marshallian general equilibrium system, I make clear why such a system is what we should be working on, rather than adding yet another detail to almost vacuous Walrasian vision.

7.4   Introducing stability through institutions

The central organizing theme of the Marshallian general equilibrium system that I am proposing is the following observation: Our economy may be messy and sometimes chaotic, but it is nowhere near as chaotic as one would expect of the solution to a general equilibrium system of simultaneous equations. Realistic assumptions about interactions would cause a system of simultaneous equations of a Walrasian type to exhibit dynamic path dependencies, nonlinearities, and strategic interdependencies, which should make it far more chaotic than the observed reality. *This means that our economy cannot be described by such a system of simultaneous equations.* It follows that accepting what might be called the Walrasian fudge is senseless – the assumption of a Walrasian auctioneer who eliminates all dynamic disequilibrium adjustment problems and brings about equilibrium. Mathematically, this fudge creates the possibility of a solution to the system, but it is a conceptually uninteresting solution to anyone who agrees with the Marshallian observation.[6]

For Marshall the question was what to do in specifying an alternative system, and given his cautiousness, he simply did nothing. He should have posited the existence of a set of equations combined with restrictions on the aggregate combinations of individual actions, and hence on individual actions themselves, that eliminated these instabilities. These restrictions are what might be the Marshallian fudge.

This Marshallian fudge involves a substantive role for existing institutions and non-market coordinating mechanisms in providing the coordination assumed in Walras. These institutions provide a framework of coordination, but they also provide systemic constraints on individuals' decision making. Any analysis of individual decision making must take into account these systemic constraints. An economy without institutions would, in this Marshallian sense, be unstable; it would be characterized by anarchy and chaos.[7] Because these restrictions embodied in institutions provide the stability necessary to prevent chaos, such restrictions must be included in the analysis. Institutions provide stability, but they also provide restrictions on individual actions. You cannot assume stability without institutions.

The Marshallian fudge follows from insights we obtain from the analysis of complex systems. Inevitably those complex systems are not organized with a single system of simultaneous equations; instead they are organized with hierarchical structures that take advantage of the computational abilities of the various levels. A metaphor for this approach is the way a computer is organized. It has an operating system, software, and nested software. Individuals operating at lower levels do not understand the workings of the entire computer; they accept the rationality of their subsystem.

The essence of my proposed Marshallian general equilibrium analysis is that it sees the interaction among sectors as being solved in a sequential manner in which nested institutions of various longevities are accepted by some set of individual decision makers. These institutions limit instability by placing a corridor around existing situations. In normal times, individual optimization is conducted given the multiple leveled constraints, but every so often, perhaps because of a large autonomous shock, or simply spontaneous dissatisfaction, individuals challenge these constraints; aggregate stability is lost, and new institutional structures, and new constraints, emerge.

Marshallian rationality is fundamentally different than Walrasian rationality, and its role in the system is different. Decisions are made sequentially, and certain decisions, once made, become operating data for lower-level systems. Marshallian rationality can mean many different things, depending on the level at which one is operating. For most decisions the institutions, and the constraints they impose on individuals' decisions, are the central feature of fixity in the Marshallian general equilibrium system, and the shorter the run, the more institutions are assumed fixed. Marshallian rationality is defined locally, not globally.[8] In fact, Marshallian systemic stability depends on individuals not exhibiting global rationality. People's limitations make it possible for institutions to develop; their bounded rationality creates a stability that could not exist if everyone pushed economic maximization to the limit.

But this Marshallian systemic stability is fragile; the economy is always bordering on chaos, and when a sufficient number of individuals try to take advantage of the niches in the system left by the prevailing set of institutions – i.e., follow economic rather than social restrictions – the institutions fail, stability is lost, and a new set of institutions must be found to provide the necessary stability. In short, the system takes advantage of people's costs of computing and whenever possible chooses an institution that provides stability.

Notice the difference between the Marshallian and Walrasian conception of the economically rational actor. In the Walrasian conception the ultra-rational economic actor drives the system to equilibrium and serves a useful purpose. In the Marshallian system such ultra-rational economic actors can destroy the system by destroying the institutions that give it stability.

7.5   A mathematical specification of Marshall's general equilibrium system

Mathematically, Marshall's jump to general equilibrium would not be a single jump, but rather a set of jumps; these intermediate jumps complicate the mathematics of general equilibrium enormously. A mathematical specification of Marshall's general equilibrium involves specifying all decisions as a system of multiple nested equations:

$$y = f(g(h(k(l(x))))).$$

One could argue that such a layered problem could be reduced to a Walrasian system by simply reducing this equation into a composite function:

$$y = f'(x).$$

That could be done, but the functional form would have no relationship to our intuition. It likely would be non-continuous, and we could not presume it to have any of the nice properties necessary to analyze it formally. The reason is that the broader optimization involves complex programming problems that cause strategies to shift substantially as the situation changes slightly.

Let's consider some micro examples. First: high sulfur and low sulfur coal. When EPA regulations were initially imposed, high sulfur coal was almost unusable since firms could not meet the regulatory standards using existing technologies. Then the standards were raised – which meant that the only way low sulfur coal could meet the standards was by installing scrubbers and high temperature furnaces. But once these systems were installed, it was equally efficient to burn high or low sulfur coal, since the sulfur would be removed in the process of burning. Capturing such a switch mathematically is complicated. The appropriate mathematical function would be discontinuous at the switch points which, in turn, would depend on the allowable level of pollution.

Alternatively, consider printing a journal. As the quantity increases, the optimal printing strategy changes from laser printing to xeroxing to offset printing. But once one has made a decision to produce by offset printing, for example, then the strategy changes since those costs will have been undertaken, and hence a higher level function will have become fixed. With multiple-level sequential decisions, the potential discontinuities expand exponentially. That's why in this Marshallian system decisions can only be considered sequentially – a timeless consideration loses much of the richness of the choice.

A macro example involves the specification of the aggregate production function. In the Walrasian system, that production function can be assumed to be characterized by diminishing marginal returns and the aggregate decision can be assumed to be made within short-run competitive markets. In a Marshallian system, the production function would be seen as needing alternative non-market coordinating mechanisms, and those mechanisms would likely place constraints on the nature of the market. Money, for example, is one such coordinating device, and an economic system that uses money would need to see that the nominal price level does not fluctuate so much that those fluctuations destroy the value of money. Since the aggregate price level is composed of individuals' nominal prices, the system would have to have constraints on the sum of individual nominal price decisions.

Marshall would argue that we can reasonably hope to understand a system only when people are operating within that system – when they are accepting the restrictions that are imposed at all but the lowest level. Our intuition doesn't go beyond that – hence, Marshall's limited, partial equilibrium, focus of analysis.

For Marshall, it is impossible to go from intuition to specification of composite functional form as is done in Walrasian general equilibrium analysis. Intuition is not presumed to correspond to functional form. The characteristics of the composite function will likely be significantly different from the characteristics one would identify intuitively.

If one uses the composite function rule, the composite function should have built into it all the constraints that would follow from the intuition of combining the various functions. One cannot continue to use one's intuition about functional relationships as if a composite function were not used. But that is precisely what is done in Walrasian general equilibrium, which is why it can use perfectly competitive assumptions when talking of aggregate equilibrium. In Marshall, by contrast, perfectly competitive markets in the aggregate cannot be assumed, nor can the aggregate production function be assumed to exhibit diminishing marginal returns. Marshall recognized the limitations of the mathematics of this multiple jump and therefore he chose the zig zags of literary exposition rather than the assured failure of incomplete mathematical specification.

The mathematical specification of such a layered equilibrium is extraordinarily difficult, and each layer involves a slight deviation from intuition. Thus, when Robert Solow points out that Alfred Marshall seems to have felt that at every level of mathematical deduction a little truth leaked out, Solow is right. But Solow is suggesting that Marshall was wrong in believing that; I am suggesting that Marshall was right. If you are trying to relate intuition and observation with formal specification, the tolerances of deviation increase with the specification of each functional form.

How does one deal with such a problem? By relying on observation, not deduction. This accounts for the Marshallian dynamics that assumes prices are fixed and quantities variable in the short-run adjustment, as opposed to Walrasian dynamics which sees prices variable and quantities fixed.

7.6   Some implications of the Marshallian approach

There are many implications of this Marshallian approach to general equilibrium for the way we do economics in the 1990s. For example, consider the justification for the dynamics. In Walrasian economics one must search for a microfoundation for such dynamics. Why don't individuals allow prices to fluctuate, since that would be optimal? Marshallian general equilibrium makes no such presumption, and thus the search for a contextless microfoundations, a search that characterizes much of modern macro, is meaningless. If institutions exhibit relatively fixed nominal prices, such fixity is a macro systemic constraint that is imposed by institutional requirements.

A related issue concerns the optimality of the market system. Since multiple institutions can be chosen, systemic optimality of a market system is not presumed. Any conclusion about systemic optimality follows only from a consideration of comparative institutions. There is no assurance that the market system coordinates better than other systems. If it does, this is an observable phenomenon, not a deduced fact. In fact, in the Marshallian system the concept "market" has no meaning without a specification of the institutions that make that market feasible.

In the long run all interactions are possible, but like a computer without an operating system, the long-run institutional structure is extremely user unfriendly. Changes in that institutional structure are made with great trouble. No omnipotent being chooses the best system but instead the choosers are individuals who work within the institutional structure they have. Existing institutions will reflect individuals' rent seeking activities, and thus they are not presumed to be optimal; in fact there is a strong presumption that they will be non-optimal. But there is no easy way to change them. Making changes in such a system can only be made in reference to existing institutions.

As a final example of a fundamentally different view of economic reality given by Marshallian general equilibrium theory compared to its Walrasian counterpart, let me consider a specific aspect of economics. It is one that has been central to distinguishing different schools of economics: the theory of distribution. In the Walrasian approach income distribution is determined by marginal productivity. Assuming a linear homogeneous production function, marginal productivity theory provides a complete theory of distribution. This theory of marginal productivity is so built into our way of thinking that it is often not questioned. Marshall, however, had serious reservations about it, and understanding Marshallian general equilibrium explains why. In the Marshallian general equilibrium approach, marginal productivity theory influences distribution, but it is in no way a theory of distribution. You can see Marshall's view when he writes:

> This doctrine (of marginal productivity) has sometimes been put forward as a theory of wages. But there is no valid ground for any such pretension. The doctrine that the earnings of a worker tend to be equal to the net product of his work has by itself no real meaning; since in order to estimate net product, we have to take for granted all the expenses of production of the commodity on which he works, other than his own wages.
>
> But though this objection is valid against a claim that it contains a theory of wages; it is not valid against a claim that the doctrine throws into clear sight the action of one of the causes that govern wages. (1961: 519)

The problem Marshall had with marginal productivity theory is that institutions have significant effects on distribution, and thus it is simply wrong to talk about marginal productivity independent of the effects of these institutions on income distribution. In game-theoretic terms the argument is that to get an acceptance of institutions, side deals must be made among participants which place constraints on individuals and change the nature of equilibrium.

Let me give an example. Say you have two types of individuals: big heads and big arms. Say also that three production techniques are possible. Two of these production techniques require acquiescence among individuals; these two techniques are equally efficient in the sense that when all workers are used, 100 units of output, Q, are brought forth by either technique. Technique A, however, gives a marginal product (MP) of 3/4 Q to big arms and 1/4 Q to big heads, while Technique B gives a MP of 3/4 Q to big heads and 1/4 Q to big arms. Techniques A and B require acceptance from both groups; if no agreement is reached, Technique C must be used, which gives a MP of 1/2 Q for both, but has a total output of only 40.

Clearly each group will be better off with choosing either Technique A or Technique B, but neither technique dominates the other. How do they decide which technique to use? One obvious answer is to make an inviolable social compact, embodied in an institution, to use one of the two techniques. But to get such a social compact agreed to would require that big arms receive certain side payments, perhaps 25 units, from big heads. (Of course, big arms would want more since no compact is inviolate, but let me ignore that complication here.) The point of this example is that what exists currently cannot be seen independent of its history, and that social norms, and even government regulations and government transfer payments, may be part of the intertemporal optimization process; they cannot be assumed to be *a priori* inefficient.

In Walrasian economics such side payments resulting from prior deals cannot be considered; there is no history and no institutions. In Marshallian economics, a theory of distribution requires both a theory of history and a theory of institutions. In Marshallian economics, to judge any outcome, it is not enough to look at marginal productivities at a point in time; production has a social and historical component, and a particular result can be interpreted only in its historical and social context. Walrasians make the implicit assumptions that all these complications do not matter – that the time inconsistency problem is not dealt with by individuals, and that somehow, all institutions are simply plopped down upon individuals. Walrasian marginal productivity distribution theory ignores all that; Marshallian general equilibrium distribution theory could not, and therefore is much more complicated.

7.7   Conclusion: a reversal of Samuelson's dictum

There is much more to be said about Marshallian general equilibrium, but I have said enough to make my point. There is some depth in Marshall that belies the many negative assessments of his work. And there is sufficient depth to warrant a reversal of the negative assessments discussed above. To make my point clear, let me refer again to Paul Samuelson's attack on Marshall with which I started this paper. Samuelson writes:

> I have come to feel that Marshall's dictum that "it seems doubtful whether any one spends his time well in reading lengthy translations of economic doctrines into mathematics, that has not been done by himself" should be exactly reversed. The laborious literary working over of essentially simple mathematical concepts such as is characteristic of much modern economic theory is not only unrewarding from the standpoint of advancing science, but involves as well mental gymnastics of a peculiarly depraved type. (1955: 6)

In the 1940s and 1950s, in certain aspects of economics Samuelson was, I have no doubt, right. At that time many issues needed to be cleared up, and his *Foundations* did clear up numerous issues. But the fact that some poor intuitive literary economic analysis existed then should not condemn all intuitive literary economics, just as the fact that today that there is some poor mathematical economics should not condemn all mathematical economics.

What I am arguing is that there is a symbiotic relationship between intuitive literary economics and formal mathematical economics. Both are necessary; both can advance our knowledge. Some aspects of good literary economics of a period become the core of good formal economics of a later period. But we will only know which aspects when the formal math catches up with the intuition.

The ideal would be a peaceful coexistence of the two. But peaceful coexistence does not seem to be a stable equilibrium, and instead the profession seems to experience these cycles when Marshall's Dictum or Samuelson's Dictum predominates. Whether Samuelson's Dictum or Marshall's Dictum is relevant depends on where we are in the cycle. The 1930s-50s was a time for formal mathematical economics to export ideas to intuitive economics. In my view, the 1990s is a time for the reverse. More and more top economists are accepting that we have come as far as we can with the static Walrasian general equilibrium model and we need good intuitive economists to guide us to a meaningful Post Walrasian model.

The new reality of the 1990s is an acceptance of the formal complexity of the general equilibrium system relevant to our economy. Because that is the case, in the 1990s Samuelson's condemnation of Marshall needs to be reversed. Thus, for the 1990s I suggest that the pendulum has swung and the following reworking of Samuelson's above quotation is relevant. Specifically: *The laborious* mathematical *working over of essentially simple* intuitive *concepts such as is characteristic of much modern economic theory is not only unrewarding from the standpoint of advancing science, but involves mental gymnastics of a peculiarly depraved type. The intuitive ambiguities of Walras's general equilibrium, and Samuelson's expansion of it, have paralyzed the best brains in economics for the last five decades.* It is only now that the profession is returning to the understanding of economic issues that Marshall had at the turn of the century.

Endnotes

This paper was first given as the Presidential Address at the 1995 Eastern Economic Conference in New York City and is reprinted from the *Eastern Economic Journal* (Vol. 21, No. 3) with permission. Changes have been made for stylistic consistency.

1. Until recently Chicago economists, especially Milton Friedman, saw themselves as working in a Marshallian tradition. More recently, however, younger Chicago economists know little of Marshall, and work within the same Walrasian general equilibrium framework as does the majority of the profession.
2. Even here Marshall's contribution is questioned. As Humphrey (1992) argues, Marshall was neither first, nor clearest, in his presentation of partial equilibrium supply and demand.
3. In a well-known letter to A. L. Bowley, Marshall wrote: "I had a growing feeling in the later years of my work at the subject that a good mathematical theorem dealing with economic hypotheses was very unlikely to be good economics; and I went more and more on the rules (1) Use mathematics as a shorthand language, rather than as an engine of inquiry. (2) Keep to them until you have done. (3) Translate into English. (4) Then illustrate by examples that are important in real life. (5) Burn the mathematics. (6) If you can't succeed in (4), burn (3). This last I did often" (Pigou, 1956: 427).
4. I want to be careful to avoid the type of unfair criticisms of Walras that I believe earlier economists have made of Marshall. I am not an expert on Walras, and what I am criticizing as Walrasian is what has been passed down as Walrasian, not necessarily what a fair interpretation

of Walras would include. I am sure that there are many subtleties in Walras, which, if given a sympathetic reading, can lead one to conclude that Walras would have opposed what came to be known as Walrasian general equilibrium – that is, analysis of the aggregate economy that assumes a unique equilibrium system in which an auctioneer sets price and no trading is done at disequilibrium prices even though the system is always in disequilibrium.

For example, Donald Walker (1994) argues that while this view of Walras follows from the fourth edition of the *Elements,* the version with which most English-speaking economists are familiar (since that was the version translated), earlier versions contained a different, and according to Walker a more meaningful system – one closer to the system I am attributing to Marshall. Walker calls this earlier version the "mature Walras" and attributes the later version to Walras's intellectual decline that began in the mid-1890s. Other Walrasian scholars with whom I have discussed this issue argue that the Walrasian system does not even follow from the fourth edition.

I leave it for historians of thought to determine whether Walras and Marshall are closer in their views of general equilibrium than my argument suggests and whether the entire development of modern general equilibrium is based on an incorrect interpretation of Walras, or on the translation of the wrong edition of his book.

5. I should make it clear that while, I believe, this conception is within a Marshallian tradition, I make no claims that it is the only general equilibrium conception consistent with Marshall. It is what we are calling in this book a Post Walrasian conception. What Marshall would have put forward, or what can be teased out of Marshall, is infinitely debatable. I do not wish to be part of that debate; my interest in the past relates primarily to its ability to generate ideas about the present and future, not to the past itself.

6. There are two reasons why I believe Marshall could not accept the Walrasian fudge. The first is that he did not believe that general equilibrium issues could be dealt with reasonably using a set of timeless interrelated simultaneous equations because individuals lack the capabilities to process the information necessary to deal with such a system. The second is that if people did have the capabilities to deal with general equilibrium analysis, the result would have been chaos since there were too many options and strategic interdependencies.

7. The irony of Marshall's general equilibrium system is that if it is taken seriously, it undermines the one contribution for which he is known – partial equilibrium analysis – because what is now known as partial equilibrium does not take into account the constraints imposed on individual decision makers by general equilibrium institutions.

8. Herbert Simon, and his bounded rationality, is the logical follower of Marshall.

References

Edgeworth, F. Y. (1925). *Paper Relating to Political Economy,* Burt Franklin, New York.

Humphrey, T. (1992). "Marshallian Cross Diagrams and Their Uses before Alfred Marshall." *Federal Reserve Bank of Richmond Economic Review.*

Keynes, J. M. (1956). *Essays and Sketches in Biography.* New York: Meridian.

Landreth, H. and D. Colander (1994). *History of Economic Thought.* Boston: Houghton Mifflin.

Leijonhufvud, A. (1995). "J. Hicks, J. M. Keynes, and A. Marshall." In Hagemann and Hamouda, eds. (1995). *The Legacy of Hicks: His Contributions to Economic Analysis.* New York and London: Routledge.

Marshall, A. (1908). Personal letter to J. B. Clark. In A.C. Pigou, ed., *Memorials of Alfred Marshall.* New York: Kelley and Millman.

(1920, 1961) *Principles of Economics,* 9th ed. London: Macmillan,.

Pigou, A.C., ed. (1956). *Memorials of Alfred Marshall.* New York: Kelley and Millman.

Rosser, B. (1991). *From Catastrophe to Chaos: A General Theory of Economic Discontinuities.* Boston: Kluwer.

Samuelson, P. (1955). *Foundations of Economic Analysis.* Cambridge, Mass.: Harvard University Press.

(1967). "The Monopolistic Competition Revolution." In R.E. Kuenne, ed., *Competition Theory.* New York: John Wiley.

Walker, D. (1994). "The Structure of Walras's Consumer Commodities Model in the Mature Phase of His Thought." *Revue Economique.*

(1994). "The Adjustment Processes in Walras's Consumer Commodities Model in the Mature Phase of his Work." *Revue Economique.*

Walras, L. (1954). *Elements of Pure Economics,* 4th ed. Tr. W. Jaffé from the 1926 edition. Homewood, Ill.: Irwin Publishers.

PART III

MODELING A POST WALRASIAN ECONOMY

CHAPTER 8

Heterogeneity, aggregation, and a meaningful macroeconomics

Robert J. Martel

8.1   Microfoundations for macroeconomics

One of the major research programs over the past two decades has been the search for microfoundations of macroeconomic theory, particularly of the New Keynesian variety. (A sampling of this work is in Mankiw and Romer (1991); for recent reviews of this research program see the articles by Colander (1992) and van Ees and Garretsen (1992) in this volume.) The hallmark of this activity has been to ascertain what economic behavior patterns operating at the level of the household and firm could be responsible for certain observed or hypothesized relationships between aggregate macroeconomic variables as GDP, inflation, real wages, productivity, and unemployment. An impressive array of competing behavioral hypotheses have been modeled formally and plausibly argued on choice-theoretic grounds. The empirical track record is somewhat less compelling. Most of these models have not been tested with aggregate data; for those that have, clear victories have been few and many puzzles remain. At this point in time it seems that more foundations than houses have been built, and a coherent, progressive direction to this research program is not at all obvious. There may be good reasons for this.

It has been known for some time (e. g., beginning with Leontief (1947), Gorman (1953), and Theil (1954), and later Eisenberg (1961) and Green (1964) that the logical requirements of consistent linear aggregation are so restrictive on functional forms that choice-theoretic microfoundations at the level of the individual agent have few implications for the behavior of large-scale aggregates *unless* one is prepared to make a number of auxiliary assumptions.[1] These include:

127

a. homothetic preferences;
b. weakly separable and linearly homogenous production functions, identical for all firms;
c. homogenous and infinitely divisible commodities and factors of production;
d. a common set of prices with constant relative ratios;
e. fixed distributions of income and endowments over time.

These auxiliary assumptions are necessary in order to justify the construction of aggregate quantity and price indices over commodities, factors, firms, individuals, and time in a logically consistent way. They also define the analysis space as a linear, homogenous manifold in which the operative preferences of all individuals, and the optimizing plans of all firms, are *identical* at the margin. Since all of the agents within each sector are marginally identical actors, only one from each sector needs to be identified at the aggregate level: an individually optimizing "representative agent" household or firm. The quantum leap from micro-behavior to an *assumed corresponding macro-behavior* is usually made by invoking the representative agent assumption and all that it entails.

The theme of this paper is that the representative agent methodology described above is a gross fallacy of composition which disqualifies *any* kind of microfoundation from being a logically consistent and complete foundation for macroeconomics. The main points in support of this thesis are:

1. The auxiliary assumptions above, individually and collectively, are patently false for a real-life national economy and therefore any correspondence between the predictions of representative agent models and actual aggregates is fortuitous;[2]
2. *Walrasian* representative agent models are *inherently* incapable of portraying the essential differences that exist between social and individual economic behavior that emerge in the aggregate;
3. Macroeconomics needs to have its own axiomatic foundations for aggregate behavior, which should include micro-level specifications to the extent that they survive the aggregation process.

8.2   The nonrepresentative agent

The representative firm was invented by Marshall (1920) as a rhetorical and pedagogical device to reconcile his static mechanical mode of partial equilibrium analysis with the underlying heterogeneity he observed among firms in an industry with respect to increasing and decreasing returns. Marshall's notion was misinterpreted, criticized (Robbins, 1928), debated (Shove, 1930; Robertson, 1930), and mutated (Pigou, 1928), and under Joan Robinson (1933) and others subsequently became a collection of *identical* firms. The modern version of the representative "agent," which includes individuals or households, has been strongly criticized by contemporary authors (Geweke, 1985; Lewbel, 1989; Grandmont, 1992; Kirman, 1992; Stoker, 1993; Fisher, 1982; Deaton, 1992), who have left little more to be said. I offer two additional points:

1. The representative agent assumption may be analytically convenient but is not essential for developing a rigorous foundation for macroeconomic analysis. Most choice-theoretic micro models are under-specified for macro purposes,[3] and applying them directly to large aggregates via the representative agent method ignores potentially useful information about functional heterogeneity and aggregative structure that tend to make aggregates behave differently than individuals

2. The representative agent methodology, carried to its extreme, *is contributing to the devolution of macroeconomics*. Mainstream macro has become micro with an extra commodity called money.[4] The theoretical macro models in most textbooks and many journal articles can easily be interpreted as recapitulations of Robinson Crusoe's *micro*-economic problem in which coordination failure was impossible and money was useless.

The representative agent method of aggregation is the hallmark of Walrasian macro-theorizing. Except for having to rationalize money and government (surprisingly difficult to do), doing mainstream macro nowadays is not much different than doing Walrasian micro.[5] Those who do it should recognize that they are implicitly buying into the underlying New Classical vision of the economy, the construction of which denies any significant differences between the behavior of aggregates and the behavior of individually optimizing agents.

The issue is not whether economics should be or can be a unified science, but whether it is reasonable to assume, upon the evidence, that the large-scale aggregated systems which are the subject of macro-level analysis and the market systems of micro-level analysis share the simplifying property of *homotheticity*. If that proposition is unreasonable then the representative agent methodology as currently practiced is a gross fallacy of composition (Caballero, 1992) and the legitimacy of microfoundations (New-anything) is very much in doubt.

Some examples may serve to demonstrate these points and illustrate how the representative agent methodology tries (unsuccessfully) to finesse the aggregation problem.

8.3   The aggregation problem: 2 + 2 = 5

The macro-micro dichotomy is a legacy from the time of Keynes[6] and represents different levels of abstraction in analyzing relationships in an economic

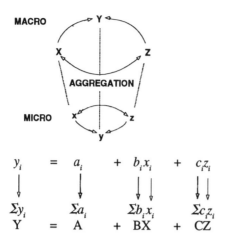

Figure 8.1 The positing of functional microrelations between a chosen set of micro-variables and functional macrorelations between a set of "corresponding" macrovariables.

system. Modeling is the art of judicious abstraction, and depending on the objective or problem at hand, economic behavior can be modeled at the level of macrostructure, microstructure, or anywhere in between. (See Figure 8.1.) The fundamental indivisible units of interest are taken to be the individual and the firm, and any grouping of these units involves either an aggregation or an abstraction. Economic analysis is not principally concerned with individuals and firms but with how they interact, particularly in groups that are organized into markets. Thus, a considerable degree of aggregation or abstraction is necessary at any level, and aggregation problems persist on a continuum. They are particularly severe in the study of national economies.

Figure 8.1 illustrates the positing of functional microrelations between a chosen set of micro-variables x, y, and z, and also functional macro-relations between a set of "corresponding" macro-variables X, Y, and Z. The correspondence is represented by aggregation relations between the two sets of variables.[7]

Now assume that we are interested in predicting at the macro-level how Y will change as X and Z change, i. e., $Y = F(X, Z)$, and that we have some historical time-series data on Y, X, and Z. We have some choices about how to proceed:

a. the statistical forecasting approach: fitting some arbitrarily lagged polynomial to the data, projecting ahead one period, and hoping for the best;

b. developing a *macro*-behavioral theory of the relationship between the aggregates Y and (X, Z), guided by any significant historical patterns in the aggregate data and partially motivated by introspection and insights gained from sub-aggregate or micro-level experience.

c. developing or appropriating a *micro*-behavioral theory of the relationship between y and (x, z), and then by analogy applying this same theory to Y and (X, Z) and testing the implications on aggregate data.

If good short-run forecasts are all that matter, method (a) may not be inferior to (b) or (c) in spite of being atheoretical. The sophisticated version is modern time-series analysis. Method (b) was the method of Keynes and his immediate followers and was considered a respectable thing for an economist to be doing until the 1970s, when Keynesian heretics began to be indicted for *ad hocery* in neoclassical courtrooms. This leaves (c), which places a lot of faith in the proposition that the microrelation will continue to hold up at the macro-level of aggregation. This implies a *homological* thesis, that relationships between elements of a system at one level of dimension or structure will be preserved at higher levels. This thesis is valid only for a system that is completely *homogeneous* and has a linear hierarchal structure that remains stable over time. The representative agent assumptions restrict a model to exactly that kind of structure. Those restrictions are inoperative in the real world.

This seems to be taking the long way around to find a behavioral relationship between Y and (X, Z) if X, Y, and Z can be observed directly. Why not model aggregate behavior directly, as is frequently done in the natural and biological sciences? The longer way is usually taken in order to comply with a methodological prescription in economic theory that all behavioral specifications must ultimately be grounded in optimizing choices of *individual* agents.[8] In economics a "theory" involving only Y, X, and Z without a logical trail back to received wisdom about y, x, and z (at least "on average") is merely descriptive, an *ad hoc* story without any "microfoundations," not to be taken seriously no matter how interesting or useful it might be. This has been a problem for macroeconomic theory, going back to Keynes.

As shown in Figure 8.1, we have a set of behavioral microrelations:[9]

$$y_i = a_i + b_i x_i + c_i z_i \tag{8.1}$$

$$i = (1, \ldots \ldots, N),$$

which I will assume are choice-theoretic, perfectly specified, and with known parameters a_i, b_i, and c_i *which may vary across individuals or groups of individuals* in a population of size N. If Y, X, and Z are simple sums or per capita averages of y, x, and z over N, we seek conditions under which the *same form* of relationship in (1) will hold at the macro-level:

$$Y = A + BX + CZ \tag{8.2}$$

$$Y = \Sigma y_i, \ X = \Sigma x_i, \ Z = \Sigma z_i.$$

Furthermore, since we are accepting the premise that the behavioral motivation of (2) must be derived from (1), in addition to carrying over the linear functional relationship we seek to completely *identify* the values of A, B, and C from the known or estimated values of a_i, b_i, and c_i. If we can accomplish that, we will have our behavioral macro-model complete with rigorous microfoundations. From inspection of (1) and (2) and Figure 8.1 it is obvious that *if* $b_i = b$ and $c_i = c$ for all $i = (1, \ldots, N)$, then the required aggregation relation is a simple adding up:

$$\Sigma y_i = \Sigma a_i + b\Sigma x_i + c\Sigma z_i \tag{8.2a}$$

$$Y = A + BX + CZ. \tag{8.2b}$$

That is, the marginal responses or elasticities of y with respect to x must be constant and identical for all individuals, and likewise with respect to z. In this special case (2) will be a consistent aggregation of (1), in the sense that the same values for Y would be produced by both (if all the x's and z's were known!).

But what if the b_i and c_i are not the same but vary across heterogenous individuals or groups, as is most certainly the case? Then B and C will be weighted sums of the micro-parameters, with the weights depending on the joint distribution of (b_i, x_i) and (c_i, z_i) in the population, i. e., on the *aggregation relations*. If x and z are distributed independently of b and c and in constant proportions to their aggregates such that $x_i = \beta_i X$, $z_i = \gamma_i Z$ with $\Sigma \beta_i = \Sigma \gamma_i = 1$, then it follows that $B = \Sigma(b_i \beta_i)$, $C = \Sigma(c_i \gamma_i)$, and A is as before. B and C will be weighted sums, with the weights depending on the proportional distributions of x and z in the aggregate. In this case, *and in all other cases where the* b'*s and* c'*s are not identical for all agents, distribution matters* in aggregation. The sufficient distribution statistics which must be known in order to construct a consistent aggregation of (1) are the vectors β and γ.

The more general case where

$$x_i = \alpha_i + \beta_{1i}X + \beta_{2i}Z$$
$$z_i = \delta_i + \gamma_{1i}X + \gamma_{2i}Z \tag{8.3}$$
$$\Sigma \alpha_i = \Sigma \delta_i = \Sigma \beta_{2i} = \Sigma \gamma_{1i} = 0, \ \Sigma \beta_{1i} = \Sigma \gamma_{2i} = 1$$

includes the possibility that x and z are not distributed independently of b and c in the population (e. g., the marginal propensity to consume goods is a function of income and age), and that their *distributions* are affected by changes in the macrovariables X and Z.[10] (See Figure 8.2.) In this case the aggregation of (1) is

$$\Sigma y_i = \Sigma a_i + \Sigma(\alpha_i b_i + \delta_i c_i) + \Sigma(b_i \beta_{1i} + c_i \gamma_{1i})X + \Sigma(c_i \gamma_{2i} + b_i \beta_{2i})Z$$
$$Y = [A] + [B]X + [C]Z \tag{8.4}$$

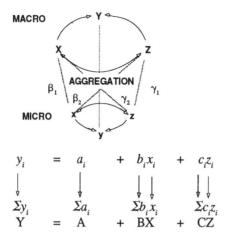

Figure 8.2 Non-homogeneous aggregation in which **b** and **c** are not distributed independently of x and z.

In (4) the values of A, B, and C depend on the cross-structural effects on the distributions of x and z. In this case, equivalent expressions for the macro-parameters in (4) are

$$A = N^{-1}\Sigma a_i + N[\text{Cov}(b, \alpha) + \text{Cov}(c, \delta)] \qquad (8.5a)$$

$$B = N^{-1}\Sigma b_i + N[\text{Cov}(b, \beta_1) + \text{Cov}(c, \gamma_1)] \qquad (8.5b)$$

$$C = N^{-1}\Sigma c_i + N[\text{Cov}(b, \beta_2) + \text{Cov}(c, \gamma_2)] \qquad (8.5c)$$

where the bracketed covariance terms represent *aggregation bias* relative to the specification in (1); when aggregation is consistent the bias is zero. Consistent aggregation of (3) in a representative agent framework means that each of the bracketed covariance terms in (5) must net out to zero. The simplest case is when **b** and **c** are constants, which is (2) above. Another possibility is that the cross-correlation effects $\text{Cov}(c,\gamma_1)$ and $\text{Cov}(b,\beta_2)$ are zero, $\alpha = \delta = 0$, and the proportional distribution vectors β_1 and γ_2 are uncorrelated with **b** and **c** respectively. Clearly these are special cases. With more than two explanatory variables almost anything is possible. It is apparent from (5) that one of more of the macro-parameters could take on values close to zero or have the opposite sign from its counterpart in (1) *due to distributional features in the economy that are not captured in the microrelation.*

If covariance exists between behavioral and structural parameters across an aggregate, there will be a *logical* distributional bias in the representative agent model *compared with the original behavioral model (1).* I refer to this as a *logi-*

cal bias because it follows deductively from the microrelations (1), the representative agent macrorelation (2), and the aggregation relations (3), and is separate from any *statistical* biases due to mis-specification and other econometric diseases[11].

The point of the previous example is that if individual agents or subaggregates behave according to (1) *ceteris paribus* but have an aggregation structure like (3) *mutatis mutandis* in a *monetary economy*, a representative agent model will throw away useful information about aggregate economic behavior. Which would be the correctly specified macro-model, (2) or some version of (4)? For most purposes it will be the one that most faithfully imitates the actual functioning of the economy, *including any distributional effects that are important to the investigation.*

"Aggregation bias" is measured relative to the consistent aggregation of (1), as in (2), which assumes no distributional affects whatsoever. So if we *assume* model (2) and test it against aggregate data from an economy that is more like (3), we should expect to get aggregation bias. *We should not infer from this that model (2) is correct and the economy is wrong!* The aggregation bias is telling us something – that the simplistic model (2) is mis-specified for the *macro*-economy it was tested on. It indicates that there are important things going on in the aggregative structure of the economy, having to do with the heterogeneity of agents, that are outside of the domain of the original micro-model (1) and that were assumed away by the representative agent approach.

Because agents have diverse tastes, endowments, and technologies, social economic behavior is not the simple sum of individual behaviors: $2 + 2 = 5$. *The homology thesis is invalid for economics.* A model such as (4) which accounts for the "bias" may be a more useful one. Grunfeld and Griliches (1960) have demonstrated that macro models with significant aggregation bias can be superior predictors to their disaggregated counterparts. They also examined sources of aggregation bias and concluded that it could be reduced by *adding missing macroeconomic variables to their behavioral microeconomic equations.* Their findings are consistent with the Lucas critique, that the behavior of individual economic agents is responsive to their observed and expected values of *macroeconomic* policy variables. The implication of the Lucas critique is that a macro-model that is constructed by simply aggregating and concatenating several individual micro-models is likely to be seriously mis-specified from a macro-behavior perspective, and thus a treacherous policy instrument.

The fallacy of composition is not merely a pedagogical device to amuse beginning students; it occupies the core of the micro-macro "foundations" debate, and is a large part of what Keynes was getting at in *The General Theory* (Leijonhufvud, 1968). Macroeconomics needs to have its *own* rigorous foundations on a par with microfoundations. Accepting this view leads one automatically to non-Walrasian macroeconomics and top-down as well as bottom-up model building.

It appears that the usual practice in theoretical work is to ignore the aggregation issue completely or leave it for the econometric exercises. This is accomplished in the formal model-building stage by introducing auxiliary assumptions from the list (a) through (e) above, often implicitly. For example, if (1) is an individual consumer demand function for a good, derived from constrained utility maximization of a particular functional form, then the assumption of homothetic preferences guarantees that (1) will be linear in x and z, and b and c will be identical for all consumers. *Those are precisely the necessary and sufficient conditions for (1) to aggregate consistently to (2) in theory.* The economic interpretation of this, of course, is that b, the marginal propensity to consume this good out of income at fixed prices, is assumed to be constant for all levels of individual income and the same for all consumers in the economy. (A family of linear and parallel Engel curves.) The same holds true for all other commodities, with different values of b and c. If Y is the composite consumption good and X is aggregate disposable income, $B = b$ is the marginal propensity to consume and is the same for all consumers. Luxury and necessity goods would be the same for all, and inferior goods are ruled out. These are strong restrictions, and are empirically counterfactual. They are acceptable if *only* averages matter.

Homothetic preferences have additional implications. Gorman (1953) proved that if Engel curves are linear with the same slope for all consumers, then there exists a *community preference field* corresponding to an aggregate demand function; this demand function has all of the properties *as if* it were generated by a representative consumer having the community preferences. (The individual Engel curves are linear and parallel to all the others, and the intercept is the average of all the others.) We know from Arrow's theorem that such a community preference function would not be democratic, but there is little room for tyranny when all agents' notional demands are homothetic. However, Kirman (1992) points out that the representative agent's "preference function" is not necessarily consistent with any individual agent's preferences, or any reasonable way of representing a group preference. In spite of surface appearances, the representative agent does not solve Arrow's problem of social choice.

An additional assumption is frequently made that all consumers have *identical* homothetic preferences. This places all of the Engel curves for a commodity through the origin, ensuring that all consumers purchase identical bundles and act in unison on price and income changes. It also guarantees that *the* set of consumer demand curves for a commodity bundle are identical to any subset of *market* demand curves for that bundle, and all such demand functions satisfy the Strong Axiom of Revealed Preference (Shafer and Sonnenschein, 1982). Such extreme versions of the representative agent model impose a utility maximization criterion on all *market demand* functions, which is more than is required for consistent aggregation and more than general equilibrium theory will support.[12] It also eliminates by assumption all sources of heterogeneity in marginal consumption and supply behavior in the model, and, it would seem the need for a "representative" agent. Here the problem of social choice is trivialized.

A similar homogenization takes place on the production side, where assumptions (b) through (e) justify a single homogenous production function for the economy (or M identical ones) producing a single composite commodity from the ratio of two homogeneous, infinitely divisible factors named K and L. The output expansion path is linear with constant returns to scale. For short-run business cycle analysis K is assumed to be fixed, producing diminishing marginal returns to L. Profit maximization results in a highly aggregated neoclassical labor demand function which interacts with the highly aggregated labor supply function of the single representative consumer. (The rest of the story you know.) Quite apart from the "Cambridge controversy" over homogeneous capital, Ackley (1978) and Fisher (1969, 1982) have been critical of the very notion of a neoclassical homogeneous aggregate production function, on both theoretical and empirical grounds. Ingenious metaphors involving waterfalls, putty-clay, and capital jelly have been evoked in its defense. We are now relearning that labor also is heterogeneous and does not aggregate so easily.

In this homogeneous world of a representative household and a representative firm, money and financial markets are introduced along with a (representative?) government budget constraint, and a particular microfoundations model is constructed, sometimes including imperfections in a composite labor market. *What kind of a microfoundations model is this?* If it is a foundation for anything, it is a foundation for a rather special case in *microeconomics*. Much of the terminology sounds like macro, sometimes even Keynesian macro. The logical content is Walras, writ small. The auctioneer and the representative agent ensure that valuation and coordination problems are pre-solved, that a (not necessarily unique) equilibrium exists, and that markets eventually clear. There are no really interesting macroeconomic problems left to analyze because they have been assumed away. With the representative agent as a jointly maintained hypothesis, it is not surprising that most empirical tests of these models on aggregate data are inconclusive.

To a macroeconomist who does not subscribe to the homology thesis, the discovery of significant aggregation bias in a representative agent model should be cause for celebration. The challenge is to discover the source of the "bias" if it is quantitatively significant, for this can only lead to a better understanding and cataloging of systemic relationships which emerge at different levels of aggregation. Heterogeneity does not always average out, and sometimes distribution matters. *It is the emergent properties of aggregate economic behavior, particularly in a monetary economy, that distinguish the field of macroeconomics from microeconomics.* (For examples, see the papers by Clower and Howitt, Leijonhufvud, and Bryant in this volume).

Stoker (1984, 1986) and Powell and Stoker (1985) have demonstrated one way of estimating aggregation bias by using cross-sectional estimates of aggregation functions to solve the identification problem characterized by (4). Geweke (1985), however, has demonstrated that aggregation relations can be just as sensitive to the macroeconomic policy regime as the formation of expectations, exposing them also to the Lucas critique. The aggregation problem in macroeconomics is a theoretical issue as well as an econometric one.

8.4   Functional heterogeneity

There is a small but growing body of research on the economic significance of *heterogeneity*, or multiple dimensions of differences among consumers, workers, and firms. Economists, like biologists and evolutionists of an earlier period, are rediscovering that heterogeneity, not homogeneity, is the prevailing characteristic of a market economy, and that some heterogeneity is fundamental to how markets actually function.

Much individual economic behavior can be explained as people simply striving to improve their circumstances at the margin against the forces of scarcity and adversity. Some people are better at it, some are luckier, and endogenous tastes and upbringing have a lot to do with it. It is a striving game of skill and chance in which the desirable payoffs (income, wealth, fame, etc.) end up being distributed non-uniformly, creating differences. It is the striving by some to maintain these differences, and by others to overcome them, that results in non-homogeneous responses of agents to the same trading opportunities. Differences in income, wealth, tastes, and opportunity sets are behind the shapes and elasticities of labor supply and commodity demand curves. Differences in technologies, cost structures, and creative and entrepreneurial skill are what create an industry of differentiated firms instead of a single monolithic firm. Exact aggregation is not possible over agents with different response elasticities, and if they are lumped together the behavior of the aggregate will not be the "sum" of the individual heterogeneous behaviors. These *differences that make a difference* I call *functional heterogeneity*. Functional heterogeneity is a social concept, and may be a more important determinant of *market* behavior than the implications of individual utility maximization. In particular, endogenous shifts in the distributions of heterogeneous agent characteristics can produce multiple equilibria.

There is no place for heterogeneity in the Walrasian representative agent paradigm, so the burden of reconciling with the data falls upon econometrics. Several researchers (Ehrenberg, 1971; Heckman and Sedlacek, 1985; Keane, Moffitt and Runkle, 1988) have used disaggregated sectoral models to analyze outcomes with heterogenous groups of representative agents. These models have been used to estimate aggregation bias in aggregate measures of wages and employment. This segmented market technique is well developed, but has been limited in practice to two or three subaggregates and still retains the representative agent assumption within each sector.

Another attempt to capture heterogeneity within the traditional framework is the extensive work in econometrics by Jorgenson, Lau and Stoker (1982), and Stoker (1984, 1985, 1993 (review)), in which additional explanatory variables representing either fractiles or moments of cross-sectional distributions are added to a linear behavioral equation (roughly equivalent to adding a vector of z's to (1) above). The coefficients on these variables are estimated cross-sectionally and a full identification of the model is made. These methods are designed to capture relevant distributional information in the presence of agent heterogeneity with a few degrees of freedom.

A different direction of research abandons the homology thesis altogether and uses heterogeneity as the primitive organizing force of market demand (Hildenbrand, 1983, 1994). In Hildenbrand's approach, heterogeneity in agents' income supports a *distribution* of agent notional demand functions for a commodity along a constant-price budget line. Individual agent demands are assumed to be generated in the conventional way (constrained utility maximization or revealed preference); it is the *degree of dispersion* in individual agents' demands (e.g., the variance of the distribution of income) that can generate a *market* demand function that satisfies the Weak Axiom of Revealed Preference. This is significant because with "sufficient heterogeneity," *a market demand function having the desirable Hicksian stability properties is created without invoking the representative agent assumptions.* The greater the metric of heterogeneity in agent demands, the stronger are the stability properties of the market demand function.

Grandmont (1988, 1992) extended Hildenbrand's results to multiple dimensions of agent characteristics and showed that a sufficient condition for the existence of a market demand function is that the conditional density functions defined over agent characteristics be continuous and relatively "flat."[13] The special case of a uniform density of agent choices along a budget line corresponds to Gary Becker's (1962) classic paper in which he showed that a downward sloping market demand curve could be derived from a uniform probability density of inconsistent agent preferences.

One implication of Hildenbrand's work is that *individual rationality (utility maximization) and market rationality (WARP and Samuelson-Hicks stability) are not essentially connected.* But if well-behaved micro markets can be rationalized without utility-maximizing agents, there is no reason why macroeconomic markets cannot be also, given enough heterogeneity. Thus the "aggregation problem" may be merely a consequence of having attempted to build macro-models in a most roundabout way. To quote Hildenbrand,

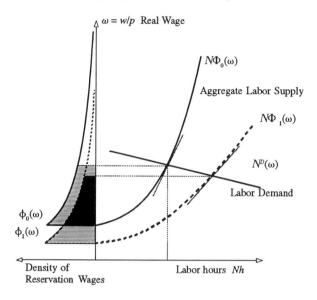

Figure 8.3 Heterogeneous wealth effect and endogenous elasticity of aggregate labor supply.

I believe that the relevant question is not to ask which properties of the individual demand behavior are *preserved* by going from individual to market demand, but rather to analyze which new properties are *created* by the aggregation procedure. (1994, emphasis in the original)

An interesting example of new properties created by an aggregation procedure is the generation of an aggregate labor supply function for indivisible labor. Suppose the demand for labor is constrained to a fixed number of hours h per worker per period, and real wealth is a shift variable in the individual's labor supply function. The individual worker is confronted with a binary choice of accepting employment of h hours per period or none at the offered real wage. The utility-maximizing choice is to accept an employment offer if the offered wage is greater than the individual's reservation wage ω_r for h hours of work, otherwise to reject the offer. The proportion of the labor force willing to accept the standard unit of employment at the offered wage is given by the cumulative distribution of reservation wages $\Phi(\omega)$ in the available workforce. Thus the aggregate supply of labor is the labor force voluntary participation rate. It is self-evident that reservation wages vary even among workers with similar qualifications, and depend (among other things) on non-labor sources of purchasing power, including real *wealth*. It is well known that the distribution of household wealth in the U. S. labor force is positively skewed (Wolff and Marley, 1989), and can be fitted well by a family of exponential density functions. An exponential density function on wealth would produce an exponential density function $\phi(\omega)$ of reservation wages and a corresponding aggregate labor supply curve $N\phi_0(\omega)$ similar to that shown in Figure 8.3. This aggregate labor supply curve results from a non-convex opportunity set, an imposed quantity constraint, and the distribution of wealth in the labor force; it is not the labor supply curve of a representative agent having average wealth.

With the distribution of reservation wages determined by the distribution of real wealth, a reverse wealth effect due to an increase in the actual or expected price level would reduce the mean of $\phi(\omega)$ and shift the labor supply curve down and to the right. More significantly, with a positive lower bound on reservation wages, and a significant fraction of the workforce owning negligible wealth, the *dispersion or second moment* of $\phi(\omega)$ will also decrease, increasing the elasticity of the labor supply curve as it shifts out. (See Figure 8.3.) In this example the wage-elasticity of labor supply depends upon the *distribution* of real wealth, which is endogenous in a macro-model. *Endogenous elasticity* is an example of functional heterogeneity at the macro-level. It is a plausible source of non-homogeneous response that is unlikely to be found in a micro-level specification of market conditions – an emergent property of aggregation, and part of the macrofoundation for macroeconomics.

8.5   Toward a more meaningful macroeconomics

Is a more meaningful macroeconomics possible?
I predict not, if it remains stuck in the representative agent straightjacket. With all due respect for the virtues of abstraction and simplification in theoretical work, it seems absurd to perpetuate the illusion that the national economy functions like a wide-screen projection of a Robinson Crusoe micro-economy. If non-aggregatable diversity in economic behavior has no economic significance, then why is it so pervasive? A theory that is capable, at best, of making somewhat biased predictions about broad averages and cannot even discuss distributional effects is rather sterile. In particular, it is not well adapted to answer the kinds of questions that policy-makers ask, because in the design of policy and intervention programs *distributional effects definitely matter.*

There has been a misplaced emphasis on *micro*foundations. There should just be *foundations*, without field labels. The aggregation problem in macroeconomics poses important theoretical and econometric problems that need to be dealt with explicitly and not assumed away. An undiscerning obeisance to methodological individualism and the Walrasian representative agent paradigm poses two risks: the first is that most of these atomistic foundations ultimately may be turn out to be unreliable in a macroeconomic context because of nonlinear aggregation; the second is that alternative wholistic approaches to modeling the behavior of complex *economic* systems[14] may be excluded from the mainstream research and teaching agenda on ideological grounds. Either of these outcomes would retard the evolution of our understanding of how national economies actually function.

It is methodologically acceptable to theorize about and model aggregate behavior directly, without requiring *all* behavioral specifications to be derived from atomistic individual behavior.[15] All that is required for coherent scientific discourse is that wholistic theories of aggregate behavior not be inconsistent with those theoretical implications of micro-behavior that survive the aggregation process *when macrofoundations are taken into account.* The set of such implications appears to be rather small.

Moving away from the Walrasian general equilibrium framework for macroeconomics requires that we dispense once and for all with the services of both the mythical auctioneer and the equally mythical representative agent. The insular roles played by these two caricatures have now been revealed. Disbelief in the auctioneer has motivated some economists to develop theories of price and quantity determination based on the relative *market power* of imperfectly informed agents, with the possibilities of disequilibrium trading, coordination failure, and multiple equilibria. Disbelief in the representative agent is motivating others to model heterogeneity explicitly and construct theories of how the skewed distributions of income, wealth, liquidity, opportunity, and human capital both affect and are affected by macroeconomic performance. Understanding the economic function of heterogeneity and recognizing the importance of distribution are prerequisites for a true macroeconomics. There are favorable prospects for a more meaningful and relevant macroeconomics beyond the Walrasian paradigm.

Endnotes

This paper is based on the author's Ph. D. dissertation. Financial support from the Whittemore School of Business and Economics and the Graduate School at the University of New Hampshire is gratefully acknowledged. The author has had the benefit of constructive comments from the members of his dissertation committee, from participants in the UNH Economics Department Research Workshop in 1994, and from three referees and the editor of this volume. Opinions expressed are the author's.

1. The term "auxiliary" refers to the fact that they are not necessary conditions for utility or profit maximization or system stability, but are introduced (usually implicitly) for other reasons.
2. If p implies q but p is false, q may still be true but it does not follow from p; i. e., p cannot be the logical foundation for q.
3. They are usually *ceteris paribus,* whereas macro models are *mutatis mutandis.*
4. Colander's antelopes (1993, reprinted in this volume) have flown away.
5. Notable exceptions to this statement, in the author's opinion, are to be found in the recent non-Walrasian literature. See, for example, Benassy (1986, 1993), Grandmont (1988), Hildenbrand (1994), and the accompanying papers in this volume.

6. I attribute it to Keynes's era because it does not predate his *Treatise on Money* and *The General Theory*, but became a major schism in economics afterward.

7. For example, y could be annual household demand for sugar at a particular market price, x household income, z a vector of demographic characteristics; in the macrorelation Y could be national demand for sugar at the same market price, X disposable personal income from the NIPA, and Z a corresponding set of average demographic statistics from the U. S. Census Bureau or Labor Department. The relations $x{:}X$, $y{:}Y$, and $z{:}Z$ may not be simple proportions and could vary over time.

8. Boland (1986) has labeled this "methodological individualism" and gives a thorough critique.

9. There is no essential loss of generality in assuming linear functions in this example, for that is the only class for which consistent aggregation is possible, a significant restriction in itself.

10. Error terms are suppressed throughout because they are irrelevant to the present discussion.

11. Granger (1990) and Lippi and Forni (1990) found that in the presence of aggregation bias, microrelations that were static or at most AR(1) generated very long ARMA time series in the aggregate variables, and simple dynamics in the microrelations propagated perplexing dynamics at the macro-level. Both sources are critical of bottom-up representative agent modeling.

12. This strong and unwarranted assumption licenses the playing of "welfare enhancement" games with the model, since by assumption what is good for the individual is also good for the collective (and vice versa), an application of the invisible backhand.

13. Technically, large second and fourth moments (kurtosis). For an agent characteristic measured on the positive real axis, the class of density functions referred to includes the exponential, gamma, and Pareto.

14. For example, the works of Mandelbrot (1982), Prigogine (1993), Lesourne (1992), and Day (1993), as well the accompanying papers in this volume.

15. It is interesting that the practice of generalizing from the behavior of a particular individual is known as the "ecological fallacy" in the natural sciences, and in social sciences other than economics.

References

Ackley, G. (1978). *Macroeconomics: Theory and Policy*. London: Macmillan & Co.

Becker, G. (1962). "Irrational Behavior and Economic Theory." *Journal of Political Economy* 70: 1-13.

Benassy, J. (1986). *Macroeconomics: An Introduction to the Non-Walrasian Approach*. New York: Academic Press.

(1993). "Non-clearing Markets: Microeconomic Concepts and Macroeconomic Applications." *Journal of Economic Literature* 32: 732-61.

Boland, L. (1986). *Methodology for a New Macroeconomics*. Boston: Allen & Unwin.

Caballero, R. J. (1992). "A Fallacy of Composition." *American Economic Review* 82: 1279-92.

Colander, D. (1992). "New Keynesian Economics in Perspective." *Eastern Economic Journal* 18: 438-48.

(1993). "The Macrofoundations of Micro." *Eastern Economic Journal* 19: 447-58.

Day, R. H. (1993). "Nonlinear Dynamics and Evolutionary Economics." In R. H. Day and P. Chen, eds., *Nonlinear Dynamics and Evolutionary Economics*. New York: Oxford University Press.

Deaton, A. (1992). *Understanding Consumption*. New York: Clarendon/Oxford University Press.

Ehrenberg, R. (1971). "Heterogeneous Labor, the Internal Labor Markets and the Dynamics of the Employment-Hours Decision." *Journal of Economic Theory*, 3: 85-104.

Eisenberg, B. (1961). "Aggregation of Utility Functions." *Management Science* 6: 337-50.

Fisher, F. M. (1969). "The Existence of Production Functions." *Econometrica* 37: 553-477.

(1982). "Aggregate Production Functions Revisited." *Review of Economic Statistics* 49: 615-26.

Geweke, J. (1985). "Macroeconomic Modeling and the Theory of the Representative Agent." *American Economic Review* 75: 206-10.

Gorman, W. (1953). "Community Preference Fields." *Econometrica* 21: 63-80.

(1959). "Separating Utility and Aggregation." *Econometrica* 27: 469-81

Grandmont, J. (1988). *Temporary Equilibrium.* New York: Academic Press.

(1992). "Transformations of the Commodity Space, Behavioral Heterogeneity, and the Aggregation Problem." *Journal of Economic Theory* 57: 1-35.

Granger, W. (1990). "Aggregation of Time-Series Variables." In T. Barker and M. H. Pesaran, ed., *Disaggregation in Econometric Modeling*. London: Routledge, Ch. 2, 17-34.

Green, H. A. J. (1964). *Aggregation in Economic Analysis.* Princeton, N.J.: Princeton University Press.

Grunfeld, Y. and Z. Griliches (1960). "Is Aggregation Necessarily Bad?" *Review of Economic Statistics* 42: 1-13.

Heckman, J. and G. Sedlacek (1985). "Heterogeneity, Aggregation, and Market Wage Functions: An Empirical Model of Self-Selection in the Labor Market." *Journal of Political Economy* 93: 1077-1125.

Hildenbrand, W. (1983). "On the Law of Demand." *Econometrica* 51: 997-1019.

(1994). *Market Demand.* Princeton, N.J.: Princeton University Press.

Jorgenson, D. W., L. J. Lau, and T. M. Stoker (1982). "The Transcendental Logarithmic Model of Aggregate Consumer Behavior." In Basmann and Rhodes, eds., *Advances in Econometrics*. Greenwich, Conn. JAI Press.

Keane, J., R. Moffitt and D. Runkle (1988). "Real Wages over the Business Cycle: Estimating the Impact of Heterogeneity with Micro Data." *Journal of Political Economy* 96: 1232-65.

Kirman, A. P. (1992). "Whom or What Does the Representative Agent Represent? *Journal of Economic Perspectives* 6: 117-36.

Leijonhufvud, A. (1968). *On Keynesian Economics and the Economics of Keynes.* London: Oxford University Press.

Leontief, W. W. (1947). "Introduction to a Theory of the Internal Structure of Functional Relationships." *Econometrica* 15: 361-73.

Lesourne, J. (1992). "Self-Organization as a Process in Evolution of Economic Systems." In R. H. Day and P. Chen, eds., *Nonlinear Dynamics and Evolutionary Economics*. New York: Oxford University Press.

Lewbel, A. (1989). "Exact Aggregation and a Representative Consumer." *Econometrica* 57: 701-06.

Lippi, M. and M. Forni (1990). "On the Dynamic Specification of Aggregated Models." In Barker and Pesaran, eds., *Disaggregation in Economic Analysis.* London: Routledge.

Mandelbrot, B. (1982). *The Fractal Geometry of Nature.* New York: W. H. Freeman.

Mankiw, N. G. and D. Romer, eds. (1991). *New Keynesian Economics,* 2 Vols. Cambridge, Mass.: MIT Press.

Marshall, A. (1920). *Principles of Economics,* 8th ed. London: Macmillan.

Pigou, A. C. (1928). "An Analysis of Supply." *Economic Journal* 38: 238-57.

Powell, J. L. and T. M. Stoker (1985). "The Estimation of Complete Aggregation Structures." *Journal of Econometrics* 30: 317-44.

Prigogine, I. (1993). "Bounded Rationality: From Dynamical Systems to Socio-Economic Models." In R. H. Day and P. Chen, eds., *Nonlinear Dynamics and Evolutionary Economics.* New York: Oxford University Press.

Robertson, D.H. (1930). "The Trees of the Forest." *Economic Journal* 40: 80-9.

Robbins, L. (1928). "The Representative Firm." *Economic Journal* 37: 387-404.

Robinson, J. (1933). *The Economics of Imperfect Competition.* London: MacMillan.

Shafer, W. and H. Sonnenschein (1982). "Market Demand and Excess Demand Functions." In *Handbook of Mathematical Economics.* Amsterdam: North-Holland.

Shove, G. E. (1930). "The Representative Firm and Increasing Returns." *Economic Journal* 40: 94-116.

Stoker, T. M. (1984). "Completeness, Distribution Restrictions, and the Form of Aggregate Functions." *Econometrica* 52: 887-907.

——— (1985). "Aggregation, Efficiency, and Cross-Section Regression." *Econometrica* 54: 171-86.

——— (1986). "Simple Tests of Distributional Effects on Macroeconomic Equations." *Journal of Political Economy* 94: 763-95.

——— (1993). "Empirical Approaches to the Problem of Aggregation Over Individuals." *Journal of Economic Literature* 32: 1827-74.

Theil, H. (1954). *Linear Aggregation of Economic Relations.* Amsterdam: North-Holland.

van Ees, H. and H. Garretsen, (1992). "On the Contribution of New Keynesian Economics." *Eastern Economic Journal* 18: 465-77.

Wolff, E. N. and M. Marley (1989). "Long-term Trends in U.S. Wealth Inequality: Methodological Issues and Results." In R. E. Lipsey and H.S. Tice, eds., *The Measurement of Saving, Investment, and Wealth. NBER Studies in Income and Wealth* 52: 765-839.

CHAPTER 9

Walras, complexity, and Post Walrasian macroeconomics

David M. Reaume

The version of macroeconomics that is taught in most schools today depends on three assumptions that have recently come under renewed attack. Two of the three are "structural" in that they assert that the macro economy is intrinsically non-complex and analytically tractable. The third of the three assumptions is methodological and, as such, justifies current practice in the approximation of unknown macroeconomic functions. The first two make it possible to deduce the correct model from axioms of individual behavior (at least with respect to the names of the variables within each equation), while the third enables the analyst to quantify parameters and to find closed form solutions.

> Assumption #1 (structural): *An understanding of the macroeconomy can be achieved by studying its microfoundations in abstraction from institutional details, feedback effects, and externalities.* Colander (1992) refers to this as the "Independence Assumption."

> Assumption #2 (structural): *Issues of aggregation are a bother but not a deterrent to understanding the linkages between micro and macro.* Martel criticizes this contention at some length in a companion piece in this volume.

> Assumption #3 (methodological): *Key macroeconomic functions can be locally approximated within acceptable levels of tolerance by either linear statistical estimators or low order Taylor's polynomials.* A critique of this assumption is a central focus of this paper. If it cannot be maintained, closed form solutions to even relatively simple macroeconomic models become substantially more difficult, if not impossible, to derive.

All three of these assumptions have been challenged in the past but to little avail, in part because the points made by critics have been viewed as quantitatively unimportant and therefore as unproductive counsels of perfection. The mainstream has observed that mathematical models quickly become intractable as the level of abstraction is reduced[1] and that, given the presumed quantitative unimportance of the criticisms, maintenance of all three assumptions is not only acceptable but analytically necessary.

Although it may not seem so at first glance, methodological Assumption #3 is absolutely essential to the profession's continued attachment to pure analysis and its unwillingness to confront head on the nonlinearities and dynamic feedbacks that characterize real-world economies. If Assumption #3 is maintained, Assumptions #1 and #2 can be discarded without seriously challenging the supremacy of pure analytics. Assumption #3 allows one to argue that at least for "small" changes the dynamics of the system are not greatly distorted by linear models and, therefore, that the resultant gain in analytic simplicity and rigor more than offsets the loss from any distortions that might be introduced.

This paper and its companions in the present volume make the case not only for the quantitative importance of feedback effects, coordination failures, and other features of a complex economy, but also for a substantial loosening of the profession's attachment to pure analysis. The thrust of the challenge is that the quantitative importance of the points made by critics has been greatly underestimated. The common theme of the volume's papers is that economics likely has gone as far as it can without explicitly confronting the complexity of economic interactions and the limited ability of pure analysis to deal with it. Although the economy's broad outlines have been illuminated by generations of economists working in the pure analytical, rational man tradition, important details remain obscure.[2]

What has changed is the technology of analysis. With the enormous advances in computer science that we have seen in the past 20 years, the profession's long-standing aversion to computer-generated proofs of mathematical theorems and its associated distrust of computer simulations has been called into question, as has its emphasis on pure analysis. The new reality is that even highly nonlinear models can now be solved by computer at reasonable cost in both real time and money.

9.1   Complexity and the microfoundations of macroeconomics

At least since the time of Walras (1874), mainstream theorists have shared a common belief in the potential fruitfulness of the partial equilibrium search for what we now call the microeconomic foundations of macroeconomics. The structure of the Walrasian model together with the device of recontracting has seemed to validate such a search for many economists. In the canonical Walrasian world the tatonnement process assures that aggregate demand and supply equations are simple combinations of individual demand and supply because the prices called out by the auctioneer are "given" to individuals and because no other macro variables appear in the individual demand and supply equations. Once an equilibrium is achieved, aggregate demand and supply (read: macroeconomic variables) are determined in blocks of the Walrasian model which are recursively appended to the set of individual demand and supply functions.

In this sense, the canonical Walrasian "whole" is just the sum of its parts, or can at least be recursively appended to its parts. In order to understand macroeconomic phenomena in a Walrasian world one must get right the equations which describe individual behavior and then either add them up or aggregate them in some other well defined way. Herbert Scarf's work on computational economic equilibria (1973) capped a century of research along these lines.

Although few economists hold a strict Walrasian view of the world, many accept the Walrasian model as a reasonable approximation to reality.[3] For better or for worse the Walrasian model has been burned into our brains and has conditioned our approach to macroeconomics to the point where the partial equilibrium search for the microfoundations of macroeconomics just seems like the right thing to do. But is the world enough like the Walrasian model to validate the search for the microfoundations of macroeconomics on present terms? Can aggregate demand and supply functions be deduced from individual behavior with minimal regard for institutions, macroeconomic externalities, and feedback from the macro to the micro?

Recent work, including a number of the papers in this volume, suggests not. A diverse body of research including early work by Lucas (1976) and Diamond (1982) has raised several issues which suggest the possibility that the present search for the microfoundations of macroeconomics may be too limited in its scope. For example, building on the prior work of Williamson (1985), Clower and Howitt in this volume call for a new and more institutionally detailed theory of the firm, one which recognizes that "firms make markets" and that their willingness and ability to do so may depend rather heavily on institutional details and interrelationships not well considered in the Walrasian world (wherein markets arise as a *deus ex machina*).

Colander (1986,1992) has argued that any attempt to build a consensus macroeconomic theory from microeconomic principles will fail unless a companion search is joined for the "macroeconomic foundations of microeconomics." His point is that the burgeoning literature on coordination failures suggests an avenue of feedback from the macro to the micro that is too important to be ignored. The gist of his argument is that coordination failures, which may arise for a number of reasons, imply the possibility of multiple equilibria, some of which may exhibit Keynesian unemployment;[4] and that given the possibility of multiple equilibria, policymakers must either accept the equilibrium that turns up or choose among the alternatives. The link to individual behavior is completed because changes in policy regimes change the structural parameters within which individual agents optimize (Lucas, 1976; Farmer, 1993). Through these linkages, coordination failures and policy related institutional change constitute what Colander calls the macrofoundations of microeconomics.

9.2   Aggregation and complexity

At the same time that Colander and others have been emphasizing one aspect of our complex environment, namely the need to consider coordination failures and feedback from the macro to the micro, a second set of theorists[5] has reasserted the relevance of aggregation problems to the understanding of micromacro linkages. Their work asserts that even if macro to micro feedback loops could be safely ignored, the linkages from the micro to the macro may be indiscernible at levels of abstraction that do not leave out essential elements of reality.

Although often discussed separately from issues of complexity, aggregation problems are simply one aspect of the phenomenon. The implausibility of perfect aggregation of functions has been well known at least since Leontief's (1947) piece on functional separability.[6] As in the case of coordination failures, the profession has noted the problem and then largely ignored it. Franklin Fisher concluded his article in the *New Palgrave* on the "aggregation problem" with the following, somewhat sarcastic, remark.

> Such results show that the analytic use of such aggregates as 'capital,' 'output,' 'labour,' or 'investment' as though the production side of the economy could be treated as a single firm is without foundation. This has not discouraged macroeconomists from continuing to work in such terms. Fisher (1987: 55)

9.3   Is approximation the way out?

Good mainstream macro theorists accept these criticisms as troubling, but because of their radical implications argue that in normal cases we can rely on linear models that approximate the workings of the "true" model. But, can we ?

Suppose for the moment that we concede that the economy is deeply nonlinear and beset by feedback effects, coordination failures, and aggregation problems, can we not still expect to approximate key macroeconomic relationships well enough to get on with analysis as usual using, say, Taylor's theorem, linear regression, or any of several other large sample statistical techniques?[7] If we can, then all this fuss about complexity may well be much ado about nothing. If, on the other hand, linear approximation is not a way out, then the deductions of pure theory lose much of their policy relevance and the issue of the economy's complexity is clearly on the table in terms it would not otherwise be. In this section I suggest two reasons for holding out little hope that linear approximation or, more generally, low order approximation is a promising way out.

9.3.1   Functional instability inhibits statistical estimation

As is shown below, certain aspects of complexity imply that macroeconomic functional forms are themselves unstable, and not just unstable in the parameters.[8] If it is true that key macroeconomic functions are unstable, then they are not amenable to approximation via large sample statistical techniques (including those targeted at the problem of variable parameters), for the simple reason that regime changes may well be too rapid or because different agents' expectations may be functionally distinct and not readily aggregated.[9]

Examples can often be clearer than abstractions, so let me begin with an example. Suppose that each agent's expected value of a particular macroeconomic variable Y is a sinusoidal function of time over some finite horizon. Also suppose that there are N agents whose expectations "matter" in some sense, and that these N agents do not always share the same expectation. In particular, suppose that when individual expectations differ, they do so with respect to the amplitude and frequency of the sinusoidal function of time. It is quite easy to show that aggregate expectations (defined as some weighted average of each individual's expected value of Y) can range from a straight line, to sinusoidal functions of differing frequencies and amplitudes, to a square wave; and that the precise functional form representing aggregate expectations will change from time to time.

At one extreme, if one of the N agents is an opinion maker,[10] or if a combination of several influential agents share the same expectations and act together as an opinion maker, then every agent's expected value of Y (viewed as a function of time) will have the same amplitude and frequency, as will the aggregate of these expectations. At another extreme, if expectations are perfectly out of phase, the aggregate expectation of Y will be a horizontal straight line. At yet a third extreme, if N is large enough and if individual expectations are suitably diverse, the aggregate expectation of Y is a square wave.[11,12]

The result of all of this is that the equation expressing aggregate expectations as a function of time, at least in this example, may be unstable both in the parameters and in its functional form, at one time taking the shape of a square wave, at another a straight line and at yet another a sinusoidal curve (however one weights individual expectations). Unstable macroeconomic functions cannot be confidently estimated using known statistical techniques if the time is short between changes in parameters or functional form (i.e., between regime changes). In a sense, this is the Lucas Critique writ large. In order to understand how aggregate expectations are formed in this example, one must model individual expectations, the process by which one or more agents become opinion makers, and the events that trigger regime changes. In brief, one must confront the economy's inherent complexity.

Arthur, Ermoliev, and Kaniovski (1994) have suggested yet another reason why macroeconomic functions may be unstable and, therefore, not amenable to known techniques of statistical approximation. They observe that the state of aggregate expectations at any point in time may be dependent upon chance in a way not usually considered. In particular, it is not implausible that agents formulate their expectations about the future at least in part by conducting informal opinion polls among their peers.[13] If they do so, then consensus may be achieved via a Polya process. The final result would then be path dependent in the sense that it would be determined largely by which "islands of opinion" first gain prominence, events that themselves may be heavily determined by chance.[14] Shocks to the economy may then lead to periodic changes in aggregate expectations (changes in expectational regimes) with no necessary relationship between the functional forms describing aggregate expectations in one regime or another. Once again, statistical estimation (approximation) would be inhibited by the brevity of each regime and the functional dissimilarity of individual expectations at any point in time.

9.3.2   Taylor's theorem is not the way out

The second reason for discounting linear approximation as a way out is a seemingly mundane, but, upon reflection, crucial problem with standard reasoning. The problem is that the most commonly invoked non-statistical approximation theorem, namely Taylor's Theorem, is badly suited to the task of approximating what needs to be approximated. Not only are the informational requirements for Taylor's Theorem distressingly high, but, with probability approaching 0.5, even rigorously formulated low order Taylor's approximations will be badly behaved on a finite (possibly quite large) interval containing a maximum or minimum. Given the centrality of such intervals to the neoclassical paradigm of constrained optimization, this suggests that one cannot both stay within the paradigm and employ Taylor's Theorem in the manner in which it is usually employed.

In brief, Taylor's Theorem says that under certain conditions an unknown function, $F(x)$, can be approximated on a closed interval to an arbitrary degree of exactness by a certain type of polynomial of sufficiently high order. In particular, the coefficients of the variables in a Taylor's approximation are the first and higher order derivatives of $F(x)$ itself.[15, 16] For this reason the information requirements needed to make a Taylor's approximation are quite stringent.

Now if macroeconomic functions are unknown and, *a fortiori*, if they are not only unknown but unstable in the sense discussed in the previous subsection, then there is little reason to believe that knowledge of their derivatives is somehow at hand. Unknown functions, at least in economics, usually have unknown first and higher order derivatives.

For this reason, the invocation of Taylor's Theorem to justify the linearization of unknown macroeconomic functions would appear in those cases where the function's derivatives are also unknown to entail two separate steps. First, the analyst calls upon Taylor's Theorem to justify non-statistical approximation and then, second, implicitly relies upon a statistical estimate of the unknown coefficients in the Taylor's approximation to produce the linear (or low order) equation used in the subsequent analysis. Of course, what we have in such cases is not a Taylor's approximation per se, but rather a statistical estimate of a Taylor's approximation, which is to say, an estimate of an estimate. As such its accuracy is in doubt given the regime change problem noted above.

Furthermore, it is well known that approximation of $F(x)$ by statistical methods and approximation by a genuine Taylor's series will in many cases produce two different approximating equations (often radically different).[17] In either case, however, if the function to be approximated is both unknown and unstable neither approximator has any compelling claim to accuracy unless somehow its derivatives are known. The conclusion is clear that if key macroeconomic functions are both unknown and unstable, neither statistical techniques nor Taylor's Theorem can generally be relied upon to produce suitable approximations.

But that is not the end of it. Suppose that, in fact, certain key nonlinear macroeconomic functions are unknown and unstable as considered above (so that statistical estimation of Taylor's polynomials is ruled out of the approximation game), but that through some special insight their derivatives just happen to be known.[18] It would seem, would it not, that at least under these conditions one could use Taylor's Theorem to closely approximate those equations with low order polynomials? The answer is NO! Even under these stringent conditions a Taylor's approximation may be badly behaved on an interval that contains a local maximum or minimum. To see this we must review a little mathematics.

A Taylor's representation is a Taylor's series with a remainder within an arbitrarily small neighborhood of zero. A Taylor's approximation (a "truncated" Taylor's representation) is a Taylor's series that is not a representation. For concreteness we say that a Taylor's representation is of order N and that a Taylor's approximation is of order $K < N$.

> *Definition:* A Taylor's representation is badly behaved if it exhibits any of the following three problems. (1) The sign of the estimated change in the function is wrong for an approximation of order K for any $K < N$. (2) The first order terms are smaller in absolute value than the second order terms, the second order terms smaller in absolute value than the third order terms,..., than the $(N-1)$st order terms; with the Nth order term the largest in absolute value. (3) The sum of the first N-1 terms is

smaller in absolute value than the Nth term, with only the Nth order term having the correct algebraic sign.

As an example of bad behavior, consider the second order polynomial defined on the interval $[b,a] = [0.5, 2.5]$ having a local minimum at $c = 2.0$. The function is quadratic, and given by $F(x) = x^2 - 4x + 4$. If we define

$$\Delta F = F(b) - F(a)$$

we can calculate exactly that $\Delta F = 2$.

The Taylor's representation of ΔF in an expansion about $a = 2.5$ is exact with the first order term equal to -2 and the second order term equal to $+4$. Notice, however, that this particular Taylor's representation is badly behaved, in that only the second order term is of the same sign as ΔF and is, in fact, larger in absolute value than the first order term.

An example of a cubic which yields a badly behaved Taylor's representation is $F(P) = P^3 + 1.75P^2 + P$. This function has a local minimum at $P = -1/2$ and a local maximum at $P = -2/3$. The inflection point is at $P = -7/12$. If, for example, we select $a = -5/8$ and $b = -1/6$, we find that each of the first two Taylor's terms in an expansion about a is negative and only the third positive. With $F(b) - F(a)$ positive and equal to about 0.6, we again see that the Taylor's expansion becomes progressively worse as we add terms until we get to the highest order non-zero term.

Reaume (1994) demonstrates that the behavior described here may occur with probability approaching 0.50 if the interval of approximation, however small, contains a local maximum or minimum on its interior. In brief, consider a quadratic $F(x)$ with a strictly positive coefficient on x^2 and an arbitrary closed interval $[b,a]$. The unconditional (prior) probability that we have $F(b) > F(a)$ approaches 0.5 since either $F(b) > F(a)$ or $F(b) < F(a)$, or $F(b) = F(a)$. For any interval $[b,a]$ that contains the local minimum, an expansion about "a" will be badly behaved if $F(b) > F(a)$ because $F'(a) > 0$ while $(b-a) < 0$.[19] Under these circumstances the first order term in the Taylor's representation is negative and of the opposite sign from $F(b) - F(a)$.

The neoclassical paradigm of optimization subject to constraint would seem to just about guarantee that such instances will regularly occur. If so, one cannot justify low order polynomial approximation just by invoking Taylor's Theorem if one is doing macroeconomics within the neoclassical representative agent paradigm. The potential for not only being wrong but very wrong is just too great.[20]

9.4   Conclusion: a new paradigm?

A diverse and burgeoning literature on subjects such as chaos, sunspot equilibria, speculative bubbles, aggregation problems, coordination failures, and other themes has as its common thread the realization that economic relationships are complex in a way that is quantitatively important and, therefore, that complexity can no longer be assumed away. If these phenomena are important individually, then it would seem that a world in which all coexist can only be understood if they are confronted head on. In doing so, their complexity forces us to consider rules of thumb, irrationality, bounded rationality, game assisted learning, inherent nonlinearity, and other challenges to the hegemony of pure analysis. In brief, dealing with complexity can be as inelegant and messy as everyday decision making.

Prior to the early 1960s, when computers had names like MANIAC and calculators sounded like cement mixers, the absolute technological requirement that models be amenable to analytic dissection dictated our choice of methodology. Small scale linear models or models with few and tractable nonlinearities were the *sine qua non* of economic research for the simple reason that more realistic models quickly become unmanageable. Even after the computer became available, a prejudice against computer simulation continued to dictate the use of simplified models, largely because peer review of simulation results was at best costly, cumbersome, and indecisive, but also because old ways die hard. We are now coming to realize that an understanding of the linkages between the individual and the aggregate may well require a change of paradigm.

If a change is to come, surely the new paradigm must embrace certain minimal standards of rigor, in particular verifiability and replicability. In addition, it would seem that some restrictions must be placed on freedom of choice with regard to behavioral assumptions. One should not, for example, be free to specify either extreme rationality or extreme irrationality in an entirely *ad hoc* manner. Pure *ad hocery* is likely to be a poor substitute for pure analysis.

In a companion paper appearing in this volume, Leijonhufvud offers an interesting suggestion along these lines. He argues the case for what he calls "computable economics," and proposes that "algorithmic man" replace rational economic man. The constraint on rationality is that Leijonhufvud's algorithmic man can be made as rational as one cares to make him, provided only that his decision making process be specified as an implementable algorithm. In effect, an upper bound is placed on rationality.

Leijonhufvud's algorithmic man may offer part of a solution to the problem of just how to approximate the workings of a complex interactive economy. In this regard he and his cohorts are following the lead of Nelson and Winter (1982) in exploring the ways in which computer simulation can be used to complement the purely analytical approach that has dominated economic reasoning for over 300 years. Although it is much too early to tell, one gets the sense even today that something like the ideas of Leijonhufvud, Nelson and Winter, and other successors to Herbert Simon will soon have their day.

Endnotes

David Colander gets much thanks for the clarity and perception of the comments he has offered during several revisions. If this paper is still not clear, blame me, not him.

1. Put simply, systems of simultaneous dynamic nonlinear equations cannot, in general, be solved with pad and pencil.
2. The current state of affairs in economics is not unlike that which meteorologist Edward Lorenz (1993) ascribes to the science of weather forecasting. Lorenz observes that within broad general outlines meteorology is quite good at prediction, but that weather forecasters nevertheless receive bad grades for their efforts because they cannot seem to get important details correct.
3. Computational general equilibrium models such as those described by Scarf (1973) have been applied to policy issues on numerous instances by his former students.
4. See, for example, Diamond (1982), Bryant (this volume), van Ees and Garretsen (1992), Cooper et al. (1990), Farmer (1993), and the papers in Mankiw and Romer (1991). Coordination failures have been shown to arise in a world of imperfect information and uncertainty if different agents adopt different objective functions or if cooperation is costly to achieve; and in a world where expectations are rational if expectations are self-fulfilling.
5. For example Fisher (1987) and Martel (this volume).
6. Green (1964) provides an excellent treatment of consistent aggregation both of functions and of variables.
7. A discussion of approximation, an empirical technique, is relevant here because a theorist's ability to claim policy relevance depends in part on his or her ability to build a reasonably accurate empirical model. If it had not been possible to estimate an empirical consumption function that bore a reasonable similarity to its theoretical counterpart, Keynes's *General Theory* would have had limited policy relevance.
8. Colander (1992) makes much the same point with his inclusion of a *coordination* variable in the production function. As the institutional framework changes, so might the way in which the coordination variable enters the production function.
9. By "regime change" I mean a change in either the parameters of or the functional form of one or more key macroeconomic relationships.
10. Here I define an "opinion maker" as a group, possibly of size one, which perfectly determines the expectations of the other N-1 individuals.
11. All of these results are well known to students of electrical engineering. A square wave contains an infinity of component sine waves. The relationship between individual and aggregate expectations in this example is a Fourier series.
12. Broze, Gourieroux and Szafarz (1989) provide an interesting analytic treatment of nonlinear expectational models under very simplified assumptions. A related and potentially fruitful line of research that deserves further investigation is the relationship between optimal inventory management at the level of the individual agent and the performance of aggregate inventory investment.
13. Surely economic forecasters do the same. Else why the narrow range of opinion among them? Indeed, it is well known that a risk-averse forecaster will disdain the extremes.
14. By an "island of opinion" I mean a group of individuals whose expectations are closely related.
15. All of which is well known, but possibly not well appreciated in this context.
16. I refer here to Taylor's Theorem for functions of one variable. The critique offered here extends to functions of several variables in an obvious way.
17. See, for example, Davis (1975).
18. Individual demand functions are the reduced form derived from a set of first order conditions to a constrained maximization problem. Therefore, in standard theory the derivatives of the

utility function are known (or at least observable) even though the utility function itself is unknown. Recall, however, that standard theory requires that the utility function be stable from time period to time period if one is to validly estimate demand functions from time series data, and that it be the same for a set of individuals if they are to be estimated cross sectionally.

19. The example of a quadratic given here is not quite as restrictive as it may seem at first. For more general nonlinear functions, consider an interval $[b,a]$ upon which the function is well approximated by a quadratic. Of course, this still does not address the general case.

20. As an example, consider a local Taylor's approximation to an unknown industry average cost function, $C(q)$. If it were badly behaved in the sense described here, the true effect on average cost of a change in output would be opposite in sign from the effect given by the Taylor's approximation. The quadratic example shown above illustrates this point.

References

Arthur W. A., Y. M. Ermoliev and Y. M. Kaniovski (1994). "Path Dependent Processes and the Emergence of Macrostructure." In W. A. Arthur, *Increasing Returns and Path Dependence in the Economy*. Ann Arbor: University of Michigan Press.

Barnett W. A., J. Geweke, and K. Shell, eds. (1989). *Economic Complexity, Chaos, Sunspots, Bubbles, and Nonlinearity*. Cambridge: Cambridge University Press.

Broze L., C. Gourieroux and A. Szafarz (1989). "Speculative Bubbles and Exchange Of Information On the Market of a Storable Good." In Barnett et al., *Economic Complexity, Chaos, Sunspots, Bubbles, and Nonlinearity*. Cambridge: Cambridge University Press, 101-18.

Bryant, John (1995). "Coordination Theory, The Stag Hunt And Macroeconomics." This volume.

Clower R. and P. Howitt (1995). "Taking Markets Seriously." This volume.

Colander, D. (1986). *Macroeconomic Theory and Policy*. Chicago: Scott Foresman.

(1992). "New Keynesian Economics In Perspective." *Eastern Economic Journal* 18: 438-48.

Cooper R. W., D. V. DeJong, R. Forsythe, and T. W. Ross (1990). "Selection Criteria In Coordination Games." *American Economic Review* 80: 218-33

Davis, P. J. (1975). *Interpolation and Approximation*. New York: Dover Publications.

Diamond, P. A. (1982). "Aggregate Demand Management In Search Equilibrium." *Journal of Political Economy* 90: 881-94

Farmer, Roger E. A. (1993). *The Macroeconomics of Self-fulfilling Prophecies*. Cambridge, Mass.: MIT Press.

Fisher, F. M. (1987). "Aggregation Problem." *In The New Palgrave, A Dictionary of Economics*, Vol. 1. New York: Stockton Press, 53-5.

Green, H. A. J. (1964). *Aggregation in Economic Analysis, An Introductory Survey*. Princeton, N.J.: Princeton University Press.

Leijonhufvud, A. (1995). "Towards A Not-Too-Rational Macroeconomics." This volume.

Leontief, W. (1947). "Introduction To a Thoery of Internal Structure of Functional Relationships." *Econometrica* 15: 361-73.

Lorenz, E. N. (1993). *The Essence of Chaos*. Seattle, Wash.: University of Washington Press.

Lucas, R. E. (1976). "Econometric Policy Revaluation: A Critique." In K. Brunner and A. Meltzer, eds., *The Phillips Curve and Labor Markets, Carnegie Rochester Conference Series On Public Policy*. New York: North Holland, 19-46.

Mankiw, N. G. and D. Romer, eds. (1991). *New Keynesian Economics*, 2 Vols. Cambridge, Mass.: MIT Press.

Martel, R. (1995). "Heterogeneity, Aggregation, and a Meaningful Macroeconomics." This volume.

Nelson R. R., and S. G. Winter (1982). *An Evolutionary Theory of Economic Change*. Cambridge, Mass.: Belknap Press of Harvard University Press.

Reaume, D. M. (1994). "On The Use And Misuse Of Taylor's Theorem In Economics." Unpublished manuscript, revision of April 1994.

Rosser, J. B. (1990). "Chaos Theory and the New Keynesian Economics." *The Manchester School*, September: 265-91.

Scarf, H. (1973). *The Computation of Economic Equilibria*. Cowles Foundation Monograph No. 24. New Haven, Conn.: Yale University Press.

van Ees, H. and H. Garretsen (1992). "On The Contribution Of New Keynesian Economics." *Eastern Economic Journal* 18: 465-77.

Waldrop, M. M. (1992). *Complexity, the Emerging Science at the Edge of Order and Chaos*. New York: Touchstone.

Walras, L. (1874). *Elements d'économie politique pure*. Tr. W. Jaffe (1954). *Elements of Pure Economics*. London: George Allen and Unwin, London.

Williamson, O. E. (1985). *The Economic Institutions of Capitalism*. New York: The Free Press.

CHAPTER 10

Team coordination problems and macroeconomic models

John Bryant

10.1   Introduction

The analytic foundations of the approach to macroeconomics described in the essays in this book lie in game theory, and, more specifically, in coordination problems that can exist even in an equilibrium setting. The existence of coordination problems provides a reasonable explanation of how macroeconomic problems can come into existence, even as all individuals are rational.

Coordination problems have received increasing attention of late in game theory and industrial organization, as well as in macroeconomics (see, for example, James Friedman (c. 1994)). These game-theoretic coordination developments may be particularly promising for providing a PostWalrasian approach to macroeconomics, and ultimately for elucidating the role of the macroeconomic context and institutions in determining microeconomic behavior.

In this paper I consider some simple examples of coordination failure, which make the basic concept clearer, and, hopefully, more intuitively satisfying. Specifically, I develop the concept of team coordination failure which lies at the heart of Colander's proposed Marshallian aggregate production function $x = f(K, L; C)$, where C is the "new" variable reflecting degree of coordination in the economy. In doing so I further some arguments I made in Bryant (1983, 1987, 1992, 1994).

Leigh Tesfatsion provides a clear definition of the sort of coordination failure emphasized in this paper.

> A *coordination failure* is said to occur when mutual gains, potentially attainable from a feasible all-around change in agent behavior (strategies) are not realized because no *individual* agent has an incentive to deviate from his [sic] current behavior. (1994)

157

Notice what this says about aggregate output – it can be lower than potential output, even though each individual is at a local optimum. Such a result can only occur in a multiple equilibria model, and serious consideration of the possibilities of such occurrences is what distinguishes the Post Walrasian macroeconomics work of this volume from Walrasian approaches to macroeconomics.

While some of the essays in this book depart from the rational agent specification, it is important to note that this departure is *not* important to the central message of coordination problems. In my view, it is important to first describe coordination problems within the context of the rational agent specification, so that one does not convolute the effects of coordination problems with the effects of non-rationality of economic agents. It is important to isolate exactly what feature of the economy is driving what economic phenomena. Counter to popular belief, "rational expectations" does *not* eliminate the problem of macroeconomics, and render all macro into micro, as this analysis of coordination problems, within the rational agent specification, demonstrates. Thus, the approach I will follow in this paper is to take the minimal departure from the Classical model necessary to arrive at a Post Walrasian macroeconomics. Why resort to the exotic to make one's main point, when straightforward economics will do the trick? Finally, one should not forget the importance of the marketing of ideas. There are many economists who are ready to entertain the notion of some limitations on the applicability of Walrasian equilibrium, but who are not in the least sympathetic to abandoning rationality as a working hypothesis.[1]

By taking this approach I am not saying that non-rational behavior is irrelevant. Non-rational, or near-rational, behavior may be interesting in its own right. What I am saying is that non-rational behavior is neither necessary nor sufficient for coordination failure, rationing equilibria, or, more specifically, involuntary unemployment. Indeed, I would hazard the guess that non-rational behavior is more or less orthogonal to these phenomena. This is an important point, as some authors take rationing equilibria, without wage rigidity, to be a defining characteristic of Keynes's contribution to economics (see, e.g., Phelps (1990); Phelps, esp. the Introduction (1991); Jones and Manuelli (1992))[2]. Mainstream economics models rationing equilibria by assuming nominal rigidities of various sorts. However, as Phelps (1990) demonstrates, this clearly was not Keynes's own intent. If one accepts the erroneous popular belief that "rational expectations" eliminates the problem of macroeconomics, one concludes that to be true to Keynes one must resort to non-rational behavior to explain rationing equilibria. Given the great influence of Keynes's work, it is important to emphasize that non-rational behavior, whatever its independent interest, is neither necessary nor sufficient for Keynes's results. Non-rationality is not the central message of Keynes, it is not driving Keynes's results. In short, Keynes was a game theorist mired in the pre-game theory age.

10.2   Some examples

An intuitive understanding of how and why coordination failures occur can be gained by considering production as a team effort. Individuals not only produce, given an institutional structure, but they simultaneously decide on what that institutional structure will be. The decisions they reach about institutional structure impose constraints on the technical nature of production. These are the structural constraints Colander discussed in the macrofoundations approach. The existence of these structural constraints means that there is a social or political dimension to production, and it is this dimension that often leads to coordination failures.

To give the idea some concreteness, let us consider a simple example of team production. Suppose a number of identical individuals work together as a team to produce an output, which they have decided will be divided equally. In this simple example, equal division is the simple "institutional structure" which they have arrived at by social or political means.[3] Further, suppose that the technical nature of production is that the total amount of output produced is determined by the lowest effort level, expended by any individual in the team. Any effort above the lowest level, expended by other team members, is wasted. Suppose the more effort one makes, the less pleasant it is, but that, if all individuals work equally, the additional output produced by increased effort more than compensates for the added pain of the effort. In this case, all individuals are best off if all exert the maximal effort possible. However, if some individual exerts less than the maximal effort level, it is best for all other individuals to match that reduced effort level, so as not to waste any effort. Consequently all, equal across individuals, effort levels are equilibria. Effort levels below the maximal effort level possible are coordination failures. This simple specification contains the central elements that one needs to arrive at Colander's proposed Marshallian aggregate production function. It has multiple Pareto ranked equilibria, making it possible to define the economy's potential income separate from its actual income, and the welfare of individuals is dependent upon how well individuals coordinate their actions.

Despite the example's simplicity, it is useful. The example captures tendencies of production which are manifest in the economy. Coordination matters, and the institutions that provide coordination become a central element in the analysis of the economy. This is the essence of Post Walrasian macroeconomics.[4]

Translating this conception of team production into standard concepts, we see some fundamental differences with traditional analysis. Each specific team application will differ in detail, but not, one would expect, in qualitative properties. At equal effort levels, the technology, in the simple example of team production, has the sum of the "downwards" marginal products exceeding the total product. At equal effort levels, the technology also has a kink, that is, the "upwards" marginal product (zero) is less than the "downwards" marginal product, and the sum of the "upwards" marginal products (zero) falls short of the total product. These features can be stated in a more economically intuitive way. Team production in general has innately unowned rents, and individuals are not "small" in a large economy, even in the limit.

One way to view the problem of team production is that there is an innately unowned scarce "factor," the right to get together, and this scarce "factor" accounts for all the rents in this particular case. At this level of abstraction, in any involuntary unemployment, or, more generally, rationing equilibrium, the employed are getting rents. If this rent were a return on a real factor of production, which had been ignored in the analysis, then the involuntary unemployment equilibrium is not really an involuntary unemployment equilibrium at all, but has merely been misinterpreted. The unemployed just own a factor which is not scarce (or at least is more productive at home, in leisure), and the employed are getting the rents on the ignored real factor. However, this seems an unappealing explanation of involuntary unemployment. Thus, at this level of abstraction, any appealing model of involuntary unemployment must be essentially the same as the simple example of team production, that is, it must have rents on an innately unowned scarce "factor," which is not a "real" factor of production. Individuals are not "small" in a large team production economy, even in the limit, because of their share in generating these unowned rents.[5]

These features of the "downwards" and "upwards" marginal products capture the essential features of teams in general. In a team, if a single individual deviates from a mutually consistent solution, it "pulls everyone down," and this is true for all team members. Similarly, in a team, if a single individual moves to what could be a mutually consistent solution, this does not generate the benefits of all team members simultaneously moving to that mutually consistent solution. The continuity of the simple example of team production certainly is not general, but that continuity is not important to the basic message. It does, however, replicate the continuity of Colander's proposed Marshallian aggregate production function, and in a very simple context. In addition, the feature of the simple example of team production that excess effort yields exactly zero product is special, but this also is not important to the basic message. Similarly, the feature of the simple example of team production that the total amount of output produced is determined only by the lowest effort level expended by any individual in the team, while appealing and of practical economic interest, is special, but not important to the basic message.[6]

Team production coordination can be interpreted broadly; a point that reinforces the usefulness of the simple example of team production. Indeed, observation suggests that production teams, broadly interpreted, are a pervasive phenomenon in the economy. They are what makes an economy an economy! Thus the concept of team production coordination ties in with the different papers presented in this volume, for example, Clower and Howitt, "Taking Markets Seriously."

An individual is a member of many different teams, in the several aspects of her life; teams performing various functions have overlapping memberships; and teams can, themselves, for some purposes, be members of yet larger teams. Teams also doubtless can vary substantially in the intensity of the interdependence of their members, with the simple example of team production exhibiting a strong degree of interdependence, perfect complementarity.

10.2.1 A goods interpretation

The above discussion was broad and sociological, and will, I suspect, not seem natural to many traditional economists, who think in terms of real goods. Therefore, let me relate team production coordination to something that may be more sympathetic to the traditional economist. Suppose the individuals are endowed with leisure, and like consuming just two goods, the leisure and a single commodity. The commodity is made in a two-stage production process. In the first stage of production, individuals work, sacrificing leisure, to produce intermediate goods. In the second stage of production, intermediate goods are combined effortlessly to make the commodity.

For simplicity, let there be an equal number of individuals and intermediate goods, N, say. Each of the intermediate goods can be made by one preassigned individual. Assume that an hour of work produces a pound of the respective intermediate good. When combined together in the second stage of production, the intermediate goods must be mixed in exactly equal amounts, and a surplus of any of the intermediate goods is costlessly discarded as waste. One pound of each of the ingredients produces N pounds of the commodity, one pound for each pound of intermediate good. So our commodity is like a pound cake (which does not weigh a pound, but has a pound of each ingredient!), where the recipe must be followed exactly. This is, then, a version of the familiar Leontief production technology. Under usual assumptions on tastes, given that equal amounts of intermediate goods are produced, there will be a unique optimal amount of work, and production of the commodity. This optimal amount of work corresponds to the "maximal effort level possible" in the above simple example of team production. All, equal across individuals, amounts of work, at or below the optimal amount, are equilibria. Work amounts below the optimal amount are coordination failures.

Figure 10.1 shows the optimal amounts of work and commodity production. Under the assumption that individuals are endowed with 24 hours of leisure, the line running from 24 on the Leisure axis to 24 on the Commodity axis represents the combinations of leisure and commodity available, assuming that equal amounts of intermediate goods are produced. Alternatively, this line represents

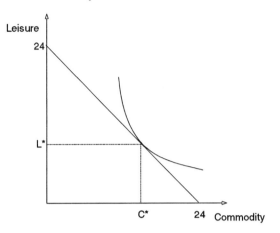

Figure 10.1 Optimal amounts of work and commodity production

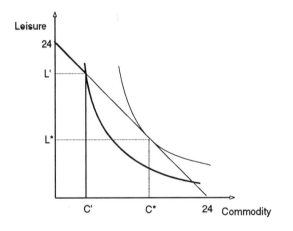

Figure 10.2 Coordination failure

the combinations of leisure and commodity available to a given individual, as-suming that all the other individuals work 24 hours to produce 24 pounds of their respective intermediate goods. The optimal amounts of leisure and com-modity, L^* and C^*, are represented by the tangency of the indifference curve with this line. The optimal amount of work is 24 minus L^*. Although the goods interpretation of team production coordination is not Walrasian, it is natural to interpret the tradeoff available between leisure and the commodity, one, to be the real wage. This tradeoff, one, is also naturally interpreted as the commodity price of intermediate good, because of the way the example is rigged, having one hour of work yield one pound of intermediate good.

Figure 10.2 shows a coordination failure, that is, an underemployment equilibrium. The kinked bold line running from 24 on the Leisure axis to C' on the Commodity axis represents the combinations of leisure and commodity available to a given individual, assuming the minimal hours worked by any other individual is 24 minus L'. The sloped portion of the kinked bold line represents the tradeoff available between leisure and the commodity, one, with the given individual working the minimal hours in the team. The vertical portion of the kinked bold line reflects the assumption that, with the given individual working more than another individual, the product of her surplus hours is just costlessly discarded as waste. The equilibrium amounts of leisure and commodity, L' and C', given that all individuals share this assumption that the minimal hours worked by any other individual are 24 minus L', are represented by the tangency of the bold indifference curve with this kinked bold line. The equilibrium amount of work is 24 minus L'. It is natural to interpret the kinked bold line as representing a real wage, or a commodity price of the intermediate good, subject to a quantity constraint. Indeed, this interpretation makes the particular structure of the simple example of team production seem less arbitrary. The use of the minimum rule is dictated by the price interpretation, hence continuity and constant returns, subject to a quantity constraint.

The goods interpretation of team production coordination illustrates that prices may not be the problem in a market coordination failure. This is a central element of the Post Walrasian macroeconomic story: the real wage is not the problem it focuses on. In a coordination failure, an underemployment equilibrium, the real wage, and the commodity price of the intermediate good are at their "competitive" market clearing levels, one. It is the self validating perception of institutional or systems quantity constraints that is the source of the problem, not prices.[7] The real wage and the commodity price of the intermediate good are not too high in an underemployment equilibrium. It is not clear that in such an environment there is any pressure for prices to fall. Nor is it clear that a reduction in the real wage, or in the commodity price of the intermediate good, would move the economy towards the full employment equilibrium, as this would be a price distortion.

10.2.2   The integration of aggregate supply and demand: the systems approach

In his proposed textbook model, Colander argues that the model will include an interrelated aggregate supply and demand analysis. The goods interpretation of team production coordination illustrates that supply and demand are not easily separated in a general equilibrium model. Team production coordination failure is usually viewed as a supply side problem. However, one can view the individuals, in the goods interpretation of team production coordination, as sellers of the intermediate good. With this view, individuals are expecting inadequate demand for their product, and, because of that expectation, underproduce. Expectations are not being optimally coordinated. This anticipation of inadequate demand is self-validating. Hence, the goods interpretation of team production coordination can be viewed as a model of effective demand. In Figure 10.2, the "effective" demand is C' and the "notional" demand is C^*. The goods interpretation of team production coordination may also capture the essence of Keynes's notion of a rigid world, as opposed to the fluid world of the Classicals. Thus, the team production coordination problem allows a possible role of inadequate effective demand in equilibrium.

The team production coordination approach is motivated by a fundamental outlook on the basic structure of the economy. Individuals are members of teams. As suggested above, these teams may sometimes be independent, and sometimes overlapping or horizontally interactive, as when intermediate goods are used in many products or functions, or when common transportation, communication, marketing, and wholesaling and retailing systems are used.[8] When the output of a particular group takes the form of an independently tradable commodity or service, as in the goods interpretation of team production coordination, the production processes can be multi-staged, decentralized, and interactive; and can thereby gain increased flexibility, selection and pooling, reduced moral hazard, and increased entrepreneurial initiative, at the possible cost of increased difficulty of coordination. At the end of the line, as it were, all individuals put on their consumer hats, and purchase an array of consumer goods and services from the retail outlets. In short, because of the overlapping and interactive teams, the economy itself is a complex interactive system, a complex team. This is what makes the economy an economy.

This is a fundamentally different outlook on the basic structure of the economy from that which motivates Walrasian equilibrium. The basic Walrasian starting point is that of endowed traders, or individual producers of individual goods, meeting in a grand bazaar.[9] Perhaps one telling example of this difference is that in Walrasian approaches, increased specialization is treated as just a finer grid of goods, whereas in the team production coordination approach, specialization involves more complex production and distribution processes.

10.2.3 "Money"

So far, the simple example of team production is purely a real-side phenomenon. It might be tempting to conclude from this that the approach observes the Classical dichotomy. However, when the approach is fully developed, this conclusion may well prove to be 180 degrees from the truth. Coming from a Walrasian perspective, money theorists have encountered a great deal of difficulty in generating models with an explicit role for money. Indeed, the difficulty of the project has been a source of some embarrassment, given the seeming pervasiveness of money in advanced economies. The basic source of the difficulty comes from the question of why barter alone will not do the trick. In turn, it may be that, as Clower and Howitt suggest, the difficulty in finding a flaw with barter may ultimately stem from the basic Walrasian starting point of the grand bazaar.

With all due respect to the efforts of the money theorists, with any complexity in commercial and industrial organization, barter is just, well, simply impractical. Of course, at the most brute level, not much complexity at all is required! It is just not practical to run my white water rafting experience through your fine French dining ambiance, no matter that I am dying for some refinement, and you really could use some excitement. (That is, even with a perfect double coincidence of wants). Similarly, if, for example, retail outlets customize the product, or offer a broad array of styles or selection, direct barter does not work well. At a minimum, the good offered in trade would have to be costlily taken to an appropriate retail outlet (in return for what?), after having costlily, and equally uselessly, been brought in by the customer. Primary and intermediate goods and services offered in trade would have similar, likely more severe, difficulties. Clearly some kind of claims are called for.

So we immediately have a role for the various kinds of claims that have been used throughout the history of advancing economies, and have, perhaps rather carelessly, been lumped together in the term "money." At times, claims to final product have been used. Even if these can be handled through a central clearing house, to facilitate exchange, one still has to worry about what relative price will be used, whether that price can be manipulated, and the much cited information cost of not knowing customary prices and qualities of goods that one does not naturally deal in as a producer or consumer. Of course, one has to worry about insolvency and fraud as well. In some cases, for example industrial wholesalers, who may not know how, or where, the product they buy will be used, claims on final products are not possible. The great fairs of Europe, in part, functioned as a traveling clearing house for bills of exchange in gold, used in wholesale trade. Massive volumes of transactions were supported with only trivial quantities of gold present; gold used just to "make change," that is, to settle small net balances. With bills of exchange in gold, one does still have to worry about insolvency and fraud. Perhaps banks emerged because of the greater ease of evaluating the monitoring capabilities of banks, in comparison to monitoring individual firms themselves, and to pool risks.

In any case, the team production coordination approach may help in the analysis of such monetary matters. Bryant (1992) just starts to scratch the surface of this topic of the role of money in coordination. In short, theorists looking for the source of money in individuals randomly bashing into each other in the Brazilian jungle may be looking in the wrong place. The source of money, and monetary innovation, may be in the increasing complexity of advancing commercial and industrial economies.[10] Team production coordination and money may be intimately intertwined.

In fact, this intimate link between team production coordination and money is a particular manifestation of the general observations on money, firms, and markets made by Clower and Howitt in their paper in this volume. Indeed, the link between team production coordination and money strongly supports, and is in perfect alignment with, the important points made in their insightful discussion.

10.2.4   Increasing returns as a team coordination problem

Increasing returns provides another common model of coordination failure, which is really a team production coordination problem. As with the goods interpretation of team production coordination, the increasing returns model reinforces the usefulness of the simple example of team production. A simple example illustrates that increasing returns can be a source of coordination failure. Suppose the individuals are two-period lived, and are endowed with a single commodity in the first period, and with nothing in the second period. The individuals desire to consume the single commodity in both periods. The individuals have two ways to get consumption in the second period. They can costlessly store any amount of the commodity, on their own, between periods, in order to get the commodity in the second period for consumption. Alternatively, the individuals can, together, in the first period, input any amount of the commodity into an increasing returns production technology that produces the commodity in the second period. The second, increasing returns, production technology has average returns less than one for low levels of input, and average returns greater than one for high levels of input. If tastes and endowments are rigged appropriately,[11] there are two equilibria in this example. There is a "bad" equilibrium, bad in the sense that it is dominated by another equilibrium, where everyone stores some of their commodity on their own, and no one uses the increasing returns production technology. There is a Pareto superior equilibrium, where everyone inputs some of their commodity into the increasing returns production technology, and no one stores any.

The increasing returns production (or investment) technology is, of course, the team activity. While for infinitesimal changes increasing returns does not have the essential features of teams in general, for discrete changes it does. If a single individual moves from the increasing returns production technology to storage, everyone else in the increasing returns production technology is pulled down. Similarly, if a single individual moves from storage to the increasing returns production technology, this does not generate the benefits of all individuals simultaneously moving to the increasing returns production technology.

This increasing returns example, itself, can be viewed as a perhaps more compelling model of inadequate effective demand. This may seem a bit paradoxical, as it is, if anything, even harder to separate supply and demand in the increasing returns example than it is in the goods interpretation of team production coordination. However, the increasing returns example exhibits Keynes's paradox of thrift, which he viewed as a crucial element in explaining inadequate effective demand. In Keynes's view, keeping in mind Say's law, for a decrease in consumption demand to influence aggregate demand, one must break the link that a greater taste for saving is a greater demand for investment. In the increasing returns example, storage can be interpreted as money holding. Greater thrift on the part of individuals, in the sense of moving to money, yields less consumption later, as the increasing returns production technology is abandoned. This is, indeed, akin to Keynes's own explanation of the paradox of thrift, namely that a demand for money is not a demand for investment. (Of course, one cannot claim that this is Keynes's model.)

As suggested above, the increasing returns example illustrates that, under increasing returns, a monetary equilibrium need not be optimal. Indeed, a monetary equilibrium may be worse than a non-monetary equilibrium. This observation may explain, and support, Keynes's advocacy of closing the market for gold. Moreover, it is trivial to imbed the increasing returns example into an overlapping generations model, with storage being fiat money holding. For some readers, this overlapping generations interpretation may make the non-optimal monetary equilibrium observation more telling. Increasing returns might also be justified on a fundamental level by the version of specialization as involving more complex production processes, provided by the goods interpretation of team production coordination.

10.3   The usefulness of the team production approach

The team coordination Post Walrasian approach to macroeconomics differs substantially from Classical economics in that it emphasizes interactions that are excluded from Walrasian equilibrium. From the team coordination perspective, Walrasian equilibrium is more a description of a collection of semi-autonomous Robinson Crusoes than a model of an integrated economy. Perhaps an economically intuitive way to state this point is to observe that both the goods interpretation of team production coordination and the increasing returns interpretation violate the no surplus condition, which is imposed in production versions of Walrasian equilibrium. In emphasizing interactions, the team coordination Post Walrasian approach to macroeconomics also departs from the representative agent model, which has been so popular in macroeconomics. By definition, the representative agent model, in which the agent is considered independently of its macroeconomic context, cannot capture aspects of agent interaction. Indeed, complex production processes, as in the goods interpretation of team production coordination, call into question the very meaningfulness of aggregate production functions, and of aggregate inputs, as discussed in this volume.

10.3.1 Team production and uncertainty

The team coordination Post Walrasian approach to macroeconomics emphasizes the importance of endogenous uncertainty. Presumably, the interactions emphasized in the approach are known to the participants. How, then, do participants decide what to do, without knowing what the other participants are doing? This endogenous source of uncertainty has been termed "strategic uncertainty" in the game theory literature. There is substantial doubt that this strategic uncertainty is best modeled probabilistically. Indeed, there is doubt that it is logically consistent to do so. Consider our first simple example of team production. If it is possible for an individual to infer a probability distribution of the decisions by the others, based on the structure of the game, then every individual must infer the same probability distribution, because of the symmetry of the example. Then every individual faces the same decision problem, and should make the same decision. Because all, equal across individuals, effort levels are equilibria, each probability distribution that puts a probability of one on any single effort level is a candidate for the common probability distribution. So which of these probability distributions should the individuals all infer? Indeed, experiments show that individuals behave differently in symmetric coordination games: They do not have the same anticipations, they do not expect each other to have a common anticipation, and they do not expect (or achieve) equilibrium play.[12] Keynes, himself one of the early developers, had substantial doubts about the philosophical foundations of probability theory. Perhaps, then, the team coordination approach captures Keynes's "animal spirits," and identifies an important source of Knightian uncertainty.[13] This "animal spirits," the endogenous uncertainty of the team coordination approach, makes a sharp contrast to the real business cycle theory, which attempts to identify external sources of probabilistic shocks to the economy.

The team coordination Post Walrasian approach to macroeconomics is not nihilistic. Admittedly, the endogenous uncertainty emphasized in the approach, can leave substantial indeterminacy in models, at least when using standard modes of analysis. However, standard iterative contraction by dominance may yield very useful bounds on behavior in many specific applications, providing a macroeconomic corridor (Leijonhufvud, this volume: Ch. 3). Moreover, if, in fact, certain aspects of behavior are innately difficult to predict, a theory that identifies these difficult aspects and focuses attention on those aspects that are more easily predicted is a very positive theory. Further, with an emphasis being placed on endogenous uncertainty, a new theory of behavior under endogenous uncertainty may be developed. Such a new theory of behavior may reduce or eliminate the indeterminacy arising from using current standard modes of analysis.

Finally, the team coordination Post Walrasian approach to macroeconomics may lead to a theory of institutions. It may be institutional arrangements which determine which equilibrium, if any, is played, and which thereby eliminate the indeterminacy generated by endogenous uncertainty. Coordination may be an important function of institutions, while in Classical economics institutions are essentially functionless (and unexplained!). The team coordination Post Walrasian approach to macroeconomics emphasizes the potential importance of macroeconomic context and institutions for economic behavior, in contrast to Classical economics, a major thrust of which is to downplay their significance.

10.4   Conclusion

Macroeconomics has come a long way since its inception in the 1930s, but in many ways it has traveled that distance by implicitly or explicitly ruling out important observable elements of the economy. The concept of team production captures many of those ruled out elements, and thus provides an important building block of a Post Walrasian microfoundation to macro. Teams are what make an economy an economy. Walrasian economics is a heroic attempt to abstract away from firm, market, and institutional detail generally, in order to get to the essence of the universal factors influencing the wealth of nations. From a Post Walrasian perspective, this heroic attempt ended up abstracting away from the essence of the macroeconomic problem.

Endnotes

I am indebted to three anonymous referees, and most especially to David Colander, for very helpful comments. Errors and oversights are my responsibility alone. I am also indebted to William Baumol, Jacques Dreze, John Harsanyi, John Seater, Martin Shubik, Robert Solow, and Lawrence Summers for supportive and helpful comments on my earlier papers.

1. For example, Allan Meltzer has most emphatically taken this stand with me in personal conversation.
2. Note that, counter to their suggestion, Jones and Manuelli's analysis does not involve team production, and their negative results on rationing equilibria do not hold if team production is involved.
3. This institution of equal division is consistent with standard models of bargaining. For further discussion of institutional arrangements in this environment see Bryant (1994).
4. At another level, this statement greatly understates the author's own attachment to this example, which is referred to in the game theory literature as the stag hunt game. Twenty years ago, the author would have said that the fundamental paradigm of economics is separating

hyperplanes. Now the author is tempted to speculate that the fundamental building blocks of social science are the stag hunt, the battle of the sexes, and the prisoner's dilemma games. In this regard, see also Tesfatsion (1994).

5. That is, in such a team production economy, the core does not converge.

6. For example, games in which individuals are penalized for deviating from the team average (rather than the team minimum as in the stag hunt game of team production) are qualitatively the same, according to standard analysis, as the simple example of team production. In both problems there is a continuum of Pareto ranked Nash equilibria. (However, according to evolutionary analysis (Crawford (1991)) and experimental evidence (Van Huyck, Battalio, and Beil (1990, 1991)) the games differ qualitatively in very interesting ways.)

7. It is an open question whether the quantity constraint can arise from the institutional arrangements themselves, or whether it must stem from the technological complementarities of team production. See footnote 2 and Roberts (1987) and Jones and Manuelli (1992).

8. In the goods interpretation of team production coordination, intermediate goods themselves can be interpreted broadly. For example, transportation, communication, marketing, and wholesale and retail trade services can be interpreted as intermediate goods. Indeed, organizing transportation may be an important problem in team coordination, both because of the strong degree of interdependence in transportation technologies, and because of the geographical separation involved.

9. Admittedly, there is a great deal of discussion of decentralization in the Walrasian literature of the "price system" as a decentralization mechanism. It is not clear what one should make of these discussions, however, as Walrasian equilibrium is not, in fact, a mechanism at all. Quite the contrary, Walrasian equilibrium is an explicit attempt to abstract away from real market mechanisms, motivated by the belief that such mechanisms are inconsequential details that obscure the unifying structure. Walrasian equilibrium is an "as if" model. I suspect that the discussions of decentralization are motivated by the beliefs that Walrasian equilibrium is useful and that the real world is decentralized. However, the structure of the explicit environment in Bryant (1983) suggests that one can make sense of the term "market," as conceived in the Walrasian sense, only by having an environment without any distance in it. See also the discussion in Bryant (1994).

10. A point suggested by a reading of Braudel (1982).

11. See Bryant (1987) for details.

12. See, e.g., Van Huyck, Battalio, and Beil (1990).

13. These observations on animal spirits also naturally lead to the topic of my other paper in this volume, disequilibrium.

References

Braudel, F. (c.1982). *The Wheels of Commerce, Civilization and Capitalism 15th-18th Century*, Vol. II. New York: Harper and Row.

Bryant, J. (1983), "A Simple Rational Expectations Keynes-Type Model." *Quarterly Journal of Economics* 98: 525-28.

(1987). "The Paradox of Thrift, Liquidity Preference and Animal Spirits." *Econometrica* 55: 1231-35.

(1992). "Banking and Coordination." *Journal of Money, Credit and Banking* 24: 563-69.

(1994). "Coordination Theory, The Stag Hunt and Macroeconomics." In J. W. Friedman, ed., *Problems of Coordination in Economic Activity*. Boston/Dordrecht/London: Kluwer Academic Publishers.

Colander, D. (1993). "The Macrofoundations of Micro." *Eastern Economic Journal* 19: 447-57.

Cooper, R., D. V. DeJong, R. Forsythe, and T. W. Ross (1992). "Communication in Coordination Games." *Quarterly Journal of Economics* 107: 739-71.

Crawford, V. P. (1991). "An 'Evolutionary' Interpretation of Van Huyck, Battalio and Beil's Experimental Results on Coordination." *Games and Economic Behavor* 3: 25-59.

Friedman, J. W., ed. (c.1994). *Problems of Coordination in Economic Activity*. Boston/ Dordrecht/London:Kluwer Academic Publishers.

Guesnerie, R. (1992). "An Exploration of the Eductive Justifications of the Rational-Expectations Hypothesis." *American Economic Review* 82: 1254-78.

Jones, L. E. and R. E. Manuelli (1992). "The Coordination Problem and Equilibrium Theories of Recessions." *American Economic Review* 82: 451-71.

Keynes, J. M. (1936). *The General Theory of Employment Interest and Money*. New York: Harcourt, Brace & World.

Mankiw, N. G. and D. Romer, eds. (c. 1991). *Coordination Failures and Real Rigidities, New Keynesian Economics,* Vol. II. Cambridge Mass.: MIT Press.

Phelps, Edmund S. (1990). *Seven Schools of Macroeconomic Thought*. New York: Oxford University Press.

(1991). *Recent Developments in Macroeconomics, The International Library of Critical Writings in Economics*. London: Edward Elgar.

Roberts, J. (1987). "An Equilibrium Model with Involuntary Unemployment at Flexible, Competitive Prices and Wages." *American Economic Review* 77: 856-74.

Tesfatsion, L. (1994). "Answer Key." Unpublished work, Iowa State University.

Van Huyck, J. B., R. C. Battalio, and R. O. Beil (1990). "Tacit Coordination Games, Strategic Uncertainty, and Coordination Failure." *American Economic Review* 80: 234-48.

(1991). "Strategic Uncertainty, Equilibrium Selection, and Coordination Failure in Average Opinion Games." *Quarterly Journal of Economics* 91: 885-910.

CHAPTER 11

"Competitive" market disequilibrium: a Post Walrasian analysis of investment

John Bryant

11.1　Introduction

Many of the models in this book involve competitive equilibrium coordination failures; that is, situations in which an equilibrium outcome, which is Pareto dominated by another equilibrium, is realized by independently acting agents. In the previous paper, I explored team production and the nature of those equilibrium coordination failures. That discussion, and the other discussions in this book, may have made it seem that equilibrium coordination failures are substitutes for models of disequilibrium. That is wrong. Nothing in the equilibrium coordination failure approach rules out the possibility, or, indeed, the importance and pervasiveness, of disequilibrium. That is why I noted in the other paper that other types of coordination failures were possible.

One of those types can be found in an earlier Keynesian coordination tradition, which was concerned with disequilibrium behavior (as noted, for example, in Van Huyck, Battalio, and Beil (1990)). In this earlier tradition agents are unsure of what to do because of the multiplicity of possible equilibrium strategies, and guess differently. The traditional noneconomic example of disequilibrium is to imagine a country in which none of the drivers are sure whether the "drive on the right" or the "drive on the left" convention applies. The economic concern with disequilibium may trace back to Keynes's famous "beauty contest" example, which he suggested as a model of the stock market and used to motivate "animal spirits."

The reality is that equilibrium coordination failure and disequilibrium coordination failure are really two manifestations of the same fundamental problem; namely the difficulty for independent agents in making mutually consistent and beneficial decisions. To demonstrate, and emphasize, the point, this paper treats disequilibrium in the most familiar and simple of competitive models, the competitive price-taking firm product-market model.[1]

The simple competitive model admits a wide range of disequilibria. In fact, it really generates an embarrassment of riches. The wide range of disequilibria imaginable suggests an unbelievable degree of instability of free markets. Simple observation suggests that this doesn't happen. This observation may reflect, and strikingly emphasize, how the competitive model formulation leaves out the institutional structures which are critical for determining that an equilibrium is achieved, thereby inducing stability. In the Post Walrasian macroeconomic approach of the papers presented in this volume, institutions play key roles not in creating instability, but in preventing instability. Equilibrium cannot be understood independently of those institutions. In Leijonhufvud's terminology (this volume) institutions create a stability corridor within which the economy can operate without breakdown. The explanation for that stability, however, is not in the typical system of equations used to describe a macroeconomic model, but is, instead, in the institutional constraints imposed on individual actors.

Explicit institutional arrangements may not be the only feature of actual markets that generate a stability corridor, however. It is conceivable that technological features also can do so. To demonstrate that this is at least a possibility in real markets, we treat one simple technological feature of markets that may generate a stability corridor, namely capacity constraints. The potential of capacity constraints to induce a degree of stability stems from a basic observation on the nature of capacity. Capacity decisions take time to come on line, while output changes may just involve "flipping the switch." Adding or reducing capacity is innately a more deliberate act than changing output. This paper considers the effects of the deliberate nature of capacity decisions on production disequilibrium, and, in particular, in reducing instability.[2]

11.2   Disequilibrium

Disequilibrium in a competitive market is introduced first, and then the consequences of capacity constraints are considered. This paper uses a formulation of competitive markets in which prices do not determine who does what. This formulation draws on Meyer, Van Huyck, Battalio, and Saving (1992). Recently Milgrom and Roberts (1991) and Guesnerie (1992) have suggested a dominance approach to analyzing such disequilibrium problems, and this is the approach taken by the author. Moreover, recent experimental results in a similar market setting appear consistent with this dominance approach, (see Meyer, Van Huyck, Battalio, and Saving (1992)). In the context of this paper, a competitive market formulation dominance implies that a given level of production is not chosen by a firm if it could choose another level of production that generates higher profits for all possible price levels.

The possibility of production disequilibrium in a competitive market is easily illustrated. This illustration assumes constant returns to scale, which provides a particularly simple version of disequilibrium, and in a very familiar context. However, it may be worth mentioning that in the absence of constant returns the problem of who does what may remain. In order to facilitate the discussion some simplifying assumptions are useful. Suppose J firms decide to produce a good. Each determines a level of capacity K_j, and a level of labor L_j. Moreover, suppose $L_j \leq K_j$ by technological constraint and that each unit of labor produces one unit of output. This is a simple fixed coefficients technology which admits a straightforward definition of capacity. Normalize the price of capacity to be one, let the wage be W, and let the realized output price function be

$$P(\sum_{j=1}^{J} L_j) \,.$$

Then firm i's profit is

$$P(\sum_{j=1}^{J} L_j) \, L_i - WL_i - K_i \,.$$

If the firm assumes the competitive price $P = 1 + W$, then, of course, any values of K_i and L_i will do as well as any others (as long as $L_i = K_i$). Therefore the "perfect foresight" of $P = 1 + W$ need not necessarily generate that equilibrium result,

$$P(\sum_{j=1}^{J} L_j) = 1 + W.$$

As firm size is indeterminate, industry size and output are indeterminate, and therefore so is price indeterminate. (To further facilitate discussion it has been assumed that J is a known constant. In general, of course, the number of firms in a market is something to be determined, as well as firm size.)

In the simple competitive market sketched above, there is a wide range of disequilibria. As mentioned above, at $P = 1 + W$ any level of output generates the same level of profits (0), so any level of output is undominated. Strictly speaking, this is, of course, impossible. For one thing, there is no way to finance unlimited output. To make the point simply, suppose firms finance all their activities exclusively by borrowing from banks. Let us suppose that the firm i can get its hands on at most B dollars. Then $WL_i + K_i \leq B$. As, by construction, capacity is useless without labor, effectively this implies $K_i \leq B/(1+W) \equiv K^m$. For simplicity assume the same B and K^m for every firm. Let the price function $P(.)$ be continuous and decreasing. Clearly for production ever to be profitable $P(O) \geq 1+W$ is required ($P(O) \geq 1+W$ will be assumed). If, in addition, $P(JK^m) > 1+W$, then $K_i = L_i = K^m$ for all i is the unique dominant outcome. That is, if credit is very tight, the banking system induces equilibrium in the market. On the other hand, if $P(JK^m) \leq 1+W$, then any $K_i \leq K^m$ is undominated. For $P = 1+W$ any $K_i \leq K^m$ will do as well as any other and, moreover, as any $K_i \leq K^m$ will do,

$$P(\sum_{j=1}^{J} K_j) = (1+W)$$

is a possible outcome. In this case limitations on credit put an upper bound on capacity. While it seems most unlikely that a competitive financial system can perfectly induce equilibrium in a market, it must inevitably impose bounds on disequilibrium, and such bounds are assumed.

11.3.   Capacity

So far the simple competitive model does not distinguish between capacity and output in a meaningful way. Distinguishing between capacity and output generates two problems of disequilibrium, a capacity disequilibrium and an output disequilibrium.

A feature that distinguishes capacity from output is that capacity decisions take time to come on line, while output changes may just involve "flipping the switch." Adding or reducing capacity is innately a more deliberate act than changing output. This distinction has three consequences which are considered below: (a) capacity precedes output; (b) capacity is more orderly than output; and (c) less information of demand exists when the capacity decision is made.

11.3.1   Capacity precedes output

One consequence of this distinction between capacity and output is that a decision on capacity typically precedes the decision on the output produced utilizing that capacity. In the above simple model, that the capacity decision precedes the output decision matters only if the capacity of other firms is observed before a firm makes its output decision. Therefore, assume now that capacity decisions are made simultaneously; then total capacity is observed by all firms, and then output decisions are made simultaneously. So far, what distinguishes capacity from output is that the output decision is made with knowledge of industry capacity, but the reverse is not true.

Overbuilding of capacity can generate a subsequent output disequilibrium problem and capacity underutilization. If a firm takes price as given and chooses a level of capacity and output, it always chooses them equal, for to do otherwise is just to throw away money. However, with the capacity decision preceding the output decision and industry capacity observed, it may make sense to produce below capacity. The link between overbuilding of capacity and the output disequilibrium problem is implied by the output decision rule. Suppose

$$(\sum_{j=1}^{J} K_j)$$

is observed and

$$P(\sum_{j=1}^{J} K_j) > W.$$

Then the output level is $L_i = K_i$ for firm i. There is no output disequilibrium problem. On the other hand, if

$$P(0) \geqslant W \geqslant P(\sum_{j=1}^{J} K_j) ,$$

then any $L_i \leqslant K_i$ is undominated. For if $P = W$ then any $L_i \leqslant K_i$ will do as well as any other and, moreover, as any $L_i \leqslant K_i$ will do,

$$P(\sum_{j=1}^{J} L_j) = W$$

is a possible outcome. The output disequilibrium problem is generated by extreme overbuilding of capacity. If at full capacity the industry cannot cover variable costs, let alone total costs, there is an output disequilibrium problem; namely, who cuts output? This result suggests that output disequilibrium problems may involve extreme circumstances and be qualitatively different from normal economic behavior. In particular, disequilibrium is of greatest concern when capacity is very high.

The question remains of whether overbuilding of capacity can in fact occur. Indeed, the possibilities of both underbuilding and overbuilding of capacity remain with capacity observed. Suppose $P(0) \geqslant 1+ W \geqslant P(JK^m)$ as assumed. Also assume that the individual firm is so small (J so large and K^m so small) that each firm ignores the effect of its capacity on

$$(\sum_{j=1}^{J} K_j)$$

(this is assumed throughout). Then any $K_i \leqslant K^m$ is undominated. For if firm i expects the others to have zero capacity, then it chooses $K_i = K^m$. On the other hand, if firm i expects the others to have capacity K^m *and* firm i expects the others to react to

$$(\sum_{j=1}^{J} K_j) \cong JK^m$$

by setting $L_i = K^m$, which was shown to be possible in the previous paragraph, then firm i chooses $K_i = 0$. Any intermediate value is also undominated, for if $K_i' > K_i''$ and if the low output is realized, K_i' is the more profitable, while if the high output outcome is realized, K_i'' is the more profitable.

11.3.2   Capacity is more orderly than output

A second consequence of the capacity decision being more deliberate than the output decision is that the capacity decision may have less of a disequilibrium problem than does the output decision. Changing capacity takes time, involves contracting with suppliers, is discrete, and its timing may be largely dictated by technical considerations. Consequently firms may be unlikely to add or subtract capacity simultaneously, and when they make capacity decisions they may have a good fix on existing industry capacity. This distinction between capacity and output can be treated in a simple manner by assuming that capacity decisions are rigidly sequential and observed.

That overbuilding of capacity can generate an output disequilibrium problem and capacity underutilization remains true with capacity decisions sequential. The output decision rule presented above is unaffected by the capacity decisions being sequential rather than simultaneous. What matters is that industry capacity is observed before the output decision is made. If $P(\sum_{j=1}^{J} K_j) > W$

then $L_i = K_i$, and if $P(\sum_{j=1}^{J} K_j) \leq W$

then any $L_i \leq K_i$ is undominated.

While, with capacity decisions sequential, underbuilding of capacity is eliminated, the possibility of overbuilding of capacity remains. The elimination of underbuilding is demonstrated in Propositions 1 and 2.

Proposition 1: If $P(\sum_{j=1}^{J} K_j) > 1+W$ then $(\sum_{j=1}^{J} K_j) = JK^m$.

Proof: If $P(\sum_{j=1}^{J} K_j) > 1+W$ then $K_J = K^m$. Suppose $K_{J-i+1} = ... = K_J = K^m$. Then $P(\sum_{j=1}^{J-i+1} K_j + iK^m) \cong P(\sum_{j=1}^{J} K_j) > 1 + W$, which implies $K_{J-i} = K^m$.

Proposition 2 (No Underbuilding): If $P(JK^m) \leq 1+W$ then $P(\sum_{j=1}^{J} K_j) \leq 1 + W$.

Proof: Suppose $P(\sum_{j=1}^{J} K_j) > 1 + W$. Then by proposition 1, $(\sum_{j=1}^{J} K_j) = Jk^m$. Then $P(\sum_{j=1}^{J} K_j) = P(JK^m) \leq 1 + W$. Contradiction.

(The precondition $P(JK^m) \leq 1+W$ was assumed to assure that very tight limitations on bank credit did not force underbuilding and thereby induce equilibrium in the market.)

While underbuilding of capacity is eliminated, the possibility of overbuilding of capacity remains. Indeed, the possibility of an output disequilibrium problem makes possible the overbuilding of capacity that generates the output disequilibrium problem. This is demonstrated in Proposition 3.

Proposition 3 (Overbuilding Possible): if $P(JK^m) < 1+W$ then $\sum_{j=1}^{J} K_j = JK^m$ is an undominated outcome iff $P(JK^m) \leq W$ and $P(0) \geq 1+W$.

Proof: Suppose $P(JK^m) \leq W$ and $P(0) \geq 1+W$. $P(\sum_{j=1}^{J} K_j) < W$ implies any $L_i < K_i$ is undominated since $P(0) \geq 1+W > W$. Therefore if $\sum_{j=1}^{J} K_j = JK^m$ then

$$\sum_{j=1}^{J} L_j = 0$$

is a possible outcome and, if so, $P(0) \geq 1 + W$ implies, if so, deviating and setting $L_i = K^m$ is profitable. Therefore $\sum_{j=1}^{J} K_j = JK^m$ is undominated. On the other hand, if $P(JK^m) > W$ or if $P(0) < 1+W$, $\sum_{j=1}^{J} K_j = JK^m$ implies certain losses so the Jth firm would set $K_J = 0$ if it observed $\sum_{j=1}^{J-1} K_j \cong JK^m$.

With capacity decisions sequential, overbuilding of capacity is really a game of "chicken." A firm builds excessive capacity in the hope that the other firms will do so as well and that, moreover, when faced with the reality of excessive capacity, and the possibility of not covering variable costs, the other firms will "chicken out" and underproduce. This would allow the firm in question to reap high profits. However, this game of chicken, which is not ruled out by dominance, is "risky." The firm "on average" will lose. Firms may not purposefully choose to play such a risky game. If, in fact, firms do not choose to play chicken, then there is no overbuilding of capacity and, consequently, no output disequilibrium problem. If firms do not play chicken this would seem, then, to completely eliminate the possibility of disequilibrium (assuming capacity decisions are sequential). This conclusion does not follow in general, however, for reasons that we turn to next.

11.3.3 Less information exists in capacity decision

A third consequence of the capacity decision being more deliberate than the output decision is that less information on demand may be available when the capacity decision is made than when the output decision is made. To treat this distinction between capacity and output, it is assumed that price is a function of industry output and a random variable s. Every firm is assumed to know the value of s at the time of its output decision, but not at the time of its capacity decision. In addition, every firm is assumed to have the same probability density function, $f(s)$, on s at the time of the capacity decision, and every firm is risk neutral.

That *ex post* overbuilding of capacity can generate an output disequilibrium problem and capacity underutilization remains true with less information on demand available. The output decision rule presented above is unaffected by the capacity decision being made with less information. What matters is that industry capacity is observed before the output decision is made.

If $P(\sum_{j=1}^{J} K_j, s)$ $> W$ then $L_i = K_i$, and if $P(0, s) > W > P(\sum_{j=1}^{J} K_j, s)$ then any $L_i \leq$ K_i is undominated.

First suppose that while the capacity decision precedes the output decision, it has a similar disequilibrium problem. The possibilities of both *ex ante* underbuilding and overbuilding of capacity remain with capacity decisions observed but *simultaneous* and with less information on demand available. In fact let $S^a \equiv \{s|P(0, s) > W\}$ and $S^{-a} = \{s|P(0,s) < W\}$. Suppose $\int_{S^a} [P(0,s) - W]f(s)ds$ $\geq 1 \geq \int_{S^a} [P(JK^m,s) - W]f(s)ds$. Then any $K_i \leq K^m$ is undominated. The argument is a repeat of the argument made above.

Now suppose that the capacity decision has less of a disequilibrium problem than the output decision itself. While *ex ante* underbuilding of capacity is eliminated, the possibility of *ex ante* overbuilding of capacity remains with capacity decisions sequential and with less information on demand available. The elimination of *ex ante* underbuilding is demonstrated in Propositions 4 and 5.

Proposition 4: If $\int_{S^a} [P(\sum_{j=1}^{J} K_j, s) - W]f(s)ds > 1$, then $(\sum_{j=1}^{J} K_j) = JK^m$.

Proof: This proof exactly parallels the proof of Proposition 1.

Proposition 5 (No *Ex Ante* Underbuilding): If $\int_{S^a} [P(JK^m,s) - W]f(s)ds \leq 1$ then $\int_{S^a} P(\sum_{j=1}^{J} K_j, s) - W]f(s)ds \leq 1$.

Proof: This proof exactly parallels the proof of Proposition 2.

(There is an issue of what one means by *ex ante* underbuilding in the context of this version of the model. Proposition 5 interprets *ex ante* underbuilding to mean that if every firm produces at maximum capacity, unless it could not cover variable costs no matter what the other firms produced ($P(0,s) < W$), then profits are positive.)

While *ex ante* underbuilding of capacity is eliminated, the possibility of *ex ante* overbuilding of capacity remains. The possibility of an output disequilibrium problem makes possible the *ex ante* overbuilding of capacity that makes the output disequilibrium problem more likely. This is demonstrated in Proposition 6. Let $S^1(\sum_{j=1}^{J} K_j)) \equiv \{s | P(\sum_{j=1}^{J} K_j), s) > W\}$ and $S^2(\sum_{j=1}^{J} K_j)) = \{s | P(0,s) > W > P(\sum_{j=1}^{J} K_j, s)\}$. Notice that $S^1(\sum_{j=1}^{J} K_j)) \cup S^2(\sum_{j=1}^{J} K_j)) = S^a$ for all values of $\sum_{j=1}^{J} K_j$.

Proposition 6 (Ex Ante Overbuilding Possible): $\sum_{j=1}^{J} K_j) = JK^m$ is an undominated outcome iff (a) $\int_{S^1(JK^m)} [P(JK^m, s) - W] f(s) ds + \int_{S^2(JK^m)} [P(0,s) - W] f(s) ds \geq$ 1.

Proof: This proof parallels the proof of Proposition 3. Suppose (a) holds. $P(0,s) \geq W \geq P(\sum_{j=1}^{J} K_j, s)$ implies any $L_i \leq K_i$ is undominated. Therefore if $(\sum_{j=1}^{J} K_j) = JK^m$ and $s \varepsilon S^2(JK^m)$ then $\sum_{j=1}^{J} L_j = 0$ is a possible outcome. If $(\sum_{j=1}^{J} K_j) = JK^m$ and $s \varepsilon S^1(JK^m)$ then $\sum_{j=1}^{J} L_j = JK^m$ while if $s \varepsilon S^a$ then $\sum_{j=1}^{J} L_j = 0$. (a) implies profits from deviating from $\{\sum_{j=1}^{J} L_j = 0$ if $s \varepsilon S^2(JK^m)\}$ by using $\{L_i = K^m$ if $s \varepsilon S^2(JK^m)\}$. Therefore $(\sum_{j=1}^{J} K_j) = JK^m$ is undominated. On the other hand, not (a) implies certain losses from $(\sum_{j=1}^{J} K_j) = JK^m$ so the Jth firm would set $K_j = 0$ if it observed $\sum_{j=1}^{J-1} K_j \cong JK^m$.

The relation between Proposition 6 and Proposition 3 can be clarified. Clearly a sufficient condition for expression (a) of Proposition 6 is $P(JK^m, s) \leq W$ for all s and $P(0,s) \geq 1+W$ for all s.

Once again, with capacity decisions sequential, *ex ante* overbuilding of capacity is really a game of chicken. Expression (a) of Proposition 6 can be re-written as

$\int_{S^a} [P(JK^m,s) 2 W] f(s) ds + \int_{S^2(JK^m)} [P(0,s) 2 P(JK^m,s)] f(s) ds > 1$. If $P(JK^m,s) > W$ for all s so that $S^2(JK^m) = f$ then $\int_{S^a} [P(JK^m,s) 2 W] f(s) ds < 1$ implies not (a).

A firm builds *ex ante* excessive capacity in the hope that the other firms will do so as well and that, moreover, when faced with the reality of excessive capacity, and the possibility of not covering variable costs, the other firms will chicken out and underproduce. This would allow the firm in question to reap high profits. There is, however, an important difference in this case with less information on demand available when the capacity decision is made than when the output decision is made. While, if firms do not choose to play chicken, there is no *ex ante* overbuilding of capacity, *ex ante* overbuilding of capacity is not necessary for the existence of an output disequilibrium problem. Excessive *ex post* overbuilding (and $P(0,s) \geq W$) suffices. Very low realized demand generates an output disequilibrium problem when at full capacity the industry cannot cover variable costs, let alone total costs. Once again, this suggests that output disequilibrium problems may involve extreme circumstances, and be qualitatively different from normal economic behavior. In particular, disequilibrium is of greatest concern when demand has fallen substantially from the levels predicted when capacity decisions were made.

11.4   Interpreting the model

Although the model was a simple one, it has some conclusions which generalize beyond it. Specifically, the result that disequilibrium is of greatest concern when capacity is in excess, possibly due to an unanticipated collapse in demand, seems robust. That is, disequilibrium may be the greatest threat to an economy already under severe duress: We may have "local" stability and "global" instability. Like the explicit institutional arrangements emphasized by Leijonhufvud, and by the other papers in this volume, market structure induced by technological features themselves also can generate a stability corridor. In this latter case, the fundamental structure that engenders local stability, and substitutes for the explicit restrictions provided by institutional arrangements, is the sequencing of decisions that technology, specifically capacity constraints, can induce. The "corridor" is pierced when something occurs which breaks down the natural sequencing of decisions. As with the explicit institutional arrangements emphasized elsewhere in this volume, the sequencing of decisions is a technologically induced structure of real markets from which the Walrasian approach abstracts, but which in reality may be very important to understanding market stability. It is worth noting that this role of the sequencing of decisions in generating stability is further evidence of the close link between equilibrium coordination failure and disequilibrium. As with disequilibrium, sequencing of decisions can eliminate equilibrium coordination failure.[3]

The treatment of capacity constraints in this paper suggests a possible refinement of the role of government policy envisioned elsewhere in this volume. Government policy might be particularly important in generating stability when the economy breaks out of the corridor of stability generated by technologically induced real market structures. Perhaps such technologically induced real-market structures generate a fine corridor of stability, and government policy a coarse corridor of stability. This bears on the old monetarist-Keynesian debate of rules versus discretion. The possibility of piercing the corridor of stability suggests that government institutions should allow themselves room for discretion, rather than being locked into rules that may have been devised based on an understanding of the behavior of the economy within the stability corridor. Government institutions should be prepared to react to the qualitatively different, and more unstable, behavior encountered in the relatively infrequent circumstances in which the corridor is pierced. In any case, a theme linking the papers of this volume is the difficulty for independent agents in making mutually consistent and beneficial decisions, and the role of real-market structures and institutions in helping them do so; a role completely ignored, indeed purposefully abstracted away from, in Walrasian analysis.

11.5   Conclusions

The analysis of investment in this paper, while perhaps not macroeconomic, is at least market-wide. This contrasts to more traditional approaches to investment. The traditional investment literature evolved from the traditional flexible accelerator model of stock adjustment. One examined the problem of the single firm in isolation, and then added up. That is, it was a rigidly microeconomic tradition, in direct contrast to the papers in this book, which stress the macroeconomic aspect and how the macroeconomic environment impinges upon the individual agent. The traditional approach ignores agent interactions, whereas agent interactions are the critical feature in the analysis in this paper. It is perhaps ironic in this regard that Keynes himself believed that investment was the fundamental problem, was the point in the economy where macroeconomic considerations entered with most telling effect, and that the retail sector could safely be left to the free market. This may also help explain why the Walrasian approach has had such difficulty in engaging the observations made by Keynes. With the basic Walrasian starting point being the grand bazaar (see my previous paper), that is, the economy being viewed as essentially a naive retailing institution, there wasn't the theoretical development of a complex commercial and industrial organization that could exhibit the problems that for Keynes were the critical ones.

Doubtless Keynes was, at least in part, motivated by empirical observation. He was, of course, well aware of the fact that it is investment which is the volatile component of national income. A stock adjustment model is not well suited for addressing volatility, treating as it does a firm as a smoothing device. The traditional approach to investment addresses the volatility by introducing accelerator elements, or by a greater interest rate sensitivity for the demand for investment goods. Whether more macroeconomic approaches to investment, as suggested by Keynes and considered in this paper, will be adopted will ultimately depend upon their success in better confronting the data. It is premature to speculate whether this will prove to be the case.

Part of the empirical difficulty is suggested in the earlier discussion of stability corridors. Naturally enough, investment studies have focused on explaining investment in every period. However, the sort of model suggested in this paper has relevance to those relatively infrequent periods when the stability corridor is pierced. Perhaps such observations as the much cited volatility of the stock market and the difficulty of predicting turning points may at least suggest some room for a new approach. Certainly, it would be very speculative at this point to further suggest that the analysis of this paper applies to such events as the Great Depression, the 1984 Houston real estate collapse, or the historical instabilities described, for example, in Braudel (1982).

Endnotes

The author is grateful to Kristine L. Chase, three anonymous referees, and, most especially, David Colander for valuable comments. Also I wish to thank the Hoover Institution, Stanford University, and the Federal Reserve Bank of Dallas for stimulating research environments and for support. All errors and oversights are the author's responsibility alone, and the views expressed herein do not necessarily reflect those of the Hoover Institution, the Federal Reserve Bank of Dallas, or the Federal Reserve System.

1. The simple competitive model also has some similarities to the battle of the sexes game, rather than to the stag hunt game of team production. This may make it an even more fruitful ground for disequilibrium than is team production, as indicated by the experiments of Cooper, DeJong, Forsythe, and Ross (1994).
2. This analysis of capacity constraints inducing a degree of stability draws on Guesnerie's (1992) observation that stability increases when decisions are sequential and observed.
3. In this regard, see also, for example, Bryant (1983) and Guesnerie (1992).

References

Braudel, F. (1982). *The Wheels of Commerce, Civilization and Capitalism 15-18th Century*, Vol. II. New York: Harper and Row.

Bryant, J. (1980). "Competitive Equilibrium with Price Setting Firms and Stochastic Demand." *International Economic Review* 21: 619-26.

(1982). "Perfection, the Infinite Horizon and Dominance." *Economics Letters* 10: 223-29.

(1983). "A Simple Rational Expectations Keynes-type Model." *Quarterly Journal of Economics* 98: 525-28.

(1984). "An Example of a Dominance Approach to Rational Expectations." *Economics Letters* 16: 249-55.

(1987). "The Paradox of Thrift, Liquidity Preference and Animal Spirits." *Econometrica* 55: 1231-35.

(1992). "Banking and Coordination." *Journal of Money, Credit and Banking* 24: 563-69.

(1994). "Coordination Theory, the Stag Hunt and Macroeconomics." In J. W. Friedman, ed., *Problems of Coordination in Economic Activity.* Boston/Dordrecht, London: Kluwer Academic Publishers.

Colander, D. (1993). "The Macrofoundations of Micro." *Eastern Economic Journal* 19: 447-58.

Cooper, R., D. V. DeJong, R. Forsythe, and T. W. Ross (1990). "Selection Criteria in Coordination Games: Some Experimental Results." *American Economic Review* 80: 218-33.

(1992). "Communication in Coordination Games." *Quarterly Journal of Economics* 86: 739-71.

(1994). "Alternative Institutions for Resolving Coordination Problems: Experimental Evidence on Forward Induction and Preplay Communication." In J. W. Friedman, ed., *Problems of Coordination in Economic Activity.* Boston/Dordrecht/ London: Kluwer Academic Publishers.

Cooper, R. and A. John (1988). "Coordinating Coordination Failures in Keynesian Models." *Quarterly Journal of Economics* 82: 441-63.

Crawford, V.P. (1991). "An 'Evolutionary' Interpretation of Van Huyck, Battalio, and Beil's Experimental Results on Coordination." *Games and Economic Behavior* 3: 25-59.

Diamond, P. (1982). "Aggregate Demand Management in Search Rquilibrium." *Journal of Political Economy* 90: 881-94.

Frisch, R. (1934). "Circulation Planning." *Econometrica* 2: 258-336, 422-35.

Guesnerie, R. (1992). "An Exploration of the Eductive Justifications of the Rational-Expectations Hypothesis." *American Economic Review* 82: 1254-78.

Jovanovic, B. (1987). "Micro Shocks and Aggregate Risk." *Quarterly Journal of Economics* 81: 405-409.

Keynes, J. M. (1936). *The General Theory of Employment, Interest, and Money.* New York: Harcourt, Brace & World.

Mankiw, N. G. and D. Romer, eds. (1991). *Coordination Failures and Real Rigidities, New Keynesian Economics* Vol. II. *MIT Press Readings in Economics* (B. Friedman and L. Summers, eds.). Cambridge, Mass.: MIT Press.

Meyer, D., J. Van Huyck, R. Battalio, and T. R. Saving (1992). "History's Role in Coordinating Decentralized Allocation Decisions." *Journal of Political Economy* 100: 292-316.

Milgrom, P. and J. Roberts (1991). "Adaptive and Sophisticated Learning in Normal Form Games." *Games and Economic Behavior* 3: 82-100.

Mitchell, W. C. (1927). *Business Cycles the Problem and Its Setting.* New York: National Bureau of Economic Research.

O'Driscoll, G. P. (1977). *Economics as a Coordination Problem: the Contributions of Friedrich A. Hayek.* Kansas City, Kans.: Sheed, Andrews and McMeel.

Pearce, D.G. (1984). "Rationalizable Strategic Behavior and the Problem of Perfection." *Econometrica* 52: 1029-1050.

Roberts, J. (1987). "An Equilibrium Model with Involuntary Unemployment at Flexible, Competitive Prices and Wages." *American Economic Review* 77: 856-74.

Van Huyck, J. B., R. C. Battalio, and R. O. Beil (1990). "Tacit Coordination Games, Strategic Uncertainty, and Coordination Failure." *American Economic Review* 90: 34-248.

   (1991). "Strategic Uncertainty, Equilibrium Selection, and Coordination Failure in Average Opinion Games." *Quarterly Journal of Economics* 91: 885-910.

Weitzman, M. (1982). "Decreasing Returns and the Foundations of Unemployment Theory." *Economic Journal* 92: 787-804.

PART IV

NEW STRUCTURALIST MACRECONOMICS VS.
POST WALRASIAN MACROECONOMICS

CHAPTER 12

Endogenizing the natural rate of unemployment: Phelps's structural slumps and the Post Walrasian framework

Hans van Ees and Harry Garretsen

12.1   Introduction

A central theme in the various contributions to this book is the dissatisfaction with the mainstream or neoclassical microfoundation of macroeconomics. This dissatisfaction concerns *inter alia* the use of Walrasian general equilibrium analysis as the microfoundation of macro, the reliance upon unique, stable equilibria, and the central role of the natural rate hypothesis. In the debate between the vast majority of (new) Keynesian and (new) Classical economists about macroeconomic stabilization policy, the question of the appropriateness of the underlying neoclassic microfoundation is taken for granted. In this respect, Edmund Phelps's (1994) book *Structural Slumps: The Modern Equilibrium Theory of Unemployment, Interest, and Assets* is interesting for a number of reasons. To begin with, the main goal of the book is to endogenize the natural rate of unemployment, thereby dismissing the standard neoclassical assumption of an invariant natural rate. Secondly, Phelps explicitly addresses the policy implications of what he calls the structuralist theory of unemployment. In this respect, a "theory is a structuralist theory in the sense that it treats unemployment as the outcome of the configuration of real demands and supplies, the 'structure' of the economy in some sense" (Phelps, 1994: 157). Finally, Phelps, as one of the founding fathers of the modern microfoundations debate,[1] offers a microfoundation of this structuralist theory and claims that his theory of unemployment differs fundamentally from Keynesian as well as Classical macroeconomic approaches.

At various stages in the book the reader is told that the structuralist theory can be looked upon as a truly new approach in macroeconomics (see introductory chapter or page 375) and it is perhaps not entirely coincidental that the subtitle of the book rings a bell to anyone familiar with the title of a book published by a well-known British economist in 1936. (See Ambler (1994) for a similar observation.). Phelps's book is certainly thought-provoking and it is the aim of this paper to assess the structuralist theory and its policy implications from a Post Walrasian perspective. We will also use *Structural Slumps* as a neoclassical benchmark for (an inevitably incomplete) discussion of policy design in a Post Walrasian framework. In the end, we think that Phelps's theory is not fundamentally different from a standard neoclassical approach to macroeconomics precisely because Phelps sticks to a microfoundation of macroeconomics that is grounded upon an essentially unchanged Walrasian general equilibrium framework.

This paper is organized as follows. In the next section the main elements of the structuralist theory and its policy implications are summarized and discussed. Section 12.3 uses Phelps's approach as a benchmark model for an analysis of the question how this model should be amended in order to deal with some of the features of a Post Walrasian framework. In section 12.4 the important issue of the design of economic policy in such a framework is briefly discussed. Section 12.5 summarizes and concludes.

12.2   On structuralist theory

12.2.1   Basic model

Before we start with a discussion of the basic model it is important to say something about the definitions used by Phelps.[2] The structuralist theory is first and foremost a *non-monetary* theory about the real forces in the economy that "are capable of propagating slumps and booms" (Phelps, 1994: 1) by moving the equilibrium or natural rate of unemployment up or down. The natural rate of unemployment is defined as the current equilibrium steady-state rate of unemployment given the current state variables. Since there is no equilibrium on the labor market as long as the actual rate of unemployment causes the change in equilibrium unemployment rate path to be nonzero (ibid.: 1), any unemployment equilibrium has to be the natural rate of unemployment. Furthermore, it is assumed that this equilibrium is unique.[3] Endogenizing the natural rate of unemployment therefore turns out to mean that, equivalently, the equilibrium level of unemployment is determined by structuralist (= real) forces. These real forces, see below, are not solely labor market forces since the determination of the labor market equilibrium is very much dependent on developments on the goods and especially the capital market.

Equilibrium in any market is defined as "a state or path along which expectations are ..., absent an unanticipated shock, fulfilled" (ibid.: 9). With the excep-

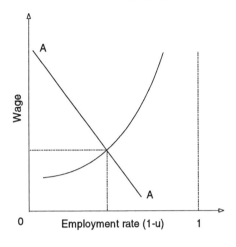

Figure 12.1   Equilibrium wage curve and the "demand-wage relation"

tion of the labor market, on which a problem of asymmetric information is explicitly modeled, this definition of equilibrium means that perfect foresight prevails in the economy. All prices are fully flexible and the goods and capital markets always clear. However, the labor market does not clear and at the equilibrium wage there exists unemployment. The latter is the result of the fact that wages are not solely determined by scarcity conditions but also by the existence of asymmetric information on the labor market.

Building upon the work of Salop (1979) and Shapiro and Stiglitz (1984), Phelps introduces a labor-turnover and a shirking model of efficiency wages to illustrate the by now well-known result that the equilibrium wage can be an increasing function of the level of the employment. The asymmetric information problem leads to an equilibrium wage that exceeds the market-clearing wage with employers having no incentive to reduce this wage.[4]

Figure 12.1 (i.e., Phelps, 1994: 40, 45, 48) allows us to discuss the essential features of the structuralist theory of unemployment (v = real wage rate; u is the level of unemployment; $1 - u$ = the level of employment). In Figure 12.1, the intersection of the positively sloped equilibrium wage curve with the negatively sloped "demand-wage relation" determines the natural rate of unemployment. The equilibrium wage curve depicts the equilibrium wage rate at each given rate of unemployment when all the firms in the economy are optimally taking into account real wage rates at other firms and other incentives to quit or shirk. The latter curve, "the derived demand for labor curve," depicts combinations of the real wage rate and employment firms are willing to choose under the assumption of equilibrium in the goods market, i.e., the situation in which firms are actually supplying those levels of output that they would have expected to supply.

Malinvaud (1994: 3) points out that since firms are always on their output supply curve (ibid.: 34), this derived demand for labor is really nothing more than the standard neoclassical firm demand for labor. It is true that firms are always on their output supply curve but there is a difference with the neoclassical demand for labor function as for instance used in real business cycle theory. In the real business cycle model the labor demand function in the $(v, 1 - u)$ space can only shift as the capital stock or the state of technology changes. In Phelps's approach to the labor demand curve, however, there are additional reasons why this curve may shift. The most important shift variable in this respect is q, the (shadow) price of firms' assets. It is here that the real innovation of *Structural Slumps* comes to the fore. The dependency of labor demand upon q and subsequently (see below) on the real rate of interest implies that the model on which Figure 12.2 is based is not a partial model like that in the New Keynesian analyses mentioned in section 12.2, but a truly general equilibrium model in which the equilibrium levels of v and $1 - u$ depend, mainly through the shadow price of firms' assets q, on the developments in the rest of the economy, that is, on the goods and capital markets.

In *Structural Slumps* Phelps explicitly distinguishes three non-financial assets: stock of employees (human capital), stock of customers (capital embodied in long-lasting relationships with customers), and physical capital. The common characteristic of these assets is that they are related to the stock of employees, i.e., they measure the present discounted value of the current stock of employees employed at a representative firm. Thus a change in q, the real (shadow) price of these assets, will affect the present discounted value of the firm's current stock of employees and hence the long-run equilibrium level of employment the firm is willing to support (*ceteris paribus*). The steady-state equilibrium in Figure 12.1 is drawn for a given value of q.

The question as to what changes the natural rate of unemployment can thus be rephrased by asking what the relevant variables are which affect the real shadow price of assets. The crux of the interdependency between the labor market and the rest of the economy is that the main determinant of q is the real rate of interest.[5] Phelps uses the real rate of interest as "new" transmission channel between the aggregate economy and the labor market. "A rise of the rate of interest, other things equal, in reducing the present discounted value (and shadow price) of the existing stock of employment, has the effect of reducing the growth of employment" (1994: 37). Thus, the argument is that a change in the real rate of interest will affect the firms' level of financial and non-financial real wealth through a change in q, which will affect the derived equilibrium demand for labor. For instance, a decline in the rate of interest will increase q, indicating an increase in future profitability, a higher willingness of firms to employ and train labor and thus a higher growth rate of employment.[6]

The labor market equilibrium may of course also be affected by other variables. Any shock (see section 12.2.2 below) that, for instance, increases non-wage income for employees increases the quit "incentive" in the labor-turnover model (or induces shirking) and leads in terms of Figure 12.1 to an inward shift of the equilibrium wage curve, thereby *ceteris paribus* increasing unemployment. Once physical capital goods are included, the story becomes somewhat reminiscent of a textbook Classical Savings/Investment diagram. The effect on (un)employment of a stock seems to depend crucially upon the source of this shock (e.g., a decrease of savings or, equivalently an increase of consumption, on the one hand, or an increase in investment, on the other). From the discussion of the model for the third asset, physical capital, it becomes clear that any shock that increases the demand for consumption goods (= decreases savings) depresses employment, whereas any shock that increases the demand for investment goods stimulates employment. This important feature of the model hinges to some extent upon the assumption (ibid.: 46) that the production of the capital good is more labor-intensive than the production of consumption goods. The claim (ibid.: 3) that the structuralist theory echoes Classical themes (under-saving as the cause of slumps) as well as Keynesian ones (under-investment as the cause of slumps) does depend on this assumption. In section 12.2.2 we will see that this assumption also drives some of the policy implications.

The partial equilibrium model, on which Figure 12.1 is based, contains a loose end because the real rate of interest and thus q still have to be determined. Phelps ties this loose end up through a general equilibrium analysis of the capital market. He assumes firms have perfect foresight and are in equilibrium when q is determined in accordance with the equilibrium real rate of interest. Households also have perfect foresight and use the same equilibrium path of the real rate of interest as do firms.[7] The equilibrium q and the equilibrium real rate of interest also ensure that the goods market is in equilibrium (ibid.: 54). Phelps states that "perhaps the centrality of the capital market is the distinctive feature of the structuralist unemployment theory" (ibid.: 58). Given the crucial role of the real rate of interest in determining unemployment, this assessment is correct in our view but this also means that it is the perfect foresight type of capital market, which is central in the structuralist theory. Even though Phelps mentions the relevance of capital market imperfections these imperfections are not incorporated in the model.

Finally, anticipating the discussion in the next section, let us briefly discuss the microfoundation of the structuralist theory (ibid.: Chs. 15 and 16). The microfoundation consists entirely of a general equilibrium foundation of the structuralist theory. Except for the microeconomic foundation of the equilibrium-wage curve this microfoundation is of the perfect foresight, perfect markets type and this microfoundation of the equilibrium-wage curve is in line with New Keynesian models of efficiency wages.

At other places the microfoundation is typically ambiguous (see also Ambler, (1994: 571; Woodford, 1994: 1804)). For instance, the absence of equilibrium price dispersion makes it unclear in *Structural Slumps* why any customer should ever accept a higher price than the average market price to begin with. Hence, the customer market model does not provide a theoretical foundation for the crucial link between the labor market and the price of assets. In as far as the main policy results of the structuralist theory differ from those derived from a neoclassical model with no market imperfections, the reason for this difference is not only to be found in the role of efficiency wages in the structuralist theory but also in the role of some far from trivial assumptions like the Blanchard-Yaari formulation of intertemporal household behavior or the assumption that the production of capital goods is relatively labor-intensive.

12.2.2   Shocks and policy implications

The crux of the effects of (policy-induced) shocks on the natural rate of employment is how such a shock affects q, the real shadow price of assets. We already have observed that a rise in the real rate of interest depresses q and hence increases equilibrium unemployment. In the context of an open economy this means, for instance, that a country confronted with a rise in the "world" interest rate sees its equilibrium unemployment level rise. Since Phelps's theory is a non-monetary theory, nominal shocks are not analyzed and monetary policy does therefore not matter for real variables.[8]

Even though some of the policy implications depend on the existence of efficiency wages,[9] Phelps's main focus is on fiscal policy, and the effects of fiscal policy depend above all on particular assumptions. In the first place, the Blanchard-Yaari model of household behavior ensures that Ricardian equivalence does not hold, which means that fiscal policy shocks can affect real variables. In the second place, the aforementioned assumption that the production of capital goods is relatively labor-intensive ensures that a policy-induced increase in the demand for capital goods stimulates the natural rate of output and employment. Any increase of the public demand for consumption goods does, however, contract the equilibrium level of output and employment. Much as in the Classical analysis in which actual output equals the natural rate, an increase of consumption raises the rate of interest and in Phelps's model this also depresses q and thus increases unemployment.

Since the present chapter is mainly concerned with theory, we make only a few theory-related remarks about the empirical part of *Structural Slumps* (Phelps, 1994: Chs. 17 and 18). First of all, even though the empirical work shows a positive relation between the real rate of interest and the level of unemployment it remains unclear to what extent the basic features of the structuralist theory are responsible for this empirical outcome. Secondly, in analyzing the data Phelps uses some arguments that are at odds with his theory.[10] Thirdly, and most importantly, it is an open question whether the main empirical results can solely be explained by the structuralist approach or also by Keynesian and Classical approaches.

This last observation touches upon the main issue in our assessment of *Structural Slumps*. Despite the attempt to endogenize the natural rate of unemployment Phelps's structuralist theory remains methodologically very close to neoclassical (Keynesian or Classical) macroeconomics grounded upon the microfoundation of Walrasian general equilibrium theory. This inevitably means that Phelps's policy conclusions are a mixture of well-known Keynesian and neoclassical policy conclusions. It also means that in order to come up with an alternative for the standard microfoundations of macroeconomics approach one has to come up with more fundamental deviations from the standard general equilibrium notions of rationality and equilibrium behavior. In the next section we will illustrate this while using Phelps's model as a benchmark.

12.3   Beyond structuralism: multiple equilibria

The preceding section offers a description of the basic ingredients of the structuralist approach to unemployment and a discussion of some of its policy implications. In this and the next section we outline an alternative analysis of economic policymaking by elaborating upon the assumption of a unique steady-state equilibrium in the structuralist approach. We think that a discussion of the assumption of unique equilibria in the structuralist theory may help to emphasize that in the structuralist approach, along with more traditional Keynesian or neoclassical approaches, some important theoretical and policy questions that ultimately originate from the multiplicity of equilibria are overlooked. Moreover, we generally believe that the discussion about the appropriate framework for macroeconomic theory can be improved upon if this discussion is not focused upon changing one or two assumptions in an otherwise unchanged general equilibrium framework. Instead, the unfounded superiority of the standard general equilibrium framework for the analysis of the structural performance of the economy should be questioned.

Phelps and the contributors to this volume share the dissatisfaction with the standard neoclassical natural rate hypothesis. Seen from this perspective, Phelps's development of a general equilibrium model in which fluctuations in the natural rate of unemployment are explained by changes in economic variables is a remarkable achievement. Moreover, and this is another shared belief, in the structuralist approach the explanation of unemployment focuses upon the underlying economic structure – the fundamentals of the aggregate demand and supply

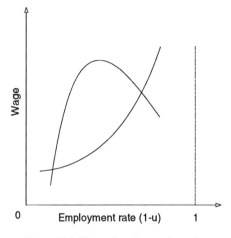

Figure 12.2 Hump-shaped wage demand curve

schedules, so to speak. Yet we argue that the Phelps structuralist approach is still "too Walrasian." In the first place, it can be concluded from the previous section that some of the results of the structuralist approach can be largely ascribed to particular assumptions that are not grounded upon economic theory, such as the absence of Ricardian equivalence. In the second place, the structuralist theory, although interesting as an extension of the Walrasian literature, is at the same time still solidly grounded in the Walrasian approach. It requires one to use a general equilibrium framework characterized by a unique steady-state equilibrium to analyze the characteristics of slumps and thereby assumes away many important issues.

Why do Post Walrasians oppose the assumption of a unique steady-state equilibrium in the structuralist approach? Because the assumption of a *unique* steady-state equilibrium, as depicted in Figure 12.1 of the preceding section, is nothing more than an assumption. In the context of the three structuralist working models of *Stuctural Slumps* this assumption is *ad hoc*. Phelps himself readily admits that the particular shape of the demand wage relation or the equilibrium-wage curve is chosen so as to guarantee uniqueness.

To start with the wage demand curve in the turnover model, given the requirement that the shadow price of trained labor uniquely determines the hiring rate, a steady-state rate of employment growth implies a constant quit rate. The latter may require that an increase in employment, which increases the quit rate, is offset by an increase in the real wage rate. On the other hand, the negative impact on cash flow of an increase in the quit rate can also be offset by a reduction in the real wage rate. Thus, the derived labor demand curve may be both upward and downward sloping. Phelps (1994: 40) argues that for sufficiently small real interest rates the derived demand for labor curve is downward sloping. Assuming for the moment an empirically plausible counter-cyclical pattern in real interest rates, this may imply that a hump-shaped derived demand for labor curve cannot be excluded in the turnover model (see Figure 12.2). In that case, at least the theoretical possibility of multiple equilibria (multiple intersections of the derived demand for labor curve and the equilibrium wage curve) cannot be ruled out so that the question as to the establishment of a particular equilibrium becomes relevant.

In the second working model of Phelps, the customer market model, the long-term value of the firm is affected by the present discounted value of long-run relationships between the firm and its customers. The firm chooses its price strategy so as to maximize the value of the firm, i.e., the present discounted value of future profits, thereby taking into account both the change in cash flow resulting from a change in prices and the gradual change in its stock of customers, following a permanent change in prices. In this model, q denotes the shadow value to the firm of a representative customer.

By taking into account the production technology, the aforementioned product market analysis can be transformed into a wage demand curve. As usual, the labor market equilibrium is achieved at the intersection of the equilibrium-wage curve and the derived demand for labor curve. Also, in the customer market model the slope of the derived demand curve is ambiguous. Phelps (ibid.: 44) carefully explains that the impact of an economy-wide wage increase on effort can be either positive or negative, depending on the impact of the increased wage/nonwage income ratio and the impact of higher wages paid at other firms. All in all, this implies that the labor demand curve can only be assumed to be downward sloping in a wage-employment space for moderate and high levels of employment. For low employment levels the curve may be upward sloping. Again, combining these features may result in a hill-shaped wage demand curve (see Figure 12.2). Finally, also in the physical capital model (introducing capital besides labor), the slope of the wage demand curve is ambiguous due to the aforementioned nonlinearities in the shirking condition. For high employment rates a negative demand curve is postulated; for low employment a positively sloped curve may be relevant (again, see Figure 12.2).[11]

Combining the aforementioned observations, it can be argued that the three "working" models of the structuralist approach potentially yield ambiguities as far as the sign of the slope-coefficients of both the equilibrium-wage curve and the wage demand curve is concerned. As a result, it can be concluded that the structuralist approach may have to cope with the existence of multiple equilibria. The interesting question is then how to acknowledge this conclusion. Phelps explicitly restricts the analysis to a unique steady state equilibrium as well as to a unique (saddlepoint stable) equilibrium path, while "throwing up our hands in the other case" (ibid.: 99). In the discussion of the customer market model explicitly, reference is even made to "a divine hand guiding the economy to that solution exhibiting the largest output level (and highest q)" (ibid.: 99).

We believe that in order to explain structural inefficiencies a different approach should be advocated. This approach rests upon the recognition of multiple equilibria or nonlinearities as basic characteristics of a market economy, which *inter alia* explains *our* dissatisfaction with the notion of an invariant natural rate. At the same time, the existence of multiple equilibria is not consistent with a Walrasian general equilibrium approach, since the associated model of microeconomic behavior is built upon the fundamental assumption that individuals do not have to take into account that the coordination of economic activities (in the best possible way) may fail.[12]

Indeed, if economic theory is grounded upon the idea that the coordination of economic activities and expectations is no longer assured, then a different kind of microeconomics is needed, based upon the notion that the required knowledge for optimal decision making is fundamentally incomplete and disseminated among agents. Moreover, in such a theory, resources, preferences, and technology can never be the necessary and sufficient ingredients of a complete model of economic behavior. Decision making is not a strictly do-it-yourself affair but dependent upon the time and place in which the decision is made, as well as upon the (expectations of) other agents. While Phelps sticks to standard Walrasian microeconomics, Post Walrasians opt for a different approach of economics, which emphasizes that economic behavior is to a large extent contextual behavior and fundamentally path-dependent as it is guided by a variety of rules and institutions.

To conclude, if the existence of multiple equilibria is not assumed away then the particular structuralist approach chosen by Phelps can only be considered as a highly special case of a more general theory, in which the problems of multiple equilibria and the associated selection of a particular equilibrium represent the core of the analysis. However, in that case Phelps's microfoundations approach is no longer consistent with the general model, since it assumes what has to be explained, i.e., how the interaction of individual activities leads to the establishment of the constrained Pareto efficient equilibrium in the three "working" models.

Similarly, it can be argued that the structuralist policy conclusions are relevant only under the assumption that a particular equilibrium has been established. Given that the economy is in a particular equilibrium, the performance of the economy can be improved upon along the lines suggested in *Structural Slumps*, provided some additional assumptions (see section 12.2) are fulfilled. In our view, this line of reasoning sidesteps a more important policy issue in the context of a multiple equilibrium framework. Rather than considering the design of policy rules for a given equilibrium situation, it may be more fruitful to consider the question how policymaking may contribute to moving the economy in the direction of the high-employment equilibria. This question will be taken up in the following section.

12.4   Institutions and the design of policy

Multiple equilibria provide very serious problems for the design of (macro)economic policy, because they leave no other option but to conclude that the coordination of economic activities implies more than simply "getting the prices right." In order to arrive at a theory of economic coordination and to assess the role of economic policy, it has to be explained why economic systems that are capable of coordinating numerous individual economic activities can at the same time produce major recessions on the one hand, and how economic policy may affect individual and aggregate economic activity on the other. We believe that this analysis requires a considerably larger amount of institutional detail than is included in the Walrasian policy analysis of, e.g., Phelps's *Structural Slumps*. The reason is that particular institutions, being the rules of the game in society, "manage" the equilibrium selection process as they order interpersonal relationships and allow people to undertake activities in a world of incomplete knowledge and uncertainty. Seen from this perspective, economic policy is first and foremost concerned with institutional change, i.e., how to assure that agents are provided with those incentives that allow them to interact toward a different equilibrium situation.[13] If there is a role for the government to interfere in the economic process, it is in affecting the rules of the game and not so much in affecting the game itself.

Obviously, such an approach represents a departure from the Classical and the (mainstream) Keynesian theory of economic policy. It is different from the Classical theory of economic policy because of the underlying idea that the "free market" will not always produce the best possible result. In a Post Walrasian framework, it's not even clear what a "free market" is. Adding distortions in an already "distorted" economy may very well improve welfare, depending upon the incentive structure before and after the introduction of the additional distortions. It is also different from a Keynesian theory of economic policy since the approach recognizes that the traditional policy instruments of (Keynesian) demand management may distort the underlying incentive structure so as to make the final result even worse than the initial situation.[14]

In our view, the most important characteristics of a theory of economic policy in such an alternative framework are the following. In the first place, it can be observed that since a theory of policy is about institutional change, an equilibrium-based, perfect markets, perfect foresight approach to economic policy, like the one in *Structural Slumps*, is not a good starting point. Indeed, the emphasis on equilibrium stated in neoclassical economics forecloses the analysis of how the rules of the game are changed.

In the second place, as institutional change has to do with learning, a theory of economic policy should incorporate some notion of learning behavior. It is well known that economic theory has a hard time dealing with learning behavior. In our view, an analysis of learning has to take into account that individual agents do have incomplete knowledge, which contradicts a fully deterministic analysis of the effects of economic policy upon the economy (see also Garretsen (1993)). Moreover, in the context of a theory of learning behavior the notion of optimal policy choice (i.e., maximizing social welfare under a given set of constraints) loses much of its relevance. If the plausible assumption is made that (learning) behavior is partly guided by conventions and institutions and partly indeterminate, then economic policy is best represented as an ongoing and irreversible process where policymakers, just like other agents, learn from their mistakes as the economy evolves.

In the third place, it should be acknowledged that since institutional change is an irreversible process, a theory of economic policy will have to be built upon the notion that economic processes are fundamentally path-dependent.[15] Path-dependency and the aforementioned idea of a limited understanding of the economy are interdependent. Incomplete knowledge helps to explain the emergence of routine behavior, which, in turn, can be considered as an important determinant of the (dis)ability of an economic system to change. For economic policy, it is important to acknowledge that path-dependency, since it is rooted in the conventional behavior of agents, determines the scope and the incentive to change. If behavior is to a considerable extent historically determined, agents will, at least initially, react to a policy change by means of established behavioral patterns. This means that institutions are to some extent inert to change.

In the fourth place, a theory of economic policy should acknowledge the complexity of institutional change and thus aim only at a rather broad and general set of policy rules. In this respect, the Austrian concept of pattern coordination (O'Driscoll and Rizzo, 1985) may be of some help. The idea of pattern coordination implies that the resulting economic order is determined partly spontaneously, i.e., determined by the free interaction of economic agents and partly by history, as certain rules that somehow came into existence in the past carry over to the present. The whole system is in a permanent state of flux, since particular combinations of spontaneous interaction and history-dependent rules and institutions define the "performance range" for the future path of the economy, i.e., the rules of the game in the future.

The objective of economic policy in such a conceptual framework is inevitably a very modest one. Generally, the complexity of interaction processes in modern economies hinders successful direct government intervention. The very notion of decentralized decision making logically prohibits the required knowledge from being collected by one particular agent. On the other hand, the government is not just any other agent on the playing field. Direct government intervention will certainly change the rules of the game (both in terms of efficiency and stability). The problem is that often only an *ex post* rationalization can be given of the "effectiveness" of a policy rule. For that reason, direct government intervention has to be applied very reluctantly.[16]

A more fruitful approach to policy may be to aim at the establishment of a rather general and broad set of rules and institutions that set the stage for the game between market participants. Government policy also, by affecting rules and institutions, may influence the equilibrium selection process and *in this way* enhance the stability in the economy.[17]

Note, however, that this notion of "stabilization policy" is different from the more restrictive interpretation in neoclassical economics, where stabilization policy stands for the use of policy instruments so as to achieve a full employment level of aggregate output. In our view, governments should aim at some notion of "corridor stability" by guiding the behavior of economic agents through a simple and general set of policy rules. Moreover, the fact that institutions are the main focus of economic policy implies, in the first place, that the design and use of policy instruments is a process of trial and error; and, in the second place, that economic policy is "institutionally specific," i.e., necessarily constrained by specific economic, social, and political conditions that exist at a particular moment in time.

Some would argue that this view on policy making is totally *ad hoc*. However, we believe that a general theory of economic policy is simply inconsistent with a notion of economics in which the ideas of path-dependency, learning processes, and rules and institutions are properly accounted for. At the end of this section we will illustrate the aforementioned conceptual framework by a preliminary discussion of some aspects of the problem of high levels of unemployment (see also Hargreaves Heap (1994)). In this respect, the general response of policymakers has been to advocate increased (wage) flexibility in the labor market, on the one hand, and, in the spirit of *Structural Slumps*, to advocate a trimming of the welfare state and a decreased impact of unions on the wage-setting process, on the other.

Obviously, this approach builds upon the belief that the "free" market will generate the constrained Pareto efficient solution. One of the issues in this discussion concerns the alleged adverse impact of centralized wage setting on (long-run) unemployment. In our view, this argument neglects some of virtues of centralized wage setting, which in the first place originate from the fact that setting wages in response to changes in economic conditions can be considered as a solution to a coordination problem. To illustrate the issue at hand, note that it can be learned from the New Keynesian literature that the individual incentive to adjust wages in response to an aggregate shock will depend on the number of other agents who adjust as well. Hence in the presence of small costs there are two equilibria, a low-employment equilibrium with sticky wages and a high-employment equilibrium in which everybody adjusts wages in response to an adverse aggregate shock. There is no natural solution to the problem of wage determination in response to an aggregate shock.

On the other hand, the selection of a particular equilibrium after an aggregate shock can be represented as a coordination game. The advantage of centralized wage setting over decentralized wage determination in this game is that it makes it easier to select the Pareto-superior solution, since individual choice is turned into collective choice and it is the latter that is required as a response to an aggregate shock.

In the second place, it can be observed that also the long-run level of unemployment can be positively affected by more centralized wage setting. The theoretical argument is that in a decentralized wage bargain the true social costs of unemployment may be underestimated because there are always perceived "outside opportunities" to bear the costs of unemployment. However, the empirical evidence on the relationship between centralization and unemployment is rather ambiguous, particularly because of the lack of objective indicators in this area (e.g., Calmfors and Driffil, 1988; Layard, Nickell and Jackman, 1991). Therefore the discussion on this relationship is still unsettled.

The example about centralized wage setting, however, is useful, first, as an illustration of the possible impact of institutions on economic performance, and, second, as an illustration of the idea that the problem of unemployment cannot be analyzed by focusing only on distortions in relative prices, as in *Structural Slumps* with the general equilibrium framework as a benchmark. But we have neglected in this example several of our earlier arguments. First of all, the aforementioned view of labor markets resembles a partial equilibrium approach. While this framework may be appropriate to illustrate the *existence* of some relationships, it does not offer many insights into how these relationships may be *changed* so as to improve welfare. Secondly, our observations with respect to path-dependency and incomplete knowledge suggest that changing institutions in specific (labor) markets may very likely not produce exactly the results that are obtained in other markets or in other economies. In his analysis of postwar economic development in Europe, Eichengreen (1994) addresses the questions of institutional change and the functioning of labor markets. He convincingly shows how institutional arrangements such as the centralization of the wage setting enabled both wage moderation and high investment growth and therewith solved the underlying coordination problems in the first decades after World War II in the majority of European countries. But, and this is the relevant point, changes in the economic environment, e.g., the gradual increase in international mobility, led to these arrangements becoming outdated. Changing previous well-functioning institutions turns out to be difficult because the path-dependency agents, at least initially, resist a change in these institutional arrangements.

12.5   Summary and conclusion

In this paper we have discussed Edmund Phelps's *Structural Slumps: The Modern Equilibrium Theory of Unemployment, Interest, and Assets* (1994). While we recognize that the development of an endogenous explanation of the natural rate of unemployment is a remarkable achievement, we also think that the analytical framework of *Structural Slumps* hinders instead of helps the development of an alternative economic theory.

The problem is that the underlying framework rests upon the *ad hoc* assumption of uniqueness of equilibria in *Structural Slumps*. If the existence of multiple equilibria is acknowledged and taken seriously, then a rather different theory of economic behavior and policy making is needed. In this paper, we have only offered a few suggestions for such an alternative analytical framework. An important element in our line of reasoning is that a more fruitful economic explanation of unemployment has to incorporate much more institutional detail.

The caveat to this argument is of course that we choose to give up the search for generally valid explanations of adverse economic conditions. The importance of institutions for economic performance implies that the scope for a general theory (and policy) is rather limited, and necessarily constrained by specific economic, social, and political conditions that exist at a particular moment in time. A general theory of economic theory and policy is simply inconsistent with a notion of economics in which the ideas of path-dependency, learning processes, and rules and institutions are properly accounted for.

Endnotes

1. In the introduction of the famous Phelps et al. (1970) collection, Phelps developed a new parable that could serve as a microfoundation for Keynesian macroeconomics. The so-called Phelps-island parable essentially allowed for demand to affect output because of imperfect coordination, i.e., the inability to communicate essential information to traders at a particular moment in time. Ironically, the island parable became associated with Classical macroeconomics as Robert Lucas (1972) sidestepped the coordination problem by restricting the information problem to monetary shocks only.
2. Some of the arguments used in this section can also be found in the discussion of *Structural Slumps* (Malinvaud, 1994; Ambler (1994); Woodford (1994)). All page references are to Phelps's book unless indicated otherwise.
3. In section 12.3 we will argue that the uniqueness of equilibria need not necessarily follow from Phelps's model.
4. Nowadays most intermediate macro texts acknowledge this explanation of unemployment based on real rigidities in labor markets. See for instance Mankiw (1994: 130).
5. Obviously, there are other determinants as well, e.g., transfer payments.
6. In explaining this model of firm behavior, Phelps develops three so-called working models, one for each asset. A full-fledged portfolio choice model which would integrate the firm's decisions with respect to the three assets is lacking. In Chapter 10 a first attempt to integrate the three working models is provided. It cannot be excluded that integration will increase the

ambiguity with respect to the slope coefficients of the derived demand for labor and the equilibrium-wage curve (see also section 3).

7. The intertemporal model of household behavior follows the Blanchard-Yaari model of maximization of present and future consumption. In adopting the Blanchard-Yaari assumption of finite lives, Phelps ensures that Ricardian equivalence does not hold.

8. Basically, this observation implies that the Classical dichotomy holds. Money (or monetary exchange) does not impinge upon the structure of the economy. Money only affects the nominal rate without affecting the real rate (the Fisher effect).

9. One example: transfer payments by the government raise the nonwage income of employees and this increases the incentive to shirk in the shirking model and the incentive to quit in the labor-turnover model. In terms of Figure 12.1.1, an increase in nonwage income leads to an inward shift of the equilibrium-wage curve and consequently to an increase of the real wage and the level of unemployment.

10. Two examples: nominal shocks do matter (Ch. 17, in line with the standard short-term Phillips curve, a change in the inflation rate has a significant negative effect on the level of unemployment); and learning-behavior and money-illusion (Ch. 18: 338) which are very much at odds with Phelps's notion of equilibrium as outlined in section 12.2.1.

11. In order to be complete, it can be observed that the equilibrium-wage curve is monotonically upward-sloping if it is assumed that quitting behavior only depends on the *difference* between the future income prospects of the employed and the unemployed and not on other related phenomena. If this assumption is not warranted, and Phelps himself provides some arguments why this may not be the case (ibid.: 27-30), then the equilibrium-wage curve may have a negative slope over relevant ranges.

12. Already Hayek (1937) argued that the analysis of coordination problems is fundamentally at odds with the standard equilibrium assumption.

13. Note that this is not to say that the equilibrium will actually be attained. It only points at the relevance of analyzing economic problems as evolutionary processes.

14. In this respect, we support the general idea of *Structural Slumps* that the demand and supply side effects of economic policy often cannot be disentangled.

15. Note that this is not to say that we are in sympathy with recent attempts to introduce the concept of path-dependency in a rational expectations equilibrium framework. In our view, this approach suffers from a major inconsistency since the question why a particular equilibrium is established in period t is only explained by *assuming* the existence of an equilibrium in period $t - 1$. Like learning behavior, the notion of path-dependency is at odds with the equilibrium framework of, e.g., Cooper (1994).

16. Obviously, government behavior is not solely guided by efficiency and stability considerations. For instance, government intervention can be motivated by equity reasons as well.

17. This line of reasoning implies that economic policy should focus on stability considerations. The issue of efficiency is best left to the market, without, however, implying that the spontaneous interaction in markets will eventually result in first best or even constrained first best solutions.

References

Ambler, S. A. (1994). "Book Review of Structural Slumps: The Modern Equilibrium Theory of Unemployment, Interest, and Assets." *Journal of Monetary Economics* 34: 507-579.

Calmfors, L. and J. Driffil (1988). "Centralisation of Wage Bargaining and Economic Performance." *Economic Policy* 6: 13-61.

Cooper, R. (1994). "Equilibrium Selection in Imperfectly Competitive Economies with Multiple Equilibria." *The Economic Journal* 104: 1106-1122.

Eichengreen, B. (1994). "Institutions and Economic Growth: Europe after World War II." CEPR Discussion Paper Series, No. 973, London.

Garretsen, H. (1993). "The Relevance of Hayek for Mainstream Economics." In J. Birner and R. van Zijp, eds., *Hayek, Coordination and Evolution*. London: Routledge.

Hargreaves Heap, S.P. (1994). "Institutions and (Short-Run) Macroeconomic Performance." *Journal of Economic Surveys* 1: 35-56.

Hayek, F.A. (1937). *Economics and Knowledge*, repr. (1949) in F.A. Hayek, *Individualism and Economic Order*. London: Routledge and Kegan, 33-54.

Layard, R., S. Nickell and R. Jackman (1991). *Unemployment: Macroeconomic Performance and the Labor Market*. Oxford: Clarendon Press.

Lucas, R. E. (1972). "Expectations and the Neutrality of Money." *Journal of Economic Theory* 4: 103-124.

Malinvaud, E. (1994). " 'About Phelps' Theory of Structural Slumps and its Policy Implications." Mimeo. CEPR Conference on Unemployment Policy, Vigo, Spain.

Mankiw, N. G. (1994). *Macroeconomics* (2nd ed.). New York: Worth Publishers.

O'Driscoll, G.P. and M.J. Rizzo (1985). *The Economics of Time and Ignorance*. Oxford: Clarendon Press.

Phelps, E.S. (1994). *Structural Slumps. The Modern Equilbrium Theory of Unemployment, Interest and Assets*. Cambridge, Mass.: Harvard University Press.

Phelps, E.S., A.A. Alchian and C.C. Holt, eds. (1970). *Microeconomic Foundation of Unemployment and Inflation Theory*, London: MacMillan.

Salop, S. (1979). "A Model of the Natural Rate of Unemployment." *American Economic Review* 69: 117-25.

Shapiro, C. and J.E. Stiglitz (1984). "Equilibrium Unemployment as a Worker Discipline Device." *American Ecnomic Review* 74: 433-44.

Woodford, M. (1994). "Structural Slump." *Journal of Economic Literature* 4: 1784-1815.

CHAPTER 13

Post Walrasian macroeconomic policy

David Colander and Hans van Ees

To most people macroeconomic theories are of interest because of the policies for which they provide support. Thus, Keynesian macroeconomic theory became popular in large part because it was seen as providing a theoretical underpinning for activist monetary and fiscal policy. Similarly, New Classical macroeconomic theory became popular because it became associated with supply side and laissez-faire macro policy.

These associations between policies and theories are, in many ways, dubious. Most theories are multifaceted and, depending on how they are interpreted, can be used to support a wide variety of policies. For example, many Classical economists, including Keynes, supported activist monetary and fiscal policy – in Keynes's case long before he presented the ideas in *The General Theory*; in *The General Theory* he never mentions monetary or fiscal policy. There, he talks about socializing investment.[1]

This need to be associated with a particular policy to gain widespread recognition presents a problem for Post Walrasian theory since a central tenet of Post Walrasian theory is that the aggregate economy is so complex that, by themselves, theoretical notions only suggest broad policy rules, not specific mechanistic rules. There is no one set of policies to which Post Walrasian theory leads. In the Post Walrasian approach, policymaking is an art, not a science.

13.1 Policy implications of the Post Walrasian view

While there is no specific policy to which the Post Walrasian view of the economy leads, it, nonetheless, has significant policy implications. Most importantly, it leads to the conclusion that definitive policy proposals *do not* flow from theoretical analysis based on noncontextual microfoundations – i.e., from the Walrasian general equilibrium models that characterize most macroeconomists' formal theory. The reason is simple; it is that those Walrasian models are far too simple to capture the complexity of economic interactions that one must understand in order to draw policy conclusions. The problem is the way Walrasian economics captures the behavior of the economy. Walrasian economics sees the economy from the perspective of a "top-down" approach (Leijonhufvud, Ch. 3, this volume). An incredibly smart "central processing unit" is able to do all the calculations necessary to replicate the behavior of the entire economy. Consequently, the issue of policymaking is addressed with a similar degree of "rigor." Post Walrasian economics, on the other hand, follows a bottom-up approach. Individuals interact, which produces results that are beyond the capacity of the individual decision units to fully predict. Following this bottom-up approach, Post Walrasian policy design starts from the fundamental idea that individuals aren't smart enough to deal with all the necessary information processing the economy requires. In making decisions, individuals do not, and cannot, completely understand the working of the economy. There is no presumption of individuals, acting separately, being led to an ideal result. If they are led to an acceptable result, it is because they have created acceptable institutions that take care of the problems individuals cannot.

Because of its underlying view of the complexity of the economy, rather than the design of actual policy, Post Walrasian macroeconomic policy focuses on broad and relatively easy understandable guidelines that may improve market and non-market coordination, helping to reduce the agents' uncertainty and thereby improve the predictability (stability) of the behavior of the economy.

This Post Walrasian view of the economy's complexity might seem non-empirical since casual observation suggests that our economy is not chaotic, but is instead relatively stable. Casual observation might lead one to believe that the Walrasian simultaneous equation approach is the correct approach. The Post Walrasian response is that the observed stability is not inherent in the economy, but is imposed by institutions which guide individual choice. Institutions create systemic stability. Since these institutions bring stability into the system, they cannot be assumed away as in Walrasian economics. Their existence fundamentally affects the scope and nature of the interrelationships among individuals.

For economic modeling, this response has two implications. First, as the stability of the system is derived from the fact that individuals exhibit bounded rationality, for any model of the economy to make sense this bounded rationality must be part of that model. Second, it is impossible to intuit the net result of established institutions or institutional change without specifically considering and modeling them, and considering as well the constraints they place on individuals. The net result of such modeling efforts is likely nonlinear jumps in solutions, and multiple solutions, which precludes simple marginal analysis.

The point is that, within a Post Walrasian framework, to have something relevant to say about policy one must understand the way institutions work, how they guide individual economic behavior, and how they evolve in response to economic activity. Without that understanding, one cannot say much about specific policies. In short, the Post Walrasian view of the relation between models and policies is quite different from the Walrasian view.

In Walrasian economics there is what might be called policy certainty. Policies follow mechanistically from equilibrium models. Walrasian models may not be sufficiently well specified for the designer to be sure that the appropriate policy is being recommended, but, in principle, if the model could be specified exactly, policies would flow mechanistically from the model.

Post Walrasian economics sees policymaking as more complicated. Models are too incomplete a description of the real world to have any specific policy implications. Formal macro models may be suggestive, and capture some interrelationships that one's intuition has missed, but a model is an aid to judgment, not a replacement of judgment.

13.2   The art of Post Walrasian policy

The complex structure of the economy is, as has been observed already, relatively stable and orderly. The sources of that orderliness can be divided into two categories: market and non-market coordination of the system. The Walrasian approach to the economy explores particularly coordination by market prices, and pictures an ideal world in which that mechanism is the only one needed for perfect coordination of individual expectations, decisions, and activities. The market is the only relevant institution in that approach. All other institutions are nonessential – the characteristics of the economy do not in any fundamental way depend on their existence. The Post Walrasian approach, on the other hand, insists that the modern economy is by no means ideally coordinated by the price-mechanism, nor could it conceivably be so coordinated. Application of the Post Walrasian view to concrete policy issues involves the search for a balance between non-market and market institutions of coordination, recognizing that there are advantages and disadvantages of each, and that the two coordinating devices are in some ways complements and in some ways substitutes.

The fundamental problem Post Walrasian economics faces in applied policy concerns the design of institutions. Many of the features of Post Walrasian theory come into that design process, including multiple equilibria, limited information, complexity, and bounded rationality. By themselves these conditions only suggest criteria, they do not by themselves lead to an optimal policy design in any mechanical way. This is where art enters in. By art we mean "informed judgment" about what the effect of policies will be. This informed judgment is based on a knowledge of history and institutions as much as on abstract theory since the institutions and history define the scope for change. Institutional design requires wisdom (a kind of art) as much as the more instrumental knowledge offered by economic modeling: it is about creating robust and practical structures consistent with known and functional design criteria. Hence, to say that no definitive policies follow from Post Walrasian theory is not to say that Post Walrasian economics is irrelevant for policy. Far from it. Appropriately constrained, a PostWalrasian model can provide a way of structuring one's thinking about the economy. Post Walrasian theory can direct one to a much broader set of transmissions mechanisms through which policy affects the economy than does Walrasian theory; it can be helpful in guiding one's policy intuition, and it can lead one to explore policies that a Walrasian theory would not.

Let us give an example: the efficiency wage literature. The efficiency wage literature arose out of the efforts of the Walrasian school to explain why wages do not move to clear labor markets. From a Walrasian point of view, the policy implications of efficiency wages involve the search for a set of taxes or subsidies, or, in general, alternative incentive structures, which may correct for the market failure. The Walrasian literature provides many examples of complicated (incentive compatible) contracts that can be designed by and enforced upon incredibly rational agents, which may overcome these market failures.

From the Post Walrasian point of view, the policy message of (in)efficiency is different. Because of the limits of the intellectual faculties of the economic actors, it is not at all clear that upgrading the degree of sophistication in the contractual agreements will work. Contracts among individuals can only be understood within their macro context. From a Post Walrasian perspective efficiency wages suggest that the nature of the labor market is such that there are inherent limitations to the market method of coordination, that alternative non-market institutional mechanisms of coordination are probably already at work. One can only talk about the relevance of efficiency wages for policy from a perspective that incorporates existing institutions and their history. From a Post Walrasian perspective market failure in competitive models has no policy implications without an understanding of existing institutions that can be presumed to have developed to partially compensate for that market failure. If market mechanisms are unable to stop workers from shirking without imposing large deadweight losses on the economy, then economies will have developed alternative mechanisms to deal with the problem. Policy suggestions must be seen within the framework of those alternative mechanisms.

The policy challenge is to figure out if institutional intervention is warranted and, if so, at what level the institutional intervention should take place. For instance, if shirking were a problem for the economy, a problem that the market mechanism does not address very well, then where might the solution lie? One place might be within the firm, in structures of promotion and retention, in the organization of production, or in alternative monitoring schemes. Other places might be within the family, the school, or the church. Still another place might be at the national level, where migration policy, incomes policy, trade policy, or even aggregate demand policy may affect the parameters of the individual firms' and workers' decisions.

Two aspects are important to note about this example. The first is the range of different levels at which institutions matter and the impossibility of conflating all these levels. The second is that, in view of the complexity of the many institutionally-determined interaction patterns, often the best economic policymakers can hope to do is to aim at a rather broad and general set of rules, not to design specific policy solutions.

In this respect, the idea of pattern coordination may be helpful. Although lacking the knowledge to understand the economy in a sufficient amount of detail, individuals may recognize distinct patterns in the economy. This is where policy can be effective. Given that the government is not just another player in the field, government policy may at times be able to set the rules of the game in a way that is understandable to the agents and that leads them collectively to a better solution. Indeed, pattern coordination implies that the resulting order will develop partly spontaneously and partly determined by history, i.e., by rules that somehow carry over from the past. The art of economic policy can be described as an attempt to guide the spontaneous interaction of agents by affecting established rules rather than an attempt to directly determine the behavior of the economy.

13.3   Walrasian and Post Walrasian structural policy

It is probably most effective to explain the difference in approach between Walrasian and Post Walrasian policy by means of a concrete example. Since the macro policy debate in the late 1990s will concern primarily structural supply side issues, we will focus on discussion of policy on these structural issues, comparing a Walrasian approach to structural policy with a Post Walrasian approach.

To avoid the confusion that would result by contrasting the Post Walrasian policy with the various strains of Walrasian policy, a comparison will be made with a representative amalgam of those theories. The amalgam we have chosen is Phelps's book on *Structural Slumps* (1994). In that book Phelps spells out a new Walrasian theory which can incorporate a shifting natural rate of unemployment (see also Ch. 12 in this volume). Phelps's book is, we believe, representative of the policy thinking of a "representative modern Walrasian macro economist."

The first thing to note about Phelps's work is that his theoretical discussion is hard to classify as either Keynesian or Classical. Phelps has called in his book the new synthesis; indeed the subtitle "The Modern Equilibrium Theory of Unemployment, Interest and Assets" is suggestive of Keynes's *General Theory*. But that makes it all the better to compare with the Post Walrasian approach since Phelps's approach to both Keynesian and Classical economics is clearly Walrasian. Thus his synthesis is a Walrasian synthesis, and it has, at its core, a conception of super rational individuals able to process sufficient information to deal with general equilibrium issues without going on overload, and a unique equilibrium, albeit a shifting one over time. It is that core that invalidates the results for Post Walrasians and hence calls into question many of the policy solutions Phelps proposes.

The better to see the differences in policy approach between the Post Walrasian and the Phelps Walrasian approach, let us try to summarize both theories in non technical terms (see also Ch. 12 in this volume).

13.4   A Phelpsian structuralist explanation of structural slumps

Phelps's new structuralist theory is a slight modification of the natural rate theory. The difference is that instead of an unchanging natural rate, Phelps sees a shifting natural rate because of Olson-type structuralist problems. It is still a unique equilibrium natural rate view, in the sense that objective conditions uniquely determine the natural rate, only now the unique equilibrium natural rate is also determined by economic conditions, in particular the real rate of interest.

In Phelps's model the unemployment that results in the economy is the direct result of individual decisions. No non-market coordination failures play a role in causing that unemployment. While there may be temporary fluctuations in the level of unemployment, the post-World War II record of the increasing persistence of high unemployment rates implies, from Phelps's view, that actual unemployment is for the most part equilibrium unemployment – unemployment that results from individual choice. This *natural rate of unemployment* is caused by structural real rigidities that characterize the supply side of the economy. The natural rate of unemployment has to do with a variety of characteristics that were explored in Phelps's earlier microfoundations work; that work, however, does not leave much room for policy to affect economic performance, nor will that work allow the existence of a structural slump, a prolonged period of low levels of economic activity.

The addition that Phelps makes in his new work is a direct consideration of the economic variables that affect the firms' hiring and firing decisions as well as the economic variables that affect the decision to supply effort. Moreover, and this feature distinguishes Phelps's analysis from earlier New Classical and New Keynesian attempts, among these economic variables are also some that describe the conditions in the other markets of the economy, in particular the commodity market and the capital market.

Shorn of all the fancy modeling, Phelps's *Structural Slumps* is an attempt to explain employment fluctuations as the result of fluctuations in relative prices. A high real wage rate paid by firms increases the natural rate, because it makes firms want to hire fewer workers. By implication, any variable that positively affects the demand price or supply price of labor has a positive impact on the natural rate of unemployment. For instance, a tax on labor increases the natural rate and causes a structural slump marked by what might be called tax-gap unemployment. Or, an increase in employment benefits reduces the incentive to supply effort, increases the supply price of labor, and increases the natural rate of unemployment. But also, an increase in the real rate of interest, for instance through an increase in the amount of government debt, increases the required markup of firms in the imperfectly competitive commodity market, which reduces sales and lowers the equilibrium amount of unemployment. Thus, we have a perception of involuntary unemployment since the equilibrium level of the real rate wage is not the one that clears the market but the one that is consistent with the agents' expectations about the conditions of the economy. Moreover, since the equilibrium level of the real wage rate is susceptible to changes in economic conditions in the labor market as well as in other markets of the economy, the involuntary equilibrium level of unemployment will also be responsive to these changes.

13.5   A Post Walrasian structuralist explanation of structural slumps

There is much in Phelps's description that a Post Walrasian could accept. Even some of the policy alternatives mentioned by Phelps can be part of a Post Walrasian policy package for structural slumps. The big difference, however, is in the conception of policy, which in a Post Walrasian view follows directly from the inherent instability of the economic system and the important role that institutions play in the maintenance of stability of the economy. As a result a Post Walrasian would see Phelps's policy advice only as a small part of the story.

Because it is only a small part of the story, a Post Walrasian would see the policy solution to which Phelps is led as too limited. The reason is that Phelps precludes what might be called *non-market structural causes* of the increase in the unemployment rate – structural causes that relate to the constraints imposed by the institutions on individual decision makers. Even if the direct effects on relative prices of market imperfections were eliminated in a Post Walrasian model there could still be structural unemployment. Moreover, it may well be possible that the removal of the "distortions" of relative prices has a detrimental impact on the stability of the system. In a Post Walrasian view, "distortions" of relative prices may very well reflect institutional characteristics that stabilize the economy, or at least enhance the predictability of the economy. In Phelps's model the assumption of a unique natural rate makes all these superfluous. The effect of removing "distortions" would be inevitably to imply an elimination of the inefficiently high level of the natural rate of unemployment.

From a Post Walrasian perspective, Phelps is significantly overstating the impact of relative prices on unemployment. The problem is his Walrasian blending of institutional constraints into reduced-form structural relationships.

The problem of this blending of institutional constraints into composite functions is that it causes Phelps to miss obvious policy possibilities that involve changes in some of the functional forms entering into the reduced-form relationships. The Walrasian approach has a tendency to see the functional form as relatively stable, i.e., determined by the fundamentals of the economy. True, problems of time-consistency, which may lead to parameter instability, are recognized, but if economic policy appropriately takes into account (rational) expectations, it will set the economy on the (constrained) Pareto efficient track; the Post Walrasian approach sees functional forms as inherently instable – sometimes small (policy) shocks cause very large changes in functional forms, for instance through interdepencies in the formation of expectations, which can lead to enormous changes in outcome, switching the economy from one equilibrium path to another.

13.6   Phelps's specific policy proposals

While Phelps's theory is hard to classify as Keynesian or Classical, his specific policy recommendations are not; they have a definite Classical (aggregate supply-side) ring. Specifically, his four policy proposals for achieving a reduction in long-run unemployment are:

1. Cut direct taxes (since they are primarily on labor).
2. Increase public expenditures, with direct taxes being held constant.
3. Balanced budget reduction.
4. Employment subsidies.

Of these four, only #2 has some Keynesian (aggregate demand-side) aspects to it, but that Keyesnsian aspect is more apparent than real. In Phelps's structuralist approach expansionary fiscal policy reduces unemployment in a particular country because the associated appreciation of the real exchange rate may lower markups, which increases production and employment. On the other hand, such a policy reduces production and employment in the rest of the world, provided that the domestic country is not too small. Furthermore, a worldwide increase in government spending only increases the world real rate of interest without any change in real exchange rates and is thus contractionary. In his discussion of the proposal, Phelps clearly downplays the expansionary effects that increasing public expenditures may have. Obviously, this is all not much of a surprise since in Phelps's view aggregate demand shifts can only create transient deviations of the actual rate of unemployment from the natural rate. To reduce the natural rate, or to change the natural rate path, in Phelps's approach only supply-side policies are effective. Thus if the desire is to reduce unemployment, the price of labor must be held down so firms hire more workers, and the reservation wage of workers must be reduced.

In Phelps's theory, Keynesian policy makes little sense. While Phelps makes continual allusions to Keynes's *General Theory*, reading Phelps's descriptions of the policy prescriptions reminds one of Pigou's policy discussion in *The Theory of Unemployment* (1933), not of Keynes's policy discussions either before or after *The General Theory*. For Phelps, as for Pigou, long-run unemployment is caused by structural rigidities of various types, but primarily those affecting the supply price or the demand price for labor. Aggregate demand policy has little or no role in Phelps's model.[2]

The *assumption* of a unique, albeit moving, natural rate simply implies that his model doesn't allow that some of the problems that countries currently are experiencing involve a mis-coordination of expectations. To put it differently, Phelps's model doesn't allow macroeconomic coordination failures so that a (coordinated) expansion of aggregate demand can reduce unemployment permanently unless that expansion lowers the real wage rate. A Post Walrasian approach to policy would be far more circumspect about the implications of policy since in a Post Walrasian model not only can the natural rate shift but it may also be susceptible to random swings having nothing to do with real interest rates or factor prices. As stated above, in a Post Walrasian approach, Keynesian aggregate demand policy may make sense, albeit only for a particular problem at a particular time.

A second example of where a Post Walrasian interpretation of the policy would differ from Phelps's Walrasian view is the way in which Phelps talks about balanced budget reductions (Phelps, 1994: 365). Phelps sees such a reduction as an unambiguously positive policy; he has no discussion of potential problems. Specifically, Phelps does not consider the possibility that such a policy might significantly change the structural characteristics of the economy and thereby reduce the degree of macroeconomic coordination (stability) in the economy. A Post Walrasian approach would require consideration of such a possibility. The point is that a world in which it is known that the government will stabilize aggregate output is a different world than one in which it is believed that it will not – for better or worse. This is an example of the lack of policy certainty in Post Walrasian theory, and the limited transmission mechanisms of effects of policies allowed for in Walrasian theory.

A third example concerns employment subsidies, which in other work, and in a private conversation with Phelps, is the policy approach that he advocates most strongly. In a Post Walrasian theory, such employment subsidies might have some positive effects. On the other hand, those positive effects may be possibly offset by the impact of other institutions in particular countries. For instance, with sufficient downward wage rigidity, employment subsidies may crowd out existing workers instead of increasing employment. Moreover, employment subsidies may negatively affect the incentive of schooling and thereby negatively affect productivity growth. More generally, in view of the actual institutional organization of many (European) labor markets, employment subsidies may only cause a substitution of "bad jobs" for "good jobs" because the existence of the subsidies creates changes making more and more firms eligible. Moreover, the financing of the employment subsidies has to be taken into account. If, as Phelps suggests, employment subsidies are financed by increasing taxes (1994: 366) then the negative incentive effects of increased taxes may largely offset the possibly positive effects of employment subsidies.

In summary, from a Post Walrasian perspective the effectiveness of a system of employment subsidies can only be judged in relation to the structure in which this policy is embedded. Thus, a policy of employment subsidies will have to be considered from an analysis of the impact on employment of all the (expected) institutional changes that are associated with such a policy, not simply from an analysis of a highly simplified model. The immediate implication is that these policies are necessarily bounded by the institutional environment of specific countries. General recipes exist only in abstract theory. Without a detailed analysis of established institutions, nothing definite can be said about the possible impact of employment subsidies on employment.

13.7   A possible explanation for structural slumps that Phelps missed

One causal explanation of structural slumps that Phelps's Walrasian framework explicitly excludes concerns the potential role of aggregate demand. In Walrasian theory equilibrium unemployment cannot be caused by a shortage of aggregate demand. In Post Walrasian economics it can; thus in contrast to Phelps a Post Walrasian would find it hard to dismiss the lack of aggregate demand as a cause of the increase in the normal level of unemployment.

In Post Walrasian theory unemployment can be caused by too low aggregate demand in the following sense. If, whenever government increases aggregate demand, existing workers and firms proportionally increase their *nominal* wages and prices, the aggregate demand increase will have no real effect. Casual observation suggests that something similar is indeed happening in the economy. Inherent in nominal price setting institutions is a tendency to put an upward push on nominal prices, and hence on the nominal price level, long before the 3% unemployment level that policymakers had in mind in the 1960s is reached.

Such an upward push on prices is unstable because it will become expected, and as it becomes expected, it leads to accelerating inflation. In this respect, there is no disagreement between the Post Walrasian and the Walrasian approach. Because of this acceleration tendency, any upward push in the price level must be offset, and, given current institutions, it can only be offset by holding unemployment at a sufficiently high level to create an offsetting downward pressure.

Putting the argument we are making another way, in our current institutional structure an equilibrium approximating a static supply demand equilibrium is never reached since the economy's use of money requires aggregate price level stability, which imposes a systemic constraint that limits expansion of aggregate demand. The binding constraint for aggregate equilibrium is the actual organization of monetized exchange, and these *monetary* characteristics require the maintenance of sufficient unemployment to prevent the price level from rising.

Individuals, acting alone, cannot provide the necessary stability since the achievement of a stable aggregate price level requires a coordinated effort. Hence, a stable aggregate price level has to be achieved by systemic characteristics of the institutional structure.

To the degree that the cost of unemployment is reduced to individuals, as it has been by government programs, the downward pressure resulting from a specified level of unemployment is reduced, and therefore a higher level of equilibrium unemployment is needed. Thus the interaction between aggregate demand characteristics that affect the inherent upward instability of the aggregate price level, and the institutional characteristics that operate on the supply side of the economy, *together* may provide a plausible Post Walrasian explanation for structural slumps.

Notice that in this version of Post Walrasian theory there is an inherent link between real and nominal in the sense that the nominal wage and price setting institutions impose structural constraints on how far aggregate demand can be expanded, given established institutions that particularly operate on the supply side of the economy. Notice furthermore that Phelps's analysis addresses only the latter, without bothering to consider how policy-induced changes of supply-side characteristics may affect the nominal wage and price setting institutions that affect the demand side of the economy. Obviously, in Phelps's view this is perfectly legitimate. Indeed, in his *Structural Slumps* aggregate demand has no role to play. But in Post Walrasian approach it has. Elsewhere, Colander (1992) has described this difference as the difference between the Post Walrasian *NAIRU*, which sees unemployment as playing a systemic role in holding down inflation, and the Walrasian *natural rate*, which sees no such systemic role for unemployment.

Notice finally that our explanation does not suggest that aggregate demand policy used alone will lower the unemployment rate. It will do so only if it is supplemented by a policy that limits the increase in nominal prices resulting from such an increase. This means that an alternative coordinating mechanism for nominal prices could change the nature of the equilibrium into one that had a much lower level of unemployment. Such a coordinating mechanism is often called an incomes policy.

An example of a coordinating mechanism that is compatible with a market economy is developed in Lerner and Colander (1980). Their proposal involved the creation of a new market to coordinate nominal price decisions directly. Specifically, the system required that any price setter increasing his or her value-added price must buy the right from some other price setter who lowers his or her value-added price by an offsetting amount. With this market in place the nominal price level is fixed, but relative prices are free to fluctuate. Because the price level is fixed, aggregate demand policy is freed from directly controlling inflation.

To get a sense of how such an incomes policy could lower structural unemployment, let us now consider two theoretical questions about this policy: At what price will this market equilibrate if inflation is constant? And, What will be the effect on the economy of this market equilibrating at a nonzero price?

In answering the first question most economists have said, "At a positive price." Almost no one has said, "At a negative price" or "At a zero price." Consider the implication of those answers. Unless the answer is zero, there will be pressure on the price level to change, which, when it becomes expected, will lead to runaway inflation (positive price) or deflation (negative price). The reason is that non-accelerating inflation, by definition, means that only expectational elements of inflation exist, and since, under this new institutional regime, by law no inflation can exist, the expectational element of inflation will be eliminated.[3]

As long as there is no pressure for inflation to accelerate, the weighted number of value-added price setters wanting to raise their price must, by definition, equal the weighted number of value-added price setters wanting to lower their price. By definition the quantity supplied of rights to raise price equals the quantity demanded of rights to lower price at a zero price under our current institutional setting. So simply adding a market in something that is already, by definition, equilibrating at a zero price should not mean that it will equilibrate at a nonzero price.

But, now, say the central bank expands the money supply, increasing aggregate demand with the plan in place. What will happen? Will the price of raising price immediately shoot up to infinity and shortages appear? Or, will the price of raising price rise only somewhat, allowing some expansion in output, and some rise in the price of raising price? In Phelps's model which doesn't include a systemic monetary constraint, the price of raising price shoots up to infinity and the program becomes the equivalent to regulatory price controls. In that perspective there is a unique equilibrium at which the aggregate economy equilibrates – that this institutional change does not affect.

In the Post Walrasian perspective, different prices of raising prices offset different amounts of nominal price pressures and hence correspond to different steady-state equilibrium levels of output. Thus, there are a variety of prices of raising prices and a variety of NAIRU equilibria to which the aggregate economy will gravitate depending on institutions. A slight increase in aggregate demand results in only a slight increase in the price of raising price (a partial incomes policy) and an increase in aggregate output.

Shortages aren't caused by the policy because the program causes unemployed factors to become employed. Thus, in the Post Walrasian approach, there are multiple equilibria at which the economy can arrive, and the institution of an incomes policy moves the economy to a new, possibly preferable, equilibrium. An incomes policy can be effective because it cuts down on aggregate slack in the economy; the higher the price of raising price (the stronger the incomes policy), the more it cuts down on aggregate slack and the higher steady-state output.

The reason such an incomes policy might work in theory has to do with the nominal price-setting constraints imposed on individuals by the use of money. Within this Post Walrasian view of a monetary economy, it is incorrect to represent the aggregate equilibrium of an economy as one in which aggregate supply equals aggregate demand, as would be the case in a monetary economy. That representation does not take into account the non-accelerating price level constraint imposed by the use of money.[4]

Before we conclude, we should make it clear that the above discussion was not an argument that an incomes policy is the way to go. There are enormous practical and political problems of implementation. Discussion and resolution of such issues must precede any advocacy of a policy. The analytic justification of policies is easy; the practical justification of policies is enormously complicated. The purpose of the discussion was to show a way in which policies that Walrasian structural models preclude might affect the economy, and to stimulate thinking about the practical problems.

Endnotes

1. The push for activist monetary and fiscal policy is much more to be found in Abba Lerner's interpretation of Keynes's ideas, and in the Committee of Economic Development's policy pronouncements which played a major role in the postwar U.S. economic scene.
2. We should point out that in a telephone conversation Phelps agreed that at times Keynesian demand policy would be appropriate, but he stated that adding a disequilibrium analysis to his shifting equilibrium analysis was simply too complicated for him to include is the book.
3. We recognize that in reality there are many caveats to this argument. For example, the law may not be followed, the law may be repealed, or the controlled inflation index may not reflect the sum of the relevant individual price indices. We assume these complications away at this point to try to bring out some salient features of the plan and of the inflation process.
4. A market-based incomes policy is not the only way to coordinate nominal prices. Regulatory and tax incentive plans can also be used. We define an incomes policy as a policy designed to directly coordinate nominal pricing decisions, and thereby reduce the amount of excess supply necessary to prevent accelerating inflation. Thus, in a Post Walrasian view the purpose of an incomes policy is not to prevent inflation but is, instead, designed to raise the level of potential output by removing some of the pressure from inflation. It's an anti-monopolization policy and is designed to make the economy operate more, not less, like the conception of a competitive economy that most economists have in their minds.

References

Colander, D. (1992). "A Real Theory of Inflation and Anti-Inflation Plans." *American Economic Review* 82: 335-46.

Lerner, A. and D. Colander (1980). *MAP: A Market Anti-Inflation Plan.* New York: Harcourt Brace Jovanovich.

Phelps, E.S. (1994). *Structural Slumps. The Modern Equilbrium Theory of Unemployment, Interest and Assets*, Cambridge, Mass.: Harvard University Press.

Pigou, A. C. (1933). *The Theory of Unemployment.* London: Frank Cass.

APPENDIX
LITERATURE SURVEY

An annotated bibliography on the (macro)foundation of Post Walrasian economics

Hans van Ees and Harry Garretsen

A.1 Introduction

The idea that microeconomics must have a macrofoundation lies at the heart of the Post Walrasian approach. What is meant by the *(Macro)foundation* of *(Post Walrasian) economics*? To some, it almost looks like a contradiction in terms, convinced as they are that micro has to be basis for macro.[1] To others, it is the only fruitful way to discuss the behavior of economic agents, convinced as they are that it makes no sense to discuss economic behavior in a non-contextual way. We hope to illustrate with this annotated bibliography that depending on the definition of micro, those two views on the proper foundation of economics can be reconciled. So this is an attempt to define and classify this field of research. Fortunately, we do not have to start from scratch. Recently, the field has already been explored quite extensively, mostly, but not solely, under the heading of what is known as New Keynesian Economics. However, the classification scheme for New Keynesian economics as suggested in the literature by, for example, Mankiw and Romer (1991) and Gordon (1990) who particularly focus on short-run price and wage stickiness, is not the one we are aiming at.

Our idea of a (macro)foundation of (Post Walrasian) economics is centered around the concept of coordination failures. Following Howitt (1988) it can be observed that the coordination of economic activity has many dimensions, which in neoClassical economics have all been embodied in the view that full price flexibility solves them all.[2] Post Walrasian macroeconomics involves a return to the notion that the coordination of economic activity has many dimensions and a recognition that the possibility of coordination failures is an inherent characteristic of a decentralized economy, no matter how flexible prices are, and sometimes is caused by prices being flexible. The following quote of Leijonhufvud nicely illustrates this position. "*Coordination* because macroeconomics, in this book at least, is the study of the coordination of economic activities in large complex economic systems" (Leijonhufvud, 1981: v.; see also Weintraub, 1979).

Seen from this perspective, a (macro)foundation of (Post Walrasian) economics can be defined as *the analysis of the implications of the coordination problem for the behavior of individual agents* (Garretsen, 1992). As such, this Post Walrasian research program competes with the Walrasian microfoundation of macro approach. In our view, the latter approach can best be understood as an attempt to ground the performance of the economy as a whole upon a Walrasian framework, in which the full coordination of economic activities and expectations is already assumed (and apparently needs no further justification). It can be argued that precisely because of the assumption of complete coordination in the Walrasian general equilibrium framework, there exists the need to provide a microfoundation of aggregate economic phenomena. In fact, the assumption of full coordination leaves the analyst no other possibility than to ground the performance of the aggregate economy upon the individual responses to exogenous states of nature. On the other hand, the (macro)foundation of (Post Walrasian) economics starts from the notion that the aggregate state of the economy affects the behavior of the individual decision unit in a way that cannot completely be reduced to given individual preferences, technology, and endowments. Individual behavior is contextual or social behavior (Bryant, 1993), conditional on time and place and on the physical as well as the social environment. At the same time, the performance of aggregates does reflect the individual activities based upon beliefs about aggregates. It is this fundamental interdependence, lying at the heart of the (macro)foundation of (Post Walrasian) economics approach, that defines the coordination problem as the core of economic analysis.

In general, the issue of *Keynesian* economic theory is to explain aggregate inefficiencies, i.e., to explain that the unhampered working of the market does not necessarily establish a unique, stable Pareto-efficient outcome. In our view, by recognizing the possibility of coordination failures as an inherent characteristic of a market economy, the (macro)foundation of (Post Walrasian) economics literature can be regarded as a reasonable interpretation of what Keynesian economics should involve.[3] At the heart of this literature is the idea that the assumptions of rational behavior (and rational expectations) and flexible prices are perfectly compatible with the existence of multiple (bootstrap) equilibria with low levels of economic activity, indeterminacy of equilibria, self-fulfilling expectations, and path-dependency of equilibria. This bibliography provides many examples of that idea. At the same time, this bibliography also illustrates that there exists more than one way to derive these results. Many of the recent publications apply an optimizing framework to explain Keynesian features, such as underemployment equilibria. In this respect, there is a difference between the concept of coordination failures in the somewhat "older" and in the more recent literature.

The recent literature focuses on what Howitt (1990) denotes as equilibrium coordination problems, i.e., the analysis of the efficiency properties of equilibria in a multiple equilibrium framework. Without doubt the modern approach has the advantage of a "rigorous" treatment of that particular subject. However, "rigor" is gained at a cost in the sense that the modern approach may not be able to analyze how an equilibrium may come about. Howitt refers to this part of the analysis as disequilibrium coordination problems, i.e., the study of how to arrive at a particular equilibrium. Particularly, economists like Clower and Leijonhufvud, although from difference angles, have emphasized the need to analyze out-of-equilibrium behavior in order to study how the coordination of economic activities is achieved. From this literature there emerges the fundamental question whether the notion of instrumentally rational decision making on which the "rigorous" approach is based is not too rational for an analysis of out-of-equilibrium behavior.

A similar argument is brought forward by economists who emphasize the importance of social institutions as coordinating devices. Their line of reasoning is that the existence of shared rules of conduct can only partly be explained by referring to explicit logical design. Nevertheless, despite these differences in the analytical treatment of the problem at hand, all analyses can be brought together under our interpretation of the (macro)foundation of (Post Walrasian) economics. As such, they represent a well identified research program. This bibliography offers a selection of articles in all mentioned directions.

Each distinguished category is preceded by a short introduction to the most important characteristics of the approach. Obviously this selection reflects the authors' own preference and prejudice, so we certainly do not claim completeness. Moreover, some areas of related, relevant, and interesting research have not been included, because we focus on the issues of economic coordination problems. An example is the vast amount of research on the rationality assumption in economics, which is complementary to the work on economic coordination problems. However, we do think that this bibliography provides ample material for the reader who wants to become acquainted with this field of economic research. Moreover, we do hope to convey some sense of coherence, the idea that this collection of articles does indeed reflect an interesting direction in economic research.

The organization of this annotated bibliography is the following. After mentioning some interesting survey articles, we explore the literature on coordination failures (section A.3). Then in section A.4 we list contributions to the literature on endogenous fluctuations. In section A.5, we extend our bibliography in the direction of empirical research. Finally, in section A.6 the literature on social institutions and coordination problems is collected.

A.2   A selected bibliography of surveys

Gordon, R. J. (1990). "What is New-Keynesian Economics." *Journal of Economic Literature* 28: 1115-71.

A very accurate survey of the recent literature on the microfoundation of short-run wage and price stickiness and the implications for macroeconomic performance. Gordon's review is noteworthy in the sense that he explicitly recognizes that with the exception of the recent work on coordination failures, "an interesting aspect of recent U.S. new-Keynesian research is the near-total lack of interest in the general equilibrium properties of non-market-clearing models," i.e., the lack of interest in interaction and spillovers among markets, which is prominent in the fixed-price disequilibrium theory of, for example, Clower and Leijonhufvud.

Grandmont, J.-M. (1989). "Keynesian Issues and Economic Theory." *Scandinavian Journal of Economics* 91: 265-93.

A survey of the recent literature on the explanation of aggregate inefficiencies with particular emphasis on fixed-price disequilibrium theory and the new literature on endogenous fluctuations.

Greenwald, B.C. and J. Stiglitz (1987). "Keynesian, New Keynesian, and New Classical Economics." *Oxford Economic Papers* 39: 119-33.

This review article on recent debates in economics is included as an example of an important branch in the profession, which tries to develop a new paradigm for macroeconomic theory from the assumptions of imperfect information and incomplete markets, particularly imperfect information in capital markets. By its focus on market imperfections, i.e., deficiencies of market institutions, it can be considered as complementary to a (macro)foundation of (Post Walrasian) economics approach.

Hargreaves Heap, S. P. (1992). *The New Keynesian Macroeconomics: Time, Belief and Social Interdependence*. Aldershot, U.K.: Edward Elgar.

An easy accessible and general introduction into the most important controversies between New Classical and Keynesian economics. After reviewing the literature, the author argues that New Classical economics can be criticized for neglecting the roles of time, beliefs, and social interdependence in their arguments. Instead, the choice of beliefs involves an additional act of coordination, which is recognized to some extent in a number of areas of New Keynesian economics.

Howitt, P. (1990). *The Keynesian Recovery and Other Essays*. Ann Arbor, Mich.: University of Michigan Press.

A collection of articles by the author preceded by an illuminating introduction on the relevance and scope of a Keynesian theory. According to Howitt the distortion of the coordination problem can be traced to the logical appeal of the Walrasian parable of perfect coordination and to the failure of Keynesian economics to provide a coherent alternative. In subsequent chapters it is argued that new developments in the theory of transactions externalities and adaptive learning behavior may help to create a Keynesian recovery.

Mankiw N. G. and D. Romer, eds. (1991). *New Keynesian Economics*, 2 Vols. Cambridge, Mass.: MIT Press.

Two volumes, which bring together major contributions to what the editors describe as New Keynesian economics. In their view, New Keynesian Economics can be distinguished from other branches in the discipline by affirmative answers on the following two questions. Does the theory violate the Classical dichotomy? Does the theory assume that real market imperfections in the economy are crucial for the understanding of economic fluctuations? Although the editors include some examples of the coordination failure literature in these volumes, the main emphasis rests upon the explanation of nominal and real price rigidities.

A.3   Coordination failures

The literature on (macroeconomic) coordination failures starts from the recognition that the spontaneous and unregulated interaction of economic agents does not always maximize social welfare. Cooper and John (1988) provide a general and abstract *game theoretic* framework for the analysis of these (macroeconomic) coordination failures, with applications to production, demand, and transactions externalities. Note that this framework restricts a discussion of coordination failures to equilibrium coordination failures, which represents a difference with some of the literature mentioned as a source of inspiration (see below). In this framework "Keynesian results," such as multiple equilibria and multiplier processes, "are generated from the inability of agents to coordinate their activities successfully in a many-person, decentralized economy" (Cooper and John, 1988: 442).

The analysis centers around the notions of externalities or spillovers, strategic complementarity, and multiple equilibria. Externalities arise if a change in the effort of one agent affects the payoffs of other agents. With strategic complementarity, the optimal level of effort of an agent increases with the level of effort chosen by other agents, i.e., reaction functions are upward sloping. In a macroeconomic context, macroeconomic complementarities denote situations where the optimal effort of an agent increases with some measure of the aggregate state of the economy. The combination of positive externalities and strategic complementarity may lead to multiple Pareto-ranked equilibria, i.e., multiple intersections of reaction functions. Multiplier effects may arise if, on the one hand, an exogenous shift stimulates an increase in individual activities and if, on the other hand, due to strategic complementarity and positive externalities, the aggregate response to the shift dominates the individual initial response to the shift. In the coordination failure literature, the observed inefficiency arises as there is no incentive for unilateral changes in strategies. Only a coordinated effort could establish a move toward a superior equilibrium. Actually, this can be denoted as a communication problem. The self-fulfilling nature of the equilibria is a consequence of the fact that the level of activity is positively dependent on the aggregate effort of all other agents but this positive interdependence cannot be effectively communicated.

Similar communication problems underly the path-dependency of equilibria, as temporary shocks may become permanent in situations where the adjustment path after the shock is to some extent determined by the reciprocal interdependence of the agents' decisions. Note that this interpretation of path-dependency is different from the less far-reaching mainstream interpretation, where the term refers to the slow adjustment toward the long-run equilibrium after a shock.

A.3.1   Annotated bibliography

A.3.1.1 Sources of inspiration/forerunners

Arrow, K. J. (1959). "Toward a Theory of Price Adjustment." In M. Abramowitz, ed., *The Allocation of Economic Resources*. Stanford, Cal.: Stanford University Press, 41-51.

In this article, Arrow formally explores the idea that in atomistic markets, a disequilibrium situation necessarily implies that agents no longer behave as price takers. It is one of the early articles in mainstream theory, which is focused on economic behavior in situations where coordination (in the sense of equilibrium) is not *a priori* imposed, although the coordination problem is not mentioned as such.

Clower, R. (1975). "The Coordination of Economic Activities: a Keynesian Perspective." Repr. (1984) in D. A. Walker, ed., *Money and Markets: Essays by Robert Clower*. Cambridge: Cambridge University Press, 209-17.

The author develops a framework in which the auctioneer is still around but in which trade no longer takes place at prices that ensure collective consistency of individual trading plans and in which the assumption that trades can be negotiated and executed at no cost to individuals is abandoned.

(1975). "Reflections on the Keynesian Perplex." Repr. (1984) in D. A. Walker, ed., *Money and Markets: Essays by Robert Clower*. Cambridge, Mass.: Cambridge University Press, 187-208.

In this essay a critical examination of the state of the art in economic theory is used to deal with the issue of how sound foundations of economic theory can be developed from the many criticisms that have been raised in this respect. Clower argues that the crucial flaw in neoWalrasian theory lies in the inability to deal with the "logistics of exchange – the absence of an explicit account of the execution as distinct from the scheduling of commodity trades." This flaw precludes among other things the development of the sound theory of monetary exchange. "A sensible first step towards the formulation of an acceptable theory of an ongoing economy is to dispense with the assumption of a central coordinator and to suppose instead that trade among individual economic agents is a strictly 'do it yourself' affair."

Hahn, F. H. (1977). "Exercises in Conjectural Equilibria." *Scandinavian Journal of Economics*: 210-26.

In this paper an economy is considered in which individuals can trade at *false* prices. When they do, agents have to conjecture the relationship between prices and quantity constraints. A conjectural equilibrium is a set of price and quantity signals under which desired trades are achieved and price adjustments are not advantageous. It is argued that economies can have conjectural equilibria even when they have a Walrasian equilibrium.

(1978). "On Non-Walrasian Equilibria." *Review of Economic Studies* 45: 1-17.

This paper considers an important problem of non-Walrasian Economics, which is the distinction between the agents' true and perceived trading possibilities. It applies the notion of a conjectural equilibrium and analyzes the implications of "the circumstance that the market signals that the agent has not made a mistake does not ensure that he is in fact not mistaken." Equilibria can be bootstrap equilibria, dependent on unexplained conjectures of agents. Generally, there will be many conjectural equilibria, depending on the agents' conjectures.

Keynes, J. M. (1936). *The General Theory of Employment, Interest and Money*. Reprinted (1973) in *The Collected Writings of John Maynard Keynes*, Vol. VII. London: MacMillan.

We in particular like to refer to chapters 12 and 19 on the state of long-term expectations and the pros and cons of flexible money wages as well as to Keynes's 1937 article in the *Quarterly Journal of Economics* entitled "The General Theory of Employment." With the benefit of hindsight it can be assumed that Chapter 12 anticipates Post Walrasian work on self-fulfilling expectations and bootstrap phenomena whereas Chapter 19 preludes the partial drawbacks of increased price flexibility. Reprinted (1973) in *The Collected Writings of John Maynard Keynes*, Vol XIV. London: MacMillan.

Leijonhufvud, A. (1981). *Information and Coordination*, New York: Oxford University Press.

A collection of articles in which the problem of coordination is taken seriously. It is maintained that the coordination of individual activities is the central problem in economics. Leijonhufvud, for instance, explicitly refers to the question of how a coherent outcome (whether cooperative or noncooperative) may be achieved. Under disequilibrium, markets fail to transmit information about desired transaction plans. Coordination fails, and prices tend to move away from equilibrium values. The Invisible Hand works in the wrong direction. (The book also contains a famous parody on our profession, "Life among the Econ.")

Young, A. (1928). "Increasing Returns and Economic Progress." *Economic Journal* 38: 527-42.

One of the first articles on the relation between increasing returns and economic progress and thus of interest to people who analyze the existence of coordination failures as a result of the interrelationships between output and demand across sectors. Moreover, this article served as an important source of inspiration for Kaldor in his work on increasing returns and cumulative causation. In turn, Kaldor clearly inspired economists like Arthur, David, and Krugman (see below).

A.3.2   (Equilibrium) coordination failures

Arthur, W. B. (1994). *Increasing Returns and Path Dependence in the Economy*. Ann Arbor, Mich.: University of Michigan Press.

This books brings together Professor Arthur's pioneering work on the implications of increasing returns and path dependence for economic behavior. It includes, among other things, an extended version of "Competing Technologies, Increasing Returns, and Lock-in by Historical Events"(*The Economic Journal* 99: 116-131), the dynamics of allocation under increasing returns in an environment where agents have to adopt new technologies and where the process of adoption is characterized by increasing returns, analyzing, and "Positive Feedbacks in the Economy" (*Scientific American* 1990: 92-99), which provides a popular and nontechnical account of the themes under discussion in this area of research.

Ball, L. and D. Romer (1991). "Sticky Prices as a Coordination Failure." *American Economic Review* 81: 539-52.

This paper is included in this bibliography because it links the menu costs approach to nominal price rigidities with the coordination failure approach. By emphasizing the possibility of coordination failures and multiple equilibria in the context of the process of determining prices, the paper illustrates that nominal rigidity arises from a failure to coordinate prices instead of from the existence of menu costs. At the same time the paper illustrates that the selection of a sticky price equilibrium has to be based on extraneous information.

Bernheim, D. (1984) "Rationalizable Strategic Behaviour." *Econometrica* 52: 1007-28.

This paper examines the nature of rational choice in strategic games. It is argued that rationality alone does not require the agents to select a Nash equilibrium strategy. A natural extension in the context of strategic choice under uncertainty would be the selection of rationalizable strategies. The properties of so-called rationalizable strategies are analyzed and refinements are considered.

Bryant, J. (1983). "A Simple Rational Expectations Keynes-Type Model." *Quarterly Journal of Economics* 98: 525-59.

The paper presents a Keynes-type model with two characteristics, specialization and imperfect information, which incorporates a continuum of rational-expectations equilibria. The model is set up in order to argue against the New Classical proposition that without further restrictions optimizing behavior will lead to a Pareto-efficient equilibrium.

(1984). "An Example of a Dominance Approach to Rational Expectations." *Economic Letters* 16: 249-55.

By applying the concepts of dominance and independence the author develops an alternative approach to rational expectations in an overlapping generations framework. It is shown that dominance and independence delimit rational behavior and allow for a coherent interpretation of multiple rational expectations equilibria.

(1987). "The Paradox of Thrift, Liquidity Preference and Animal Spirits." *Econometrica* 55: 1231-35.

A short but influential article that tries to formalize familiar Keynesian notions, such as the paradox of thrift, the liquidity trap, and animal spirits by applying an equilibrium concept weaker than the Nash equilibrium (i.e., the concept of rationalizable strategies). The "Keynesian" ingredients in this note are Tobin's specification of liquidity preference and Weitzman's use of increasing returns to scale, so as to construct a meaningful coordination problem.

Bulow, J. I., J. Geanakoplos, and P. Klemperer (1985). "Multimarket Oligopoly: Strategic Substitutes and Complements." *Journal of Political Economy* 93: 448-511.

In this paper, which clearly inspired Cooper and John (1988), the concepts of strategic complementarity and substitutability are formally developed. The general idea is that a firm's actions in one market can change competitors' strategies in other markets by affecting their marginal costs in these markets. It is demonstrated that many recent results in oligopoly theory can be understood in terms of strategic complements and substitutes.

Chatterjee, S. and R. Cooper (1989). "Multiplicity of Equilibria and Fluctuations in Dynamic Imperfectly Competitive Economies." *American Economic Review Papers and Proceedings* 79: 353-57.

This paper deals with the macroeconomic consequences of participation externalities. In this respect, the analysis focuses on the existence of multiple equilibria and on the question to what extent variations in the degree of competition, i.e., shocks in the degree of market participation, may help in understanding macroeconomic fluctuations. The analysis is used to explain the counter-intuitive idea that in the presence of strategic complementarity agents prefer to have market power in a thick market rather than in a thin market.

Cooper, R. (1994). "Equilibrium Selection in Imperfectly Competitive Economies with Multiple Equilibria." *The Economic Journal* 104: 1106-22.

In this paper a history-dependent selection criterion is applied in order to select an equilibrium in an economy with multiple, Pareto-ranked Nash equilibria. The history dependence is used to explain prolonged periods of low productivity and slumps. Only large positive productivity shocks move the economy out of a recession.

Cooper, R. and A. John (1988). "Coordinating Coordination Failures in Keynesian Models." *Quarterly Journal of Economics* 103: 441-65.

In this seminal paper, the authors develop a general (static equilibrium) framework for the analysis of macroeconomic coordination failures. In addition, some examples are presented that illustrate the idea that the theoretical concepts developed characterize a large variety of macroeconomic models.

David, P. (1985). "Clio and the Economics of QWERTY." *American Economic Review Proceedings* 75: 332-37.

Paul David's famous article on the presumption that evolutionary forces inevitably lead to the best possible solution or technology. The example of the keyboard arrangement of letters (QWERTY) is used to illustrate the coordination toward an inferior technology.

Diamond, P. (1982). "Aggregate Demand Management in Search Equilibrium." *Journal of Political Economy* 51: 881-94.

This influential paper introduces participation externalities and positive feedback as sources of multiple steady-state equilibria and local inefficiency. The central result is that the actual modelling of a competitive economy with trade frictions implies finding multiple natural rates of unemployment.

Durlauf, S. (1991). "Multiple Equilibria and Persistence in Aggregate Fluctuations." *American Economic Review, Papers and Proceedings* 81: 70-74.

Friedman, J. (c. 1993). *Problems of Coordination in Economic Activity.* Boston/Dordrecht/London: Kluwer Academic Publishers.

A collection of articles reporting on ongoing research on the economics of coordination. The volume contains original research on coordination, including game theoretic questions, particular coordination issues within specific fields of economics (industrial organization, international trade, and macroeconomics), and experimental research.

Hart, O. (1982). "A Model of Imperfect Competition with Keynesian Features." *Quarterly Journal of Economics* 97: 109-38.

This seminal paper explores the notion of imperfect competition to explain that in equilibrium the economy will generally be characterized by underemployment; and a multiplier greater than unity; also that changes in demand affect both prices and quantities; and a balanced-budget fiscal policy stimulates employment.

Heller, W. (1986). "Coordination Failure under Complete Markets with Applications to Effective Demand." In W. Heller, R. Starr, and D. Starret, *Equilibrium Analysis, Essays in Honour of Kenneth J. Arrow*, Vol II. Cambridge: Cambridge University Press.

In this essay it is shown that with complete markets there can be coordination failures of the type similar to those that occur with missing markets. Coordination failures arise due to multiple Pareto-ranked equilibria in an equilibrium model with a noncompetitive sector. The inefficiencies that emerge are the same as in a modified Prisoner's Dilemma Game. There is no incentive for unilateral changes in strategies but a coordinated effort could establish a move toward a superior equilibrium.

Howitt, P. (1988). "Business Cycles with Costly Search and Recruiting." *Quarterly Journal of Economics* 103: 177-65.

A business cycle model is developed in which output is traded on Lucas-Phelps islands and labor services on each island are exchanged through costly search and recruiting with transactions externalities. The model displays persistent involuntary unemployment and inefficient equilibria.

Howitt, P. and P. McAfee (1988). "Stability of Equilibria with Trade-Externalities." *Quarterly Journal of Economics* 103: 261-77.

This paper addresses the dynamic stability of inefficient equilibria in a framework where, due to participation externalities, multiple equilibria exist. It is shown that all stationary equilibria may be locally stable to perturbations, in the sense that there exist perfect foresight trajectories leading back to the equilibrium.

Neary, J. P. and J. E. Stiglitz (1983). "Toward a Reconstruction of Keynesian Economics: Expectations and Constrained Equilibria." *Quarterly Journal of Economics* 98: S199-S228.

In the context of a two-period fixed-price disequilibrium model it is argued that with arbitrary constraint expectations many different types of current equilibria may be consistent with the same set of wages and prices, and constraint expectations exhibit bootstrap properties.

Kiyotaki, N. (1988). "Multiple Expectational Equilibria under Monopolistic Competition." *Quarterly Journal of Economics* 103: 695-713.

This article can be considered as the multi-equilibrium extension of Blanchard and Kiyotaki, which focused on nominal rigidities. In the context of a monopolistically competitive economy, multiple rational equilibria may exist. Furthermore, these equilibria can be Pareto ranked, depending on the nature of the underlying "animal spirits." It is shown that optimistic expectations concerning future demand give rise to equilibria that dominate equilibria that are conditional on pessimistic expectations of future demand conditions.

Pearce, D. G. (1984). "Rationalizable Strategic Behaviour and the Problem of Perfection." *Econometrica* 52: 1029-50.

Like Bernheim (1984), Pearce examines the nature of strategic choice and argues that the concept of rationalizability may provide a better theoretical foundation for strategic decision making.

Roberts, J. (1987). "An Equilibrium Model with Involuntary Unemployment and Flexible, Competitive Prices and Wages." *American Economic Review* 77: 856-74.

This paper develops a general equilibrium model that admits involuntary unemployment as an equilibrium outcome. Prices and quantities are chosen by the agents. Multiple equilibria arise with perfectly competitive prices and different levels of economic activity, resulting from self-confirming expectations of inadequate effective demand.

Shleifer, A. (1986). "Implementation Cycles." *Journal of Political Economy* 94: 1163-90.

The author uses the notion that aggregate demand spillovers favor the idea of synchronizing discrete choices to illustrate the impact of the entrepreneurs' expectations about the future path of macroeconomic variables on their decisions to undertake or postpone investment projects. The model displays cyclical equilibria, with the duration of slumps largely determined by expectations.

Shleifer, A. and R. W. Vishny (1988). "The Efficiency of Investment in the Presence of Aggregate Demand Spillovers." *Journal of Political Economy* 96: 1221-31.

In this under-investment model, the presence of aggregate demand spillovers creates a positive interdependency between aggregate income and individual firms' profits. Since multipliers are ignored in individual firms' decisions, the privately optimal level of investment is too low from a social point of view.

Startz, R. (1984). "Prelude to Macroeconomics." *American Economic Review* 74: 881-92.

Weitzman, M. L. (1982). "Increasing Returns and the Foundations of Unemployment Theory." *The Economic Journal* 92: 787-804.

In this paper it is argued that a consistent theory of steady-state involuntary unemployment can be developed from the notion of increasing returns to scale. Unemployment caused by a lack of aggregate demand emerges from the failure to coordinate desired expenditure plans because the unemployed lack the means to communicate their potential demands.

A.4   Endogenous fluctuations

The literature that goes under the heading of "Endogenous fluctuations" is grounded upon the following three arguments (Guesnerie and Woodford, 1991):

1. The first argument is developed from the assessment that the coordination of economic activities as such also includes the coordination of expectations. The coordination of expectations involves two elements. In the first place, individuals have to coordinate their expectations toward a common image of the future, so called weak coordination. In the second, the common image of the future has to be the true image of

the future, the so-called true coordination. The Rational Expectations Hypothesis is built upon the assumption of true coordination. However, even if true coordination is assumed there can be additional sources of multiplicity and indeterminacy because of the following arguments.

    a. Rational expectations implies a reversal of the causation between the future and the present, which accounts for an additional multiciplicity of equilibria.

    b. Rational expectations does not exclude the possibility of stochastic equilibria in an otherwise non-stochastic world. In these so-called sunspot equilibria, the only shocks that exist are shocks on beliefs. These shocks are triggered by extrinsic uncertainty generated by some outside coordinating device, as opposed to intrinsic uncertainty generated by inside devices grounded upon fundamentals i.e., endowments, technology, and preferences. In this setting, beliefs can be self-fulfilling.

2. A second argument is provided by research into the stability of rational expectations equilibria, which focuses on the "implementation" problems of these equilibria in a general equilibrium context. The correct appraisal of tatonnement, or alternatively, the adherence to equilibrium, implies that there is no well-defined answer to the question of how expectations are formed. Economic theory has little to say on learning or any other (disequilibrium) process. On the other hand, theories of learning dynamics can be considered fundamental to the analysis of economic fluctuations.

3. The recent developments in the mathematical theory on dynamical systems provide a third argument. In this branch of mathematics analysis it is clearly established that fairly simple deterministic systems of time-independent nonlinear equations or of ordinary differential equations may have very complex dynamics. Moreover, economic theory contains many examples of such simple models.

The synthesis of these elements, learning behavior, complex dynamics, multiplicity, and sunspots, has developed into an alternative explanation of economic fluctuations, emphasizing the endogeneity of macroeconomic fluctuations, which contrasts with the exogenous approach to business cycles in the mainstream. As in the coordination failure literature, the new literature on endogenous fluctuations can be distinguished from its predecessors by its reliance on models in which the agents' behavior is explicitly derived from first principles. The aforementioned theoretical developments go under the heading of the (macro)foundation of (Post Walrasian) economics because in this literature the aggregate state of the system or aggregate beliefs drive the behavior of the economy, rather than the individual responses to exogenous shocks.

A.4.1   Annotated bibliography

A.4.1.1 Nonlinearities and the business cycle

Goodwin, R. M. (1951). "The Nonlinear Accelerator and the Persistence of Business Cycles." *Econometrica* 19: 1-17.

Kaldor, N. (1940). "A Model of the Trade Cycle." *The Economic Journal* 50: 78-92.

Kalecki, M. (1935). "A Macroeconomic Theory of Business Cycles." *Econometrica* 3: 327-44.

A.4.1.2 Expectations and the business cycle

Keynes, J. M. (1936). *The General Theory of Employment, Interest and Money.* Reprinted (1973) in *The Collected Writings of John Maynard Keynes*, Vol. VII. London: MacMillan. See particularly Chapter 12 on Keynes's theory of the determination of long-term expectations.

For a more general criticism of the use of the Rational Expectations Hypothesis and its lacking foundation as a behavioral hypothesis see:

Buiter, W. H. (1977). "The Macroeconomics of Dr Pangloss. A Critical Survey of New Classical Economics." *The Economic Journal* 90: 34-50.

Frydman, R. and E. S. Phelps, eds. (1983). *Individual Forecasting and Aggregate Outcomes: "Rational Expectations Examined."* Cambridge: Cambridge University Press.

Hoover, K. (1988). *The New Classical Macroeoconomics: A Skeptical Inquiry*, Oxford: Blackwell.

Janssen, M. C. W. (1993). *Microfoundations, a Critical Inquiry.* London: Routledge.

A.4.1.3 Interdeterminacies and self-fulfilling expectations

Azariadis, C. (1981). "Self-Fulfilling Prophecies." *Journal of Economic Theory* 25: 380-96.

A seminal paper which shows that (1) for the case of an additive separable utility function stationary sunspot equilibria can exist and (2) that the indeterminacy of a monetary steady state can be regarded as a sufficient condition for the existence of these equilibria.

Barnett, W. A., J. Geweke, and Karl Shelll, eds. (1989). *Economic Complexity: Chaos, Sunspots, Bubbles, and Nonlinearity.* Cambridge: Cambridge University Press.

This book consist of the Proceedings of the Fourth International Symposium in Economic Theory and Econometrics. It contains many relevant fairly technical articles on economic complexity, i.e., the analysis of complicated outcomes in relatively simple economic models.

Baumol, W. J. and J. Benhabib (1989). "Chaos, Significance, Mechanism and Economic Applications." *Journal of Economic Perspectives* 3: 77-107.

This article is a very readable nontechnical introduction to the most important topics in chaos theory.

Benhabib, J. and R. Day (1981). "Rational Choice and Erratic Behaviour." *Review of Economic Studies* 48: 459-72.

In this paper it is argued that rational choice in a stationary environment can lead to erratic behavior when preferences depend on experience. Cyclity in preferences may lead to erratic behavior in a deterministic environment, in a way that resembles the time pattern generated by exogenously determined random shocks.

Cass, D. and K. Shell (1983). "Do Sunspots Matter?" *Journal of Political Economy* 91: 193-227.

This seminal paper tries to identify the conditions under which extrinsic uncertainty plays a significant role in rational expectations equilibrium models. It is formally established that extrinsic uncertainty does not affect the equilibrium outcome in an Arrow-Debreu economy with complete markets, but it does in the overlapping generations model with complete markets where participation is limited to those agents who are alive when markets are open. In addition, the welfare characteristics of the different equilibria are analyzed.

Geanakoplos, J. D. and H. M. Polemarchakis (1986). "Walrasian Indeterminacy and Keynesian Macroeconomics." *Review of Economic Studies* 53: 755-79.

In the context of a perfect foresight overlapping generations model, the authors use the fundamental indeterminacy of these models to illustrate the basic Keynesian idea that changes in expectations, or animal spirits, can affect the equilibrium level of economic activity even in the context of an optimizing framework. Next it is demonstrated that in the context of this framework, both Keynesian and

Classical results can be derived from the arbitrary fixation of alternative sets of variables.

Grandmont, J.-M. (1985). "On Endogenous Competitive Business Cycles." *Econometrica* 53: 995-1045.

This paper develops an example in which persistent deterministic business cycles appear in a purely endogenous fashion under laissez-faire. The origin of these cycles is the potential conflict between the wealth effect and the intertemporal substitution effect that are associated with real interest-rate movements. The techniques to analyze business cycles come from the mathematical theory on chaotic behavior in physical, biological, or ecological systems.

Grandmont, J.-M., ed. (1987). *Nonlinear Economic Dynamics*. Boston, Mass.: Academic Press.

This book, which was originally published as a special issue of the *Journal of Economic Theory*, contains a high-quality collection of papers on nonlinear economic dynamics. Examples of nonlinear dynamic processes are given in the context of growth theory, the theory of business cycles, and the theory of market behavior, i.e., duopoly theory.

Guesnerie, R. (1992). "An Exploration of the Eductive Justifications of the Rational Expectations Hypothesis." *American Economic Review* 82: 1254-78.

The paper examines justifications of the Rational Expectations Hypothesis that rely on the analysis of the agents' mental forecasting ("educing") activity. Eductive explanations rely on the understanding of the logic of the situation by economic agents. They are associated with the activity of agents to forecast the forecasts of others (reciprocity of beliefs). The corresponding emphasis on learning processes is used within the rational expectations model. Conditions for the coordination of beliefs are discussed and economically interpreted.

(1993). "Successes and Failures in Coordinating Expectations." *European Economic Review* 37: 243-68.

In this 1992 Alfred Marshall Lecture for the European Economic Association, Roger Guesnerie provides an introductory analysis of a limited but coherent set of questions with respect to the concept of rational expectations. The analysis supports a rather pessimistic view as to the possibility of strong coordination of expectations, this in contrast with the rather common intuition among the profession that expectations are reasonably well coordinated.

Hahn, F. H., ed. (1989). *The Economics of Missing Markets and Games*. Oxford: Clarendon Press.

The book reports some of the work of a group of Cambridge (U.K.) economists (as well as of some other people) on "Information, Risk, and Quantity Signals in Economics." The book and the project were motivated by the desire to move beyond the Walrasian paradigm without abandoning the strategy of rigorous theorizing in the tradition of Arrow and Debreu. The book contains, e.g., essays on the implications of missing markets for expectations formation, on learning behavior, on strategic behavior, on history dependence, and on common knowledge.

Howitt, P. (1992). "Interest Rate Control and Nonconvergence to Rational Expectations." *Journal of Political Economy* 100: 776-800.

This paper investigates the feasibility of a monetary policy of pegging the interest rate. It shows that under general conditions such a policy produces cumulative processes, which illustrate the failure of learning to converge to rational expectations.

Howitt, P. and R. P. McAfee (1992). "Animal Spirits." *American Economic Review* 82: 493-507.

This paper develops a model of a rational-expectations animal-spirits cycle, which does not depend on the common assumption in the endogenous fluctuations literature that aggregate fluctuations are driven by inflationary expectations. Instead, cycles are driven by participation externalities that produce multiple stationary equilibria.

Iwai, K. (1981). *Disequilibrium Dynamics*, New Haven, Conn: Yale University Press.

This much-neglected book addresses stability problems of noncompetitive economies with rational expectations and full price flexibility in a very lucid way. Iwai formally illustrates that without (institutional) arrangements that peg nominal prices, it cannot be expected that these economies will converge to any equilibrium situation. Cumulative inflation will result.

Kehoe, T. J. and D. K. Levine (1985). "Comparative Statics and Perfect Foresight in Infinite Horizon Economies." *Econometrica* 53: 433-53.

The paper considers whether a pure exchange economy with an infinite horizon has determinate perfect foresight equilibria. It is shown in the context of an overlapping generations model that initial conditions and the requirement of convergence to a steady state do not locally determine the equilibrium price path. Instead, there exist many equilibria, which renders the concept of perfect foresight meaningless.

Rosser, J. B. (1991). *From Catastrophe to Chaos: A General Theory of Economic Discontinuties*. Boston, Mass.: Kluwer Academic Publishers.
An insightful book, which, after a brief outline on the mathematics of discontinuity (in the second chapter), provides an elaborate overview of the many economic theoretical and empirical implications of discontinuities in microeconomic and macroeconomic models.

Woodford, M. (1984). "Indeterminacy of Equilibrium in the Overlapping Generations Model: A Survey." Unpublished mimeo. New York: Columbia University.
A rather extensive as well as accessible survey on the analytical characteristics of the overlapping generations model with a special emphasis on the implications of the double infinity (of agents as well as commodities) characteristic of this model, which gives rise to the indeterminacy result, an independent role for beliefs, and the emergence of sunspot equilibria. Additionally, the possibilities for policy to reintroduce a determinate equilibrium are discussed.

(1988). "Self-Fulfilling Expectations and Fluctuations in Aggregate Demand." *NBER Working Paper* No. 3361.
The paper presents a rational expectations equilibrium model of the business cycle in which aggregate fluctuations occur even in the absence of any stochastic variation in preferences or technology or in government policies. The fluctuations that occur are due to changes in people's expectations in response to random events that have no effect upon fundamentals.

A.5   Some empirical research

The empirical research in this area is complicated by the fact that most of these theories rely on concepts that are not directly observable, such as self-fulfilling expectations. This in particular applies to the literature on endogenous fluctuations. With respect to this literature it can be observed that the available empirical tests hardly allow one to distinguish between endogenous and exogenous fluctuations in observed time series. Furthermore, current models of endogenous fluctuations are too simple to take as correct descriptions of actual economies. In the context of the literature on coordination failures somewhat more progress has been made in the sense that from these models a small set of testable hypotheses has been confronted rather successfully with data on business cycle behavior. These hypotheses include co-movement of choices across agents, synchronizations of discrete decisions, and the propagation and amplification of shocks. Moreover, experimental methods have been applied in order to address the issue of equilibrium selection in situations of multiple equilibria.

In addition, it can be observed that at a qualitative level, the existence of multiple equilibria is increasingly used to explain that the development of economies, industries, or individual firms over time is (partly) determined by the fact that many equilibria could have been realized but that path-dependency (history) or self-fulfilling expectations determine which equilibrium actually gets established. For instance, in international economics the concept of path-dependency of equilibria is increasingly used to explain why location matters in the determination of (international) economic activity patterns (Krugman (1991, 1994). Also in industrial economics, path-dependency and self-fulfilling expectations can be used, for instance, to explain why relatively inefficient products can dominate the market.

A.5.1   Annotated bibliography

A.5.1.1 Aggregate coordination failures

Caballero, R. and E. Engel (1993). "Microeconomic Adjustment Hazards and Aggregate Dynamics." *Quarterly Journal of Economics* 108: 359-84.

This paper provides some evidence for lumpy behavior at a microeconomic level by the application of the concept of an adjustment-hazard function. The argument is that the understanding of aggregate dynamics requires the acknowledgment of heterogeneity of agents and discontinuous adjustment to shocks.

Cooper, R. and J. Haltiwanger (1993a). "The Macroeconomic Implications of Machine Replacement: Theory and Evidence." *American Economic Review* 83: 360-82.

In this paper, the spillover effects of costly machine replacement in individual sectors are analyzed and conditions for synchronized machine replacement by multiple, independent producers are developed. The model mimics some observed fluctuations in monthly output, productivity, and employment in automobile plants. The synchronization of machine replacement in the automobile industry can have aggregate implications for the U.S. economy.

(1993b). "Autos and the National Industrial Recovery Act: Evidence on Industry Complementarities." *Quarterly Journal of Economics* 108: 1043-71.

This paper investigates the motivations for, and implications of, the Automobile Industry code negotiated in 1933 and modified in 1935 under the National Industrial Recovery Act. In the paper, two models of the annual automobile cycle are developed to examine cyclical observations in the 1920s and 1930s. In one model, the cyclical pattern is due to changes in fundamentals, and the NIRA code is regarded simply as an adaptation of regulation to these changes. The competing model incorporates a coordination problem into the determination of the equilibrium timing of new model introductions. In this model the perspective on the NIRA is that it managed to coordinate activity in the automobile industry toward an alternative more efficient equilibrium.

(1993c). "Evidence on Macroeconomic Complementarities." *NBER Working Paper* No. 4577.

The second part of the paper provides a nicely structured and elaborate survey of the empirical evidence on macroeconomic complementarities. The theoretical section identifies three empirical implications that can be studied with these types of models: co-movement of choices across agents, synchronizations of discrete decisions, and propagation and amplification of shocks. The empirical section surveys microeconomic as well as aggregate evidence consistent with these implications.

Dagsvik, J. and B. Jovanovic (1994). "Was the Great Depression a Low-Level Equilibrium?" *European Economic Review* 38: 1711-29.

The multiple equilibrium approach implies that if the Great Depression in the U.S. was a low-level equilibrium, than there was another equilibrium that the economy could have attained but for some reason didn't. On the other hand, the unique equilibrium approach implies that the fall in output and employment during the Great Depression was caused by exogenous shocks. This article tries to find evidence that allows one to discriminate between the two positions. The conclusion is that the data offer little support for the multiple equilibria story.

Jovanovic, B. (1989). "Observable Implications of Models with Multiple Equilibria." *Econometrica* 57: 1431-38.

A short technical note in which a simple theoretical framework is developed that can be used to organize the debate about the question of whether a given model with multiple equilibria is identified, and about the question of how much predictive content such a model retains.

A.5.1.2 Experimental economics
Recently quite a few papers have appeared that apply experimental methods to analyze games, which reflect in an abstract way the types of interaction present

in economic models of coordination problems. Several theories of equilibrium selection and characteristics of these theories have addressed in experimental settings the role or relevance of, for instance, payoff dominance, communication, history-dependence, beliefs, and strategic uncertainty. Except for the article by Smith, Suchanek, and Williams on bubbles, we mention some work by Cooper and Van Huyck as examples of this line of work.

Cooper, R., D. V. DeJong, R. Forsythe, and T. W. Ross (1990). "Selection Criteria in Coordination Games: Some Experimental Results." *American Economic Review* 80: 218-33.

(1992). "Communication in Coordination Games." *Quarterly Journal of Economics* 107: 739-71.

(1993). "Forward Induction in the Battle-of-the-Sexes Games." *American Economic Review* 83: 1303-16.

Smith, Suchanek, and Williams (1988), "Bubbles, Crashes, and Endogenous Expectations in Experimental Spot Assets Markets." *Econometrica* 5: 1119-51.

An important article in which the existence of bubbles followed by crashes in spot assets markets is examined in a laboratory environment in which it is possible to control for the dividend distribution and traders' knowledge of it in a market with a finite trading horizon. Fourteen out of 22 experiments exhibit price-bubbles followed by crashes relative to the intrinsic value.

Van Huyck, J., R. Battalaio, and R. Beil (1990). "Tacit Coordination Games, Strategic Uncertainty, and Coordination Failure." *American Economic Review* 80: 234-48.

(1991). "Strategic Uncertainty, Equilibrium Selection, and Coordination Failures in Average Opinion Games." *Quarterly Journal of Economics* 106: 885-910.

Van Huyck J., R. Battalaio, D. J. Meyer, and T. R. Saving (1992). "History's Role in Coordinating Decentralized Allocation Decisions." *Journal of Political Economy* 100: 292-317.

A.5.1.3 Endogenous fluctuations

Brock, W. A. (1986). "Distinguishing Random and Deterministic Systems: Abridged Version." *Journal of Economic Theory* 40: 168-95.

In this article the author develops some techniques to test whether a particular time series is more likely to have been generated by a stochastic system or instead by a regime that is chaotic, defined as a deterministic system giving rise to complicated dynamics.

Brock, W. A. and C. L. Sayers (1988). "Is the Business Cycle Characterized by Deterministic Chaos?" *Journal of Monetary Economics* 22: 71-90.

This paper reports test results on the presence of deterministic chaos. The idea is to test for evidence of endogenous instability causing the business cycle. The evidence on chaos is weak but this may be due to the limited power of the tests. Evidence on nonlinearity is present in U.S. employment, unemployment, monthly postwar industrial production, and pig-iron production data.

Frank, M. Z. and T. Stengos (1988). "Some Evidence Concerning Macroeconomic Chaos." *Journal of Monetary Economics* 22: 423-38.

This paper is an empirical assessment of a linear-stochastic perspective for Canadian macroeconomic time series. The methods used are based on the mathematics of chaos. The evidence suggests that low-order deterministic chaos does not provide a satisfactory description of the data. The absence of significant nonlinear structure for the investment and unemployment series is of particular relevance in light of past findings with American data.

Hsieh, D. A. (1989). "Testing for Nonlinear Dependence in Daily Foreign Exchange Rate Changes." *Journal of Business* 62: 339-68.

The purpose of this article is to investigate whether daily changes in five foreign exchange rates contain nonlinearities. Although the data contain no linear correlation, evidence suggests the presence of substantial nonlinearity in multiplicative rather than in additive form. Further examination reveals that a GARCH model explains a large fraction of the nonlinearities for all five exchange rates.

Sayers, C. L. (1991). "Statistical Inference Based upon Nonlinear Science." *European Economic Review, Papers and Proceedings* 35: 306-12.

This paper reviews tests for the presence of deterministic chaos and presents problems surrounding such research. Statistical inference methods are presented, along with research utilizing these methods. The paper argues that while evidence of significant nonlinear structure has been demonstrated in many economic and financial time series, precisely how important these nonlinear components are to the economics of modelling, forecasting, stability, and policy has yet to be determined.

A.6   Social institutions and coordination

At present, the contribution of much of the aforementioned literature lies in the recognition of coordination problems that may arise in the face of indeterminacy and multiple equilibria. On the other hand, the "strength" of a theory with these features represents a "weakness" at the same time as deductive equilibrium analysis often fails to provide a unique equilibrium solution in situations of strategic interdependence. Theories of multiple or even of a continuum of equilibria do provide conditions "for the existence of multiple equilibria but do not provide insights into the question which of the equilibria is more or less likely to be observed" (Cooper and John, 1988: 2). A similar argument applies with respect to indeterminacies.

In the introduction of this bibliography it is argued that in the modern approach to coordination failures the assumptions of full rationality and equilibrium may foreclose an analysis of equilibrium selection. On the other hand, earlier studies of the coordination problem are much more focused on an analysis of out-of equilibrium behavior. Economic behavior is regarded as an ongoing process, which may or may not lead toward the establishment of a new equilibrium situation. Furthermore, some tradition in theories of equilibrium selection already existed. Schelling's (1960) notion of focal points can be considered as an early attempt to shed some light on the issue of equilibrium selection. A focal point denotes a situation in which the players are able to coordinate to a particular equilibrium by using information that is not explicitly incorporated in the game itself. Usually this information depends on the agents' culture and experience, i.e., the institutions that set the stage for the game to some extent determine the outcome of the game. Others have suggested that theoretical developments in biology, focusing on the evolution of species (a game-theoretic interpretation of Darwinism), can be fruitfully applied to problems of learning and evolutionary stability in economics.

From the inability to deal with the problem of equilibrium selection there has thus emerged a growing interest in the analysis of the importance of social institutions and conventions for the coordination of activities. Institutions are nothing more (or less) than shared rules of conduct or belief, which guide individual behavior by supplementing conventional (optimal) decision making. Seen from this perspective, many institutions provide the necessary bits of (extraneous) information that enables us to coordinate (economic) behavior toward a particular equilibrium. At the same time, the introduction of institutions and conventions besides the market, which is the only institution in mainstream economic theory, brings along some fundamental question as to the nature of economic behavior. In particular, how do institutions emerge? Do they arise spontaneously? Can they be regarded as the product of explicit logical decision making? What does the recognition of the importance of institutions imply for the canonical model of the instrumentally rational agent? Does the importance of institutions make economies fundamentally path dependent? These are difficult questions, many of them yet unresolved. However, these questions perfectly fit in a research program, which starts from a (macro)foundation of (Post Walrasian) economics.

A.6.1   Annotated bibliography

A.6.1.1 Three very different sources of inspiration

Hayek, F.A. (1937). "Economics and Knowledge." Reprinted (1949) in F.A. Hayek. *Individualism and Economic Order.* London, 33-54.

Schelling, T. (1960). *The Strategy of Conflict.* New Haven, Conn.: Yale University Press. (See also his highly readable 1970 book *Micromotives and Macrobehavour.*)

Smith, M. (1974). "The Theory of Games and the Evolution of Animal Conflicts." *Journal of Theoretical Biology* 47: 209-21.

A.6.1.2 Institutions and the nature of economic behavior

Clower, R. (1967). "A Reconsideration of the Microfoundation of Monetary Theory." Repr. (1984) in D. A. Walker, ed., *Money and Markets. Essays by Robert Clower.* Cambridge: Cambridge University Press, 81-89.

It is argued that attempts to develop a theory of money and prices in the context of a competitive equilibrium model have failed as they have only produced something which is nothing more than a barter economy. In this paper it is demonstrated that the conception of a money economy in these attempts is empirically and analytically vacuous. As an alternative, a conceptual microeconomic framework for a pure theory of a money economy is developed.

Denzau, A. T. and D. C. North (1994). "Shared Mental Models: Ideologies and Institutions." *Kyklos* 47: 3-31.

This article is included as an example of the natural connection between the literature in this bibliography and the literature that deals with the fundamental assumptions underlying the theory of rational choice (for an excellent introduction to this literature, see *The Economist*, December 1994: 92-94). In this article, it is argued that path- and history-dependent institutions and beliefs imply a fundamental different notion on individual decision making, which needs to be incorporated in economic modelling efforts. By departing from the fundamental assumption of substantive rationality the authors try to proceed into the domain of cognitive science by exploring the implications of the way by which human individuals attempt to order and structure their environment and to communicate with each other. By doing this we may improve our understanding of the dynamics of economic change and development.

Hargreaves Heap, S. P. (1994). "Institutions and (Short-Run) Macroeconomic Performance." *Journal of Economic Surveys* 8: 35-56.

This paper reviews the growing interest in institutions and their impact on economic performance. This connection arises because many economic interactions resemble classic games, and the outcome of these games depends on the institutional context of human interactions. This argument is illustrated by relating it to the unemployment performance and wage-setting procedures in selected OECD countries.

Heiner, R.H. (1983). "The Origin of Predictable Behavior." *American Economic Review* 73: 560-96.

Hodgson, G. M. (1988). *Economics and Institutions*, Oxford: Polity Press.

In this monograph Hodgson provides a critique of the concept of the *homo economicus* and pinpoints the central role that institutions play in molding preferences and guiding and enabling economic activities. From this perspective, the author criticizes neoclassical and Austrian as well as neo-institutional approaches to economics because of their adherence to the laissez-faire doctrine. Instead an alternative policy perspective is provided based on structural reform and institutional intervention.

Hicks, J. (1989). *A Market Theory of Money.* Oxford: Clarendon Press.

In this book Sir John Hicks develops a rudimentary foundation for new monetary theory by starting from the notion that methods of exchange, the establishment of media of exchange, and the establishment of markets as well as the undertaking of business activities are all interrelated.

Laidler, D. (1990). *Taking Money Seriously.* Cambridge, Mass.: MIT Press.

A collection of essays on monetary theory, which, among other things, develops the idea that the explanation of monetary exchange is more or less complementary to the functioning of markets and institutions in the economy.

Mehrling, P. G. (1987). A Classical Model of the Class Struggle: A Game Theoretic Approach. *Journal of Political Economy* 96: 1280-1303.

Using dynamic game theory, the paper explores how social organization affects the incentives for economic growth and technological change.

North, D. C. (1990). *Institutions, Institutional Changes and Economic Performance*. Cambridge: Cambridge University Press.

In this book Nobel laureate D.C. North develops an analytical framework for explaining the ways in which institutions and institutional change interact with economic performance and development. The nature and origin of institutions are to be found in production and transaction costs. Subsequently, as institutions determine the incentive structure in the economy, they provide the scope for change within a given institutional environment. However, as economic change affects production and transaction costs, the process of change feeds back on the institutional environment. In the end, economic development is best described in an evolutionary framework in which institutional development leads to a path-dependent pattern of economic development.

Kregel, J. A. (1987). "Rational Spirits and the Post-Keynesian Macrotheory of Microeconomics." *De Economist* 135: 520-33.

This article is included in the annotated bibliography in order to represent a long-standing tradition in Post Keynesian economics (see also Davidson, P., 1978, *Money and the Real World*, London: MacMillan; and H.P. Minsky, 1975, *John Maynard Keynes*, New York: Columbia University Press, which takes the (macro)foundation, or better the monetary, foundation of microeconomics as a starting point. The argument is that the essential characteristics of a monetary economy, in particular the relationship between money, time, and uncertainty, which enter human decision making through the notion of liquidity preference, require a different kind of microeconomic theory as a foundation for a macroeconomic, that is, a monetary analysis.

Rowe, N. (1989). *Rules and Institutions*. New York: Philip Allan.

Rules and Institutions addresses the sociological problem of order from the economist's perspective. It asks whether the nature and existence of social facts can be compatible with the assumption of rational and self-seeking behavior. The central thesis of this book is that social institutions are nothing more than agents rationally following rules of actions, and being believed by other agents to do so. However, in order to make this argument fit into the paradigm of economic theory, the theory of rational behavior has to be amended so as to understand the rationality of rules of actions.

Schotter, A. (1981). *The Economic Theory of Social Institutions*. Cambridge: Cambridge University Press.

This important book uses game theory to analyze the creation, evolution, and function of economic and social institutions. The analysis is illustrated by a description of the spontaneous evolution of institutions and conventions such as the use of money, property rights, and oligopolistic pricing conventions.

Sugden, R. (1986). *The Economics of Rights, Cooperation and Welfare.* Oxford: Basil Blackwell.

In this book Robert Sugden uses game theory to explain how self-enforcing conventions can evolve spontaneously out of the interaction of self-interested agents. His analysis of conventions and institutions challenges the mainstream view that social choices are always driven by maximization of social welfare.

(1989). "Spontaneous Order." *Journal of Economic Perspectives* 3: 85-97.

"Spontaneous Order" is a nontechnical review article on the establishment of the many rules, conventions, and institutions that characterize the behavior of a society. The argument is that order in human affairs can arise spontaneously, in the form of these conventions. However, these rules are generally not the result of any process of collective choice, nor can they, following, e.g., Hayek, be always regarded as the explicit outcome of rational design. Finally, the observed patterns of behavior need not necessarily be efficient. They have merely emerged because they were more successful in replicating themselves than alternative rules of conduct.

Endnotes

1. For an illuminating discussion of this subject see Hicks (1979).
2. In the mainstream, Keynesian economics has been juxtaposed to this view by the idea that prices are sticky, i.e., do not always obey the laws of supply and demand.
3. This view is elaborated in Colander (1992) and van Ees and Garretsen (1992).

References

Bernheim, D. (1984) "Rationalizable Strategic Behaviour." *Econometrica* 52: 1007-28.

Bryant, J. (1993). "Coordination Theory, the Stag Hunt and Macroeconomics." In J.W. Friedman, ed., *Problems of Coordination in Economic Activity.* Boston/Dordrecht/London: Kluwer Academic Publishers, 207-226.

Colander, D. (1992). "New Keynesian Economics in Perspective." *Eastern Economic Journal* 18: 438-48.

Cooper, R. and A. John (1988). "Coordinating Coordination Failures in Keynesian Models." *Quarterly Journal of Economics* 103: 441-65.

Garretsen, H. (1992). *Keynes, Coordination and Beyond. The Development of Macroeconomic and Monetary Theory since 1945.* Aldershot: Edward Elgar.

Gordon, R J. (1990). "What is New-Keynesian Economics?" *Journal of Economic Literature* 28: 1115-71.

Guesnerie, R. and M. Woodford (1991). *Endogenous Fluctuations.* Paris: Delta Document, 91-10.

Hicks, J. (1979). *Causality in Economics.* Oxford: Basil Blackwell.

Howitt, P. (1988). "Business Cycles with Costly Search and Recruiting." *Quarterly Journal of Economics*: 177-65.

(1990). *The Keynesian Recovery and Other Essays*. New York: Philip Allan.

Howitt, P. and R. P. McAfee (1992). "Animal Spirits." *American Economic Review* 82: 493-507.

Krugman, P. (1991). *Geography and Trade*. Cambridge, Mass.: MIT Press

(1994). *Peddling Prosperity*. New York: Norton.

Leijonhufvud, A. (1981). *Information and Coordination*. New York: Oxford University Press.

Mankiw N. G. and D. Romer, eds. (1991). *New Keynesian Economics*, Vols. I and II. Cambridge, Mass.: MIT Press.

Schelling, T. (1960). *The Strategy of Conflict*. Yale.

van Ees, H. van and H. Garretsen (1992). "On the Contribution of New Keynesian Economics." *Eastern Economic Journal* 18: 465-77.

van Ees, H. van and H. Garretsen (1995). "Existence and Stability of Conventions and Institutions in a Monetary Economy." *Journal of Economic Behaviour and Organization*.

Weintraub, E. R. (1979). *Microfoundations*. Cambridge: Cambridge University Press.

Name Index

Subject Index

agents, learning by induction, 45-6
aggregate production, conception of, 14
aggregate demand, role in unemployment, 216-19
aggregate output, and potential output, 157-58
aggregation, and complexity, 148
aggregation issues, as linkages between micro/macro, 145
aggregation problems, and economic relationships, 152-53
animal spirits, and team production, 168
Arrow-Debreu
    and decision problems, 43
    model, 77, 78
assumptions and the individual agent, 127-8
Austrians, 9-10
    and aggregate economy, 62
    and pattern coordination, 200
    and self-organizing economies, 99

bottom up
    and artificial intelligence, 42-3
    relation between economy and its individual agents, 42
Brussels School, and chaos theory, 98-9

Cambridge controversy, 136
capacity
    contrasted to output, 176-82
    and investment, 183
    and overbuilding, 177-9, 180-2

cash-in-advance
    and conflict, 76
    model, 23-5, 28-9
Center for Computable Economics, 39
chaos, and economic relationships, 152-3
chaos theory, 87-101
    and Austrians, 99
    Breck, Dechert, and Scheinkman statistic, 94
    and Brussels School, 98-9
    complexity beyond chaos theory, 13, 94-9
    dealing with chaos rationally, 99-100
    defined, 88-9
    and deterministic chaos, 101 fn. 6
    and fractal basin boundaries, 95-6
    and interacting particle systems models, 96-7
    and intermittency, 101 fn. 13
    and multiple attractors, 95-6
    and rational expectations models, 89-92
        without rational expectations, 92-3
    and self-organized criticality, 97-9
chaotic dynamics, 12-13, 89
    and A. Marshall, 113
choice-theoretic
    foundations, and Walrasian model, 78
    framework, macro and micro, 58
    models, 127
choice theory
    integration of micro with macro, 59
    and predetermination, 51-3
Classical Stability Postulate, 31
closed form solutions, and macroeconomic models, 145

261